The New Roadmap for Creating Online Courses

Are you ready to create an online course but do not know where to start? Do your online learners seem isolated and disengaged? Are your online courses effective enough for the current, competitive market? Whether you are an instructor, instructional designer, or part of a team, this interactive workbook will help you create effective online courses to engage your learners.

Key features of the workbook include integrating cognitive, social, and emotional aspects of learning; explaining the central role of self-reflection, dialogue, and realistic application; the incorporation of themes, scenarios, and characters to provide relevant and meaningful learning experiences; and the use of semiotics for inclusion of diverse learners.

As you journey through the course creation process in this workbook, you will expand your ideas and discover new possibilities for the students taking your online course.

Catherine R. Barber is an associate professor at the University of St. Thomas School of Education and Human Services.

Janet K. McCollum is the director of the Quality Enhancement Program and Core Assessment at the University of St. Thomas.

Wendy L. Maboudian is a professional development design specialist for teacher training with the Houston Independent School District.

T0370895

The New Roadmap for Creating Online Courses

An Interactive Workbook

Catherine R. Barber
University of St. Thomas

Janet K. McCollum
University of St. Thomas

Wendy L. Maboudian
Houston Independent School District

CAMBRIDGE
UNIVERSITY PRESS

University Printing House, Cambridge CB2 8BS, United Kingdom

One Liberty Plaza, 20th Floor, New York, NY 10006, USA

477 Williamstown Road, Port Melbourne, VIC 3207, Australia

314–321, 3rd Floor, Plot 3, Splendor Forum, Jasola District Centre, New Delhi – 110025, India

79 Anson Road, #06-04/06, Singapore 079906

Cambridge University Press is part of the University of Cambridge.

It furthers the University's mission by disseminating knowledge in the pursuit of education, learning, and research at the highest international levels of excellence.

www.cambridge.org
Information on this title: www.cambridge.org/9781108720311
DOI: 10.1017/9781108766890

First published 2020

A catalogue record for this publication is available from the British Library.

ISBN 978-1-108-72031-1 Paperback

To Michael, Cecilia, and Fiona, with love and gratitude
C.R.B.

To Pat for always being there, with love and gratitude
To Vivienne and Xavier, may you always find delight in learning
J.K.M.

To my husband, Hamid, always my North Star, for lighting my path to this book
To my daughters, Farial and Parnaz, for their loving support
W.L.M.

Contents

Figures

Tables

Acknowledgments

As we began our journey to create this workbook, we started by talking with our colleagues who have created and taught online courses and those who are interested in online courses. We were excited by their willingness to share their wealth of experience, some cautionary and some wildly successful, much of which informed this workbook. Without these conversations, this workbook would be diminished. While these people are too numerous to name, we do want to acknowledge a wide range of contributions that informed this workbook.

We want to specifically mention the following people, who took time out of their busy schedules to share insights and, in some cases, descriptions of learning activities that added to the diversity of examples we are able to provide in this workbook. We particularly want to acknowledge Dr. Lesa Tran Lu, Lecturer at the Department of Chemistry at Rice University, and Dr. Laura Schaefer, Burton J. and Ann M. McMurtry Professor and Department Chair, Department of Mechanical Engineering, Rice University. Their passion for educating their students was inspiring. In this workbook, you will find Lesa's discussion of how self-reflection was included in an introductory chemistry exam. Laura's example of a scenario-based mechanical engineering activity is also included in this workbook, along with her description of how she chooses resources for a course. We also want to acknowledge Dr. Pooya Tabesh, Assistant Professor at the Cameron School of Business, University of St. Thomas – Houston. His description of the challenges he encountered as he developed his first online course informed several of the tips we provide.

We want to thank Dr. Kathy Broussard, editor and friend, who reviewed our first chapters and responded with enthusiasm. Darnell Miller, photographer for the University of St. Thomas – Houston, also deserves our gratitude for his professional photography. We also acknowledge Dr. Wendy Maboudian for her work as our graphic illustrator.

In addition, we wish to thank the Cambridge University Press team – Dave Repetto, Executive Publisher; Emily Watton, Editorial Assistant; and Bethany Johnson, Senior Content Manager. They were supportive and patient as they walked us through the publication process. Thank you, Dave, Emily, Bethany, and the rest of the team.

We also want to thank the University of St. Thomas – Houston for their support.

1   Start Here

WELCOME!

Whether you are an instructor, an instructional designer, or part of a team creating an online course, this workbook is for you. We are excited that you are reading our workbook, *The New Roadmap for Creating Online Courses: An Interactive Workbook*, and we are delighted to share our new course creation process with you. As you prepare and create your online course, we believe that you will find this experience to be unique and engaging.

In line with the new roadmap, we introduce the workbook theme of a *journey*, specifically your learning journey. You are embarking on a journey of discovery and learning that is truly different. This workbook is not just a step-by-step description of what to do to create an online course for adult learners. Rather, as our title promises, it is an *interactive* workbook. You are encouraged to actively participate in learning activities and connect with others, which will lead you to the creation of your online course.

The new roadmap is deeply influenced by a synthesis of learning theory, research, and our and our colleagues' personal experiences in developing and facilitating online courses. To aid your application of these ideas, this workbook is designed to mirror an online course to the extent possible. We model what we ask you to do as you prepare and create your course. In addition, we include examples of others' work from various disciplines.

In this workbook, you will find both the familiar and the new. We ask you to be curious and to keep an open mind as you explore this new information. We encourage you to reach out to others and share your thoughts about what you are learning. By connecting with others, you will reinforce the interactive aspect of learning and build a community as you create your course. Going on a journey always involves some degree of flexibility and change in the way we think and feel, and in the actions we take. It also engenders a sense of anticipation and excitement. We wish you a positive learning experience and a productive journey.

Enjoy the journey with us,

Catherine R. Barber, Janet K. McCollum, and Wendy L. Maboudian

Your Guides

Your guides: (l–r) Wendy L. Maboudian, Catherine R. Barber, Janet K. McCollum.
Photo by Darnell Miller, courtesy of University of St. Thomas.

We are a team of experienced instructors and designers who have a passion for and extensive experience in creating and teaching meaningful online courses. We have consulted, presented, and published on teaching and learning in higher education. Our online courses have been nationally recognized for their exemplary features. We provide online learning consulting to faculty and organizations that work with adult learners.

Catherine R. Barber, Ph.D., is a psychologist and associate professor in the School of Education and Human Services at the University of St. Thomas, where she has been recognized with faculty awards for teaching and research. She also serves as the chair of an online education taskforce at the University of St. Thomas. Catherine has published in the fields of both psychology and education. She is the recipient of a Blackboard Exemplary Course Award and a Blackboard Catalyst Award for Teaching and Learning.

Janet K. McCollum, Ed.D., is the director of QEP and Core Assessment at the University of St. Thomas and serves on the online education taskforce. Previously, she was director of research and assistant professor in the School of Education and Human Services. Janet has created and taught online courses in business and education and has held numerous training and development leadership positions in a variety of organizations. She has presented and published in the areas of organization behavior and education. Janet is the recipient of a Blackboard Exemplary Course Award and a Blackboard Catalyst Award for Teaching and Learning.

Wendy L. Maboudian, Ed.D., is an instructional designer in education and industry. She currently designs faculty instruction for the Houston Independent School District. She has worked with faculty at Houston Community College to help them design academic and workforce online courses, including model courses for use throughout the college system. Wendy has taught instructional design at the University of Houston and has presented her methods of online design at meetings and conferences. Her passion is the use of visual representation, scenarios, and characters in online course creation to enhance learning.

Exploring the Terrain:
Justification for Online Learning

It's in the numbers. The need for quality online courses is growing. In the United States, 31.7 percent (6,294,801) of postsecondary students enrolled in degree-granting institutions took at least one distance education course in 2016, the most recent year for which data are available. Overall, 16.7 percent (3,322,186) took at least one distance education course in conjunction with traditional classroom courses, and 15 percent (2,972,186) took only distance education courses (US Department of Education, National Center for Educational Statistics, 2018). In light of these numbers, the importance of creating high-quality online courses becomes clear from both an ethical and an educational point of view.

No difference between learning online and in classroom settings. In their literature review, Shelley, Swartz, and Cole (2007) cited multiple studies that generally found no significant differences between online and traditional classroom settings regarding student satisfaction and learning. In addition, the specific findings of Shelley et al.'s (2007) study comparing traditional and online business law classes mirrored the findings of other studies they reviewed. However, given the increasing demand for online courses and the rapidly changing online environment, continued research is warranted.

Delivery formats and learning outcomes. Another consideration that seems to be relevant to the creation and delivery of online courses is whether similar learning outcomes can be used across delivery formats: traditional classroom, a hybrid mix of classroom and online, and online only. In an attempt to shed light on this question, Drew (2014) undertook a case study of an international business course that was offered in Australia and at two international locations, Singapore and Hong Kong. Drew found that although the same student learning outcomes can apply across delivery formats, other areas may need to be modified to accommodate specific course delivery formats.

WORKBOOK OVERVIEW

This workbook is divided into three major parts that reflect our Change-adept Course Creation Process: prepare, create, and revise. This process is flexible, iterative, and non-linear.

To aid your understanding of key concepts and processes, we share helpful hints, stories, and examples along the way. We provide you with relevant learning activities to help you create your online course. In addition, we have included resources to support your understanding of the adult learning and course creation processes.

These resources include in-depth, evidence-based information and/or surprising tidbits that can be found in *Exploring the Terrain*. We share our reflections that illustrate lessons we learned in the process of writing this workbook in *Notes from Our Journey*. We include *Travel Advisories* to draw your attention to reminders, cautions, or important information.

In addition, you will be asked to jot down in *Your Travel Journal* your self-reflections about what you have learned, surprises you have encountered, and any thoughts and feelings you have about your journey. To foster deeper learning, you will be prompted to *Call a Colleague* to engage in a dialogue about your online course creation process.

Workbook Chapter Preview

The **Prepare** section includes Chapters 2–5. As the section name suggests, these chapters focus on preparing you to undertake the work of creating an online course.

In *Chapter 2: Prepare Yourself*, you will prepare yourself for your journey by exploring self-reflective practice and the role of mindfulness. Self-reflection and mindfulness are important skills that are integral to learning. You are given the opportunity to engage in self-reflection throughout the workbook. In this chapter, you will also consider the impact of instructor presence on your adult learners.

In *Chapter 3: Adult Learning Principles*, we explain that all postsecondary learners are adult learners. You will explore our view of adult learning that includes cognitive, social, and emotional aspects. These three aspects are then woven into our adult learning process. A discussion of adult learning assumptions follows, with suggestions on how to apply those assumptions in your online course. We also introduce the application of semiotics for inclusion of diverse learners. We conclude the chapter by highlighting the importance of resources and the impact of power on your learners, and addressing the validity of some commonly held beliefs about learning.

In *Chapter 4: Course Destination*, you will choose the course you will work on. You will identify the contexts of your adult learners and decide how these contexts will influence your course creation. You will also choose topics and skill areas for your course as well as a course destination and possible theme to unify your course.

In *Chapter 5: Course Map*, you will draw a course map that provides you with an overview of your course topics and helps you more easily identify missing topics, irrelevant topics, and important connections that are not easily visible in an outline. You will group topics together based on the connections you have identified and finalize your course theme.

The **Create** section includes Chapters 6–11. As the section name suggests, these chapters focus on creating the elements of your online course. By the end of this section, you will have a complete online course that is ready for your online learners.

In *Chapter 6: Milestones*, you will choose summative milestones, which provide tangible evidence of learners' knowledge of the topics and acquisition of skills at the end of a learning activity.

In *Chapter 7: Learning Activities*, you will begin creating a learning activity, which is the vehicle through which course topics are learned, skills are strengthened, and milestones are achieved, leading learners to the course destination. Learning activities involve self-reflection, dialogue, and application within the context of a realistic, relevant, and meaningful experience. In this chapter, you will explore experiential and collaborative strategies for developing learning activities.

In *Chapter 8: Resources*, you will select resources for your learning activity. Resources are sources of information that support learning. You will apply adult learning principles to the resources you select.

In *Chapter 9: Feedback*, you will choose the focus and timing of your formative and summative feedback. You will determine how peer feedback will be incorporated into your course and how learners will use the feedback. You will create or revise a feedback tool to use in your learning activity, which you will finalize in this chapter.

In *Chapter 10: Course Structure*, you will create an itinerary for your course and create additional learning activities to ensure a full but manageable itinerary. You will create a learner feedback survey for gauging learners' responses to the course. In this chapter, you will also create a layout for your course modules.

In *Chapter 11: Course Start Here*, you will create the Start Here for your course by choosing welcome and engagement strategies as well as orientation strategies. You will end the chapter by uploading all of your course items to your learning management system (LMS).

The **Revise** section includes Chapter 12. This section focuses on a critical but often overlooked part of the course creation process: revising your course based on the feedback you receive.

In *Chapter 12: Course Evaluation and Revision Plan*, you will review each module you have created, as well as your course as a whole. You will consider circumstances that may require you to revise your course during the semester, when learners are actively taking the course. You will then develop a plan for evaluating your course, drawing on various sources of feedback data.

As you can tell from the description of the chapters, you will have created an online course that is ready to upload into your LMS. Your institution's LMS support team will assist you in the process of uploading the course and making the course available to your learners.

Travel Advisory:
What's Not Included in this Workbook

Notice that the focus of this workbook is on *creating* your online course, *not* putting the course in the LMS. While we realize that putting your course in the LMS is the critical last step in the process, we do not provide specific technical information and instructions on this step because of the variety of LMSs. Each LMS has its own features, structure, and behind-the-scenes technical details that constantly change. No two LMSs are alike. In addition, many institutions have policies that dictate certain common features for all online courses. Early in the process, find out what policies your institution has for these required features so you can include them as you create your course.

WORKBOOK ORIENTATION

We have stated that this workbook is different. But how? Let's review the title, *The New Roadmap for Creating Online Courses: An Interactive Workbook*, for some hints on how it is different. "New Roadmap" sets the expectation of something new. What's new? "Creating Online Courses" indicates that one difference is the use of the term "create" rather than the traditional "design." What's that all about? Then we see the word "Interactive" paired with "workbook." How can a print-based workbook be interactive? Now, hopefully, you are intrigued. As you experience this workbook, you will discover the answers to these questions.

You will see words throughout the workbook that reinforce our theme of a journey. These carefully chosen words also serve as a reminder that this workbook presents a "new road-map" to course creation. The use of *workbook destination* and *milestones* illustrates this point.

Workbook Features: Destination, Milestones, and Skill Areas

The *workbook destination* is the overarching goal of the workbook: your creation of an online course. Everything that you do in this workbook leads to this destination.

Milestones are tangible products that you create as a result of accomplishing the learning activities. Milestones indicate your progress toward the workbook destination. There are five milestones in this workbook:

- Course Map (Chapter 5)
- Learning Activity (Chapter 9)
- Online Course (Chapter 11)
- Course Evaluation and Revision Plan (Chapter 12)
- End-of-Journey Self-Reflection (Epilogue)

To accomplish the milestones, you will gain practice in four skill areas that are not topic- or discipline-specific. These skill areas enhance and support your growth and development as an instructor:

- self-reflective practice
- dialogue and collaboration
- use of the Change-adept Course Creation Process (prepare, create, and revise)
- incorporation of adult learning principles into your course.

Other Workbook Features

Table 1.1 shows the main features you will encounter during your journey through this workbook. Taken individually, you may find some of these features in other books. However, we believe that the way we have integrated these features creates a unique workbook.

Table 1.1 Workbook features and descriptions

Features	Descriptions
Customizable workbook	By jotting down your reflections on your experiences, ideas, and summaries of your dialogues with colleagues, you will create your own personal narrative of your journey through the Change-adept Course Creation Process, noting changes and learning along the way.
Change-adept Course Creation Process	The course creation process that guides this workbook includes three parts: prepare, create, and revise; is non-linear, iterative, and flexible; and incorporates the adult learning principles.
Grounded in theory, research, and experience	The workbook applies theory, research, and our and others' experiences to inform the Change-adept Course Creation Process.
Focus on adult learners	The workbook focuses exclusively on creating courses for adult learners.
Adult learning principles	Adult learning principles include our view of learning: cognitive, social, and emotional; the reflective, dialogic learning process that leads to shared understanding; adult learning assumptions; and semiotics for inclusion of diverse learners.
Mirrors an online course to the extent possible	The workbook structure, destination, theme, milestones, and learning activities are similar to those found in an online course.
One coherent, concrete example used throughout	One example throughout the workbook provides a coherent way to follow the thought process and actions involved in course creation.
Examples of course elements from various disciplines	Examples from a variety of disciplines demonstrate the potential and broad applicability of the Change-adept Course Creation Process.

Table 1.1   (*cont.*)

Features	Descriptions
Semiotics	We recognize the multiple meanings of words, images, and other symbolic aspects, and how those meanings affect learners' experiences. Application of semiotics is integral to creating a learning community in which diverse learners are appreciated and included.
Your Travel Journal (self-reflective practice)	The workbook supports the development of your mindful reflective practice. A space is provided for you to jot down your self-reflection on your ideas, concerns, feelings, and ah-ha moments. This feature models a self-reflective technique you can use with your learners to encourage them to develop their own reflective practice.
Call a Colleague (dialogue)	The workbook supports the process of learning through dialogue. A space is provided for you to jot down a summary of key points that you learn during your dialogues with colleagues about the course creation process.
Notes from Our Journey	We provide descriptions of our experiences creating and facilitating our own online courses and experiences from our journey as we created this workbook.
Exploring the Terrain	We share research-based information relevant to the course creation process. You may find some surprises along the way.
Travel Advisory	The workbook includes reminders, cautions, and other important information that may require your attention as you create your course.

We encourage you to identify these workbook features as you progress through the workbook and consider how they may inform your own course creation.

Terminology: Your Translation Guide

As you may have noticed in this chapter, sometimes we use different words to express familiar meanings (e.g., *destination* means the overarching course goal). Our rationale is twofold. First, using words that relate to a journey helps to unify the workbook and serves the additional purpose of reinforcing our theme of a journey – something special and out of the ordinary, but with a specific destination.

The second, and perhaps more important, reason is to promote your mindful reading of and engagement with the workbook. Changing words to fit the theme of a journey serves to remind you (the reader) and us (your guides) to pause and consider the intended meaning. This pause to consider the intended meaning is important because many of the ideas presented in this workbook may be new or, if familiar, incorporate new nuances in their meaning. Please note that our chosen words have been carefully considered, debated, and, ultimately, agreed upon as necessary to convey our intended meaning and to promote your mindful attention. Table 1.2 presents the terms and definitions used in this workbook.

Table 1.2 Workbook terms and definitions

Terms	Definitions
Actions	Elements of a learning activity: self-reflection, dialogue, application
Adult Learning – Our View	Cognitive, social, and emotional aspects, all of which are required for learning to occur
Adult Learning Principles	Our view of adult learning, including cognitive, social, and emotional aspects; the adult learning process; adult learning assumptions; and semiotics for inclusion of diverse learners
Adult Learning Process	Begins with a question or statement to a group of two or more learners, generating a dialogue that can lead to the emergence of shared understanding
Character	Visual representation of a fictional person or object that supports and/or guides learners throughout the course
Course Destination	Overarching course goal
Course Map	A mind map that shows the connections among the main topics of the course
Course Structure	The way the course is organized
Essential Information	Information that all learners are expected to learn
Feedback (formative and summative)	Information provided to learners about their progress (formative feedback) or final result (summative feedback)
Itinerary	Sequence and timing of learning activities that informs the course structure
Learning Activity	A combination of actions taken to learn course topics and practice skill areas, resulting in the accomplishment of milestone(s)
Milestones	Tangible results of a learning activity that represent learners' progress toward the course destination
Resources	Sources of information that support learning
Scenario	Realistic, relevant, and meaningful context for a learning activity, milestone, and/or entire course
Semiotics	Examination of important, differing interpretations of meaning
Skill Areas	Broad skills that cut across topics (e.g., critical thinking, teamwork, writing)

Table 1.2 *(cont.)*

Terms	Definitions
Theme	A unifying idea, meaningful metaphor, or storyline that engages learners and helps them see connections among the topics
Topics	Broad areas of information

Icons

You are probably already familiar with the use of emoticons when you send a text message to someone. Just as emoticons quickly convey information in a graphical form, icons serve the same function in a book or course: quick identification of repeated important information or features. Notice how we use icons throughout this workbook to convey meaning.

One other consideration about icons is that they can support your course theme, thereby providing continuity throughout your course. Once we identified our theme of a journey, we began to consider what icons would support the theme, organize information, and create visual interest. We designed our own icons to support our theme.

Table 1.3 presents an icon key for this workbook. As you review the icons and their meanings in the table, think about how the icons also support the theme of a journey.

Table 1.3   Icon key

Icons	Resources	Descriptions
	Exploring the Terrain	Research-based information relevant to the Change-adept Course Creation Process
	Notes from Our Journey	Our course creation experiences and experiences from our journey of creating the workbook
	Travel Advisory	Important information, such as reminders and cautionary notes
Icons	**Actions and Milestones**	**Descriptions**
	Your Travel Journal	Questions and space for self-reflection
	Call a Colleague	Questions and space for dialogue with a colleague
	Application	Actions you take to apply what you learn to creating your own course
	Milestone	A tangible product that demonstrates your learning

THE CHANGE-ADEPT COURSE CREATION PROCESS

The Change-adept Course Creation Process is central to this workbook. You will use this process throughout this workbook as you create your course. A visual depiction (Figure 1.1) and description of the process follows.

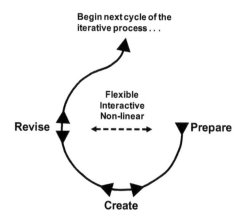

Figure 1.1 The Change-adept Course Creation Process © 2020.

First, we want to call your attention to the name of the process: "The Change-adept Course Creation Process." It is of the utmost importance that you understand the words in the name of this process. The term "change-adept" is made up of two words. The word "adept" means "skilled." Thus, we are interested in becoming "change-adept" or "skilled at changing" and to use that skill to create successful online courses.

"Course Creation" is the second part of the name of the process. We chose "course creation" rather than the traditional term "course design" because course creation holds the promise of possibilities, allowing new, creative ideas to emerge within the course, which leads to greater learning.

Last but not least, the word "process" indicates movement and change that occur naturally. This particular process has the additional characteristics of being iterative, non-linear, and flexible. Although the process follows the general pattern of prepare, create, and revise, it can just as easily move in different directions depending on what you discover from your self-reflection and dialogue with others.

Let's take a moment to consider the difference between the Change-adept Course Creation Process and a traditional instructional design model such as the ADDIE model (Branson et al., 1975; Schlegel, 1995).

 Exploring the Terrain:
ADDIE and the Change-adept Course Creation Process

ADDIE (Analysis, Design, Development, Implementation, and Evaluation) was originally developed for the US Army by the Center for Educational Technology at Florida State University in 1975 (Clark, 2015). As this model evolved over the years, its use spread beyond designing training for the military to designing training for businesses and large-scale academic programs (e.g., the Open University programs in the UK). At this point, ADDIE is one of the most widespread models of instructional design and is the foundation of various other instructional design models modified to address ADDIE's perceived weaknesses.

ADDIE is viewed as the professional standard for instructional design because it has been successful in ensuring

> good quality design, with clear objectives, carefully structured content, controlled workloads for faculty and students, integrated media, relevant student activities, and assessment strongly tied to desired learning outcomes ... [ADDIE] allows these design principles to be identified and implemented on a systematic and thorough basis. (Bates, 2019, "Benefits," para. 1)

If ADDIE is the professional standard for instructional design, why are we suggesting a change in the way we approach instructional design? We believe that ADDIE has served us well in the past, but we are now entering an era in which the learning landscape is complex, rapidly changing, and, at times, uncertain and ambiguous. In addition, our adult learners are more diverse and expect relevant experiences and choices in how they learn. This dynamic environment requires flexibility as we create online courses. Flexibility is not inherently part of ADDIE. This recognized weakness has led to modifications that include rapid prototyping, agile approaches, and other remedies.

Even though ADDIE has evolved over time, it is still influenced by its roots: designing large-scale projects that tend to be formal and mechanistic, including many moving parts and many people performing specialized functions to manage. Given this history and the current speed of change, we believe that ADDIE may no longer effectively address the course creation needs of postsecondary institutions.

We believe that the Change-adept Course Creation Process better fits your needs because it allows you to respond swiftly and flexibly when course changes are required.

THE ROLE OF SELF-REFLECTION IN THIS WORKBOOK

Reflection gives you time to stop and consider. Periodically, we will ask you to reflect on various aspects of what you have learned or actions you have taken. You can jot down your thoughts, ideas, and feelings in *Your Travel Journal*. Our rationale for asking you to jot down your reflections throughout the workbook is twofold:

- By noting your reflections throughout your journey, you will create a historical narrative of your thoughts and insights, and how they developed and changed over time. At the end of the workbook, after your course is created, we will suggest that you review your reflection notes to see if you can identify patterns that emerged and/or changed. By creating your own personal narrative of your reflections during your journey, you may discover ways to customize this process to help you create even more robust online courses.
- You are more likely to jot something down if it is easy to do and a natural part of the flow of engaging with the information in the workbook. This technique to encourage reflection can be adapted for use in your course.

Furthermore, we will provide questions to help guide your reflection. As you progress in your self-reflective practice, you may decide to create your own reflection questions that are more meaningful to you. Self-reflection is all about you exploring and learning about you!

Your Travel Journal:
A Reflection at the Beginning of Your Journey

In the space provided, jot down your reflections. As you go through the workbook, come back to this initial reflection to see what has changed as a result of your journey.

What is your initial reaction to what you have read?

What do you consider valuable, new, and/or significant?

What thoughts or concerns do you have about using the Change-adept Course Creation Process to create your online course?

Call a Colleague:
Your Colleague Contact List

Throughout this workbook, you will be prompted to *Call a Colleague*. We encourage you to engage with your colleagues because dialogue is a necessary part of the learning process. Take a moment to identify who you might call for a conversation about the following topics. Then jot down their names and contact information in the space provided.

Topic	Colleague(s) and contact information
Your learners – who they are and what they might need	
Resources – what colleagues use, why, what is available online	
Technical support – where you can go for help	
Course creation ideas – what might work in your course	
Other topics (e.g., media, resources)	

WORKBOOK ROADMAP

The workbook roadmap gives you a different view of the information in the workbook. The workbook roadmap (Figure 1.2) illustrates the connections among the topics covered in this workbook. This view provides a different perspective than the linear view provided by the table of contents.

Looking at Figure 1.2, you can see that the workbook destination is placed at the center of the map. The three main topics – prepare, create, and revise – are shown, along with the important information presented in each topic. The lines and arrows show the connections between the information within each topic and across topics. You will create a course map similar to the workbook roadmap.

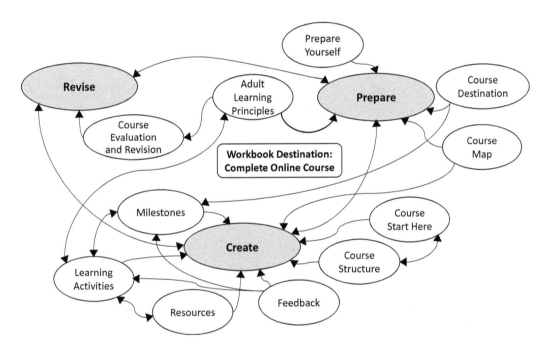

Figure 1.2 Workbook roadmap.

START HERE: SUMMARY

In this first chapter, you have experienced a version of *Start Here*, an introductory strategy that we use in our online courses to welcome and orient learners to the course. Recall that you have experienced the following introductory information and activities:

- a welcome letter
- an introduction to the authors (guides)
- a discussion of the justification for online courses
- an overview of the workbook
- an orientation to the workbook that included workbook destination (overarching goal), skill areas, milestones, and other features
- the new approach to course creation (the Change-adept Course Creation Process)

- an orientation to the workbook including terminology, icons and their meanings, and the workbook roadmap illustrating the topics and their connections
- a *Travel Journal* self-reflection and *Call a Colleague* preparation for engaging with colleagues.

As you can tell from the list of information and activities above, the overall purpose of *Start Here* is to welcome you, set expectations, provide a general orientation to the workbook, and provide a clear view of the journey ahead and your destination.

You are now ready to begin *Chapter 2: Prepare Yourself!*

PREPARE

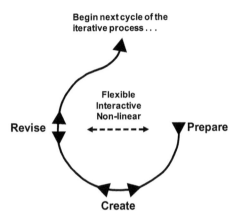

Change-adept Course Creation Process. © 2020

The *Prepare* section focuses on the preparation you will undertake as you begin the journey of creating your online course. As you proceed through the five chapters in this section, you will accomplish the following:

- Chapter 2: Prepare Yourself: Learn about and use mindful reflective practice.
- Chapter 3: Adult Learning Principles: Explore adult learning principles that underlie this workbook.
- Chapter 4: Course Destination: Choose your course, identify your adult learners' contexts and how their contexts impact your course decisions, describe the course destination (overarching goal), and identify a possible course theme.
- Chapter 5: Course Map: Create a course map that shows the connections among the topics (broad areas of knowledge) in your course and cluster connected topics in light of your theme.

You have experienced reflection opportunities in *Start Here*, which you will continue throughout the workbook in *Your Travel Journal*. In addition, you will use your *Start Here* preparation to *Call a Colleague* as you engage in dialogue with others. Two additional features that will also be present throughout the workbook are *Exploring the Terrain* and *Notes from Our Journey*. *Exploring the Terrain* provides you with additional evidence-based information for your consideration, and *Notes from Our Journey* contains relevant stories that illustrate lessons we learned in the process of writing this workbook and reinforces key points in the chapters. In this section, you will also begin to apply what you are learning through *Applications*.

By the end of the *Prepare* section, you will have prepared the journey learners will take through your course. As you develop your knowledge and skills for creating online courses and as you dialogue with others, your perspective may change; therefore, flexibility in your approach is also important. Give yourself permission to make changes. Actively seek opportunities to apply what you are learning. By applying your foundational knowledge, you will create a course that fosters your learners' success.

2   Prepare Yourself!

PREPARE YOURSELF: INTRODUCTION

This chapter is all about you! It may seem odd that the first thing we ask you to do as you begin your journey to create an online course is to prepare yourself. However, preparing yourself first makes sense because your values, beliefs, culture, and background all inform your view of learning and how you approach your learners, your course topics, and online learning. By being who you are, you shape your learners and their experience, *especially* in an online course. Therefore, we begin with *Prepare Yourself!*

> **Travel Advisory:**
> **The Use of "You"**
>
> Throughout this workbook, "you" refers to anyone who works on creating a course: an instructor, an instructional designer, or a group of instructors and/or instructional designers.

In this chapter, we invite you to develop a deeper awareness of your own approach to learning and your beliefs about your learners. At the same time, we offer you an opportunity to engage with new or different perspectives on learning and learners through mindful self-reflection. We hope you take advantage of this opportunity to reflect on and try new or different ideas, even though you may find them a bit outside your comfort zone. To complete your learning process, we encourage you to talk with others about your experiences as you create your course.

REFLECTIVE PRACTICE

You have already experienced reflective practice in *Chapter 1: Start Here* in *Your Travel Journal* as you reflected on the beginning of your journey – initial reaction, valuable or significant information, and other thoughts and concerns. By continuing to reflect on the ideas presented in this workbook and what you are learning, you are taking the time to clarify your thoughts and ideas, realize your biases and assumptions, identify your emotional responses to relationships and events, and ascertain the potential implications of your actions.

In addition, based on our experience and the experiences of our colleagues, we believe that mindfulness and reflection are an integral part of learning and a necessary first step in preparing yourself for the journey of creating your online course. By considering the ideas presented in this workbook and conversing with others, you will be able to mindfully reflect upon and integrate these ideas into your own view of learning and the learning process. Without mindfulness, learning becomes rote.

You may have noticed in the previous paragraph that we added the word "mindfully" to the idea of reflection. If you noticed the insertion of this word, kudos to you! You were mindfully reading the paragraph.

Mindlessness and Mindfulness

Langer (1989, 1997, 2000) and her colleagues have researched the phenomena of mindlessness and mindfulness. Based on this work, we will discuss and juxtapose these two phenomena, their impact on our behavior, and implications for learning.

Mindlessness

The scenarios below depict different types of mindless behavior all of us have most likely engaged in at one time or another. As you read the scenarios, think about times when you or someone you know engaged in mindless behavior. Consider the outcome of mindlessness in teaching and learning.

Have you ever intended to go to the grocery store, and instead started in the direction of work before catching yourself? This example of mindlessness illustrates how repetition can lead to ineffective but automatic behavior. How might you create learning activities that avoid learners' development of ineffective but automatic behavior?

Have you ever watched a webinar and at the end wondered what was presented? Zoning out in this way illustrates "not there" mindlessness. How might you create a video lecture that avoids learners zoning out?

Have you ever tried to solve the puzzle in which you must create a star by connecting dots within a box on a piece of paper and found you were unable to do so? When you were shown the solution, it was clear that by crossing the boundary of the box when drawing one of the lines, the star was easily created. The instructions never said that you must stay within the lines of the box, so why did you think you must? Following rules or routines that limit our options is another example of mindlessness. How might you guide your learners to look beyond perceived boundaries?

Have you ever made a pasta dish that calls for a certain type of pasta, and as you were in the process of making the dish, you realized you didn't have the "right" pasta in the pantry? So, you rushed to the store without considering that you had another type of pasta that was a perfectly acceptable substitute. In this situation, mindlessness occurs because you focused on rigidly following the recipe (rules) without exploring alternative solutions. How might you set up instructions that give learners permission to consider alternatives/possibilities?

If you have experienced situations similar to these, then you have experienced mindlessness, commonly known as "being on autopilot." Learning also suffers from mindlessness when it becomes rote learning. Rote learning occurs when the information is presented as a rigid set of rules to follow or absolutes to memorize. One common technique used to foster this type of learning is drill and practice in the absence of application. Purely rote learning predisposes the learner to follow the rules automatically regardless of the circumstances. Focusing on rules and absolutes makes it difficult for learners to consider alternative actions or different perspectives as situations change. And as we all know, in today's world, change is constant!

Mindfulness

In contrast, mindful learning encourages learners to consider alternative actions or different perspectives as situations change. *Mindfulness* is the "rich awareness of discriminatory detail" (Langer, 1997, p. 23). Langer (1997) further characterizes mindfulness as "openness to novelty and actively noticing differences, contexts, and perspectives ... [that] make[s] us receptive to changes in an ongoing situation ... and guide[s] our behavior in the present" (p. 23). In other words, mindful learning is about being involved in the present situation by actively noticing what is familiar, new, or different. Mindful learning enables us to be able to take advantage of opportunities and avoid potentially dangerous situations.

As an example of the importance of mindfulness and learning, Langer (1997) conducted a study with her colleagues that compared the exam results of two randomly assigned groups of students. One group read a chapter that was written using rule-based and absolute, factual statements (e.g., is, must) about the topic. The second group read the same chapter, but it was written to encourage mindfulness of the topic by using conditional statements (e.g., may, probably, in most cases).

The two groups of students were given a two-part test: One part of the test included multiple-choice items covering the factual material; the second part of the test went beyond facts and asked students to list multiple options or ways to approach the issue. Both groups performed similarly on the factual multiple-choice section. For the second part of the test, the students who read the conditionally written (mindful) chapter listed more options and thus performed better than the students who read the chapter written as rules and absolute factual statements. Note that words and how they are interpreted are part of semiotics, which will be addressed throughout the workbook. When students in both groups were asked how well they liked the material they read, the students who read the conditionally written chapter liked the material better than the group who read the chapter that was written using absolute statements. Consider what the findings from this study might mean for the way you choose resources and develop learning activities.

In this workbook, when we ask you to apply what you learned or when we present information using conditional statements (e.g., may, could, in some cases) rather than using absolute statements (e.g., is, must), we are encouraging you to participate in mindful learning. When you are mindfully involved, you are able to take advantage of opportunities and become more open to possibilities. This approach holds true for your learners as well.

Mindful Self-Reflection

Mindfulness is part of reflection (Mezirow, 1991) and leads you to a deeper level of learning. Through mindful self-reflection, you become more open to new information and more willing to consider other perspectives, build consensus, and be more self-aware (Kuechler & Stedham, 2018). Of particular importance is the development of your ability to mindfully observe situations and integrate those external observations with your internal experiences (thoughts and emotions). As you become more adept at including these elements as part of your reflection, your perceptions become more accurate, and you experience greater flexibility in responding to the world around you.

In addition, Mezirow (1991) saw reflective learning as transformative and, therefore, critical to learning. We agree with Mezirow's assessment of the importance of self-reflective learning and propose an approach to reflection that is based primarily on the works of Mezirow (1991) and Stacey (2001), although many others have contributed to the field (e.g., Argyris, Putnam, & Smith, 1985; Langer, 1997; Kolb, 1984; Schon, 1983).

Self-reflection focuses on past experiences and is an intentional attempt to understand what has happened; therefore, it is retrospective. Included as part of the self-reflection are the cognitive, social, and emotional responses tied to an experience. By exploring these three aspects through self-reflection, you can better understand what you learn and how you learn from the experience, and how you might change your approach to be more effective. Self-reflection on the ways in which your assumptions, biases, and personal history influence your interpretation of an experience encourages deeper learning.

Therefore, *self-reflection* is a retrospective, internal conversation with yourself that helps you assess, interpret, and/or create meaning. You may find self-reflection useful in several ways:

- clarifying your thoughts and ideas
- examining the accuracy of your knowledge
- reviewing the effectiveness of your approach to knowledge acquisition, to an issue, or to relationships
- examining your biases and assumptions and their impact on you and others
- identifying your emotional responses to relationships, information, and situations
- identifying alternative perspectives/actions and determine possible implications.

Your Travel Journal:
Mindfulness and Reflective Practice

Consider what you have learned about reflective practice and mindfulness. Jot down your thoughts and feelings in the space provided.

What are some actions you might take as you create your course to reduce your learners' mindlessness and support mindful learning?

What is your response to the practice of self-reflection for yourself? How might your response influence your use of reflection in your course?

What was your reaction to the assertion that rote learning decreases learners' ability to be more open to alternative perspectives and explanations?

Think back to a specific example where we used conditional statements rather than absolutes in this section and asked you to apply what you read. How did this approach change your willingness to consider or try something new?

Travel Advisory:
Self-Reflection and Questions

To engage in self-reflection, we must be mindful of the questions we ask, since questions are the framework that shapes our reflection.

Just as we have provided you with reflective questions to guide your self-reflective practice, you may want to provide your students with guiding questions for cognitive, social, and emotional self-reflection. As your learners become more adept at self-reflection, you may want to ask broader questions and over time allow your learners to develop their own questions. Here are examples of questions you might ask:

- What is your process for learning information, and how well is that process working for you? (cognitive)
- What might you do differently, making your learning process more effective? (cognitive)
- How do you feel about this information, and why? (emotional)
- How might you engage with a peer from this class to support your learning? (social)

Three Aspects of Self-Reflection: Cognitive, Social, and Emotional

Self-reflection includes cognitive, social, and emotional aspects. While a separate description of each aspect follows, each aspect's complementary characteristics occur together and influence each other.

- Cognitive reflection focuses on information and process – that is, reflecting on what knowledge has been acquired, the accuracy of the knowledge acquired, and the efficacy of the approach to knowledge acquisition (strategies and procedures).
- Social reflection considers societal contexts (e.g., culture, values, assumptions and biases, historical background, recent experience), social interaction with others (e.g., relationships, collaboration), and how these social elements influence our responses to situations and/or learning.
- Emotional reflection identifies feelings about the cognitive and social aspects of a learning experience, explores whether certain feelings help or hinder learning or relationships, and considers ways to address the potential influence of those feelings about an experience.

Through self-reflection that integrates all three aspects, you become more aware, develop greater understanding, and can change learning processes/strategies to be more effective when needed. This ability to respond to changing situations prepares you for lifelong learning success (Carroll, 2017).

The same is true for your learners. As you prepare and create your course, consider how you can offer your learners opportunities to self-reflect on how to develop/strengthen their cognitive, social, and emotional involvement in and responses to learning. From our perspective, cognitive, social, and emotional aspects of self-reflection are tightly connected; therefore, as you reflect on one aspect, your perceptions of the other aspects may change.

Exploring the Terrain:
Metacognition and Learning

Metacognition is defined in many ways (Schoenfield, 2016/1992). Metacognition can be defined as "knowledge and understanding of your own thinking" (*Cambridge Dictionary*), or more simply put, "thinking about thinking." Martinez (2006) suggests that the role of metacognition is "the monitoring and control of thought" (p. 696); therefore, people with more complex metacognitive skills demonstrate "abilities to predict their performances on various tasks . . . and to monitor their current levels of mastery and understanding" (National Research Council [NRC], 2000, p. 12). These views of metacognition assume that one is aware of her/his own metacognition, but this awareness does not always exist. As Girash (2014) pointed out, "metacognitive knowledge [metacognition] is not the equivalent to metacognitive awareness" (p. 155).

Metacognitive awareness. Metacognitive awareness arises from "the process of reflecting upon which learning concepts one has already mastered, what still needs to be learned, and how best to approach the task of learning" (Ehrlinger & Shain, 2014, p. 142). In other words, metacognitive awareness occurs as learners reflect on the following:

• how well they understand course material
• how well they have mastered the concepts or tasks
• the effectiveness of their approach to learning
• their willingness to change their approach to learning, if necessary, to be more successful.

Herein lies the challenge for you and your learners: Researchers found that college-aged learners lack metacognitive awareness (Girash, 2014; Schoenfield, 2016/1992).

But don't despair; Schoenfield (2016/1992) studied how students developed their ability to accurately engage in metacognition in college math classes. He created guided metacognitive reflection questions (e.g., "What [exactly] are you doing?" "Why are you doing it?" "How does it help you?" [p. 24]) and gave specific feedback to the students on their answers. Schoenfield (2016/1992) found that students who engaged in guided metacognitive reflection exhibited higher performance than those who did not. Girash (2014) reported similar findings in subsequent studies.

While the necessity of developing metacognitive awareness of learners is of critical importance, missing from these studies were reflection questions that included the social and emotional aspects of learning. While the importance of the social and emotional aspects of learning are acknowledged in the metacognitive literature (e.g., Girash, 2014; Schoenfield, 2016/1992), the narrow focus of metacognition on cognitive aspects of learning remains.

 Travel Advisory:
Terminology – Cognition and Metacognition

From our perspective, metacognition and metacognitive awareness are part of the cognitive aspect of self-reflection, which includes reflecting on your knowledge of the topics and awareness of your thinking process. In the interest of simplicity, throughout this workbook we will use *cognitive* to refer to cognitive knowledge, metacognition, and metacognitive awareness.

INSTRUCTOR PRESENCE IN AN ONLINE COURSE

As you consider your self-reflective practice, one important area to consider is your presence in your online course. Your presence is felt by your learners as you:

- establish information, learning activities, and timelines
- guide your learners
- facilitate productive dialogue
- offer support and mentor learners
- establish clear standards of behavior (including netiquette)
- create an inclusive, diverse learning environment.

(See Garrison, Cleveland-Innes, & Fung, 2010; Shea, Li, & Pickett, 2006; Shedroff, 2001.)

Part of your presence in the course includes the influence of your point of view. Shedroff (2001) emphasized the importance of the implied point of view that you, as the instructor, embed throughout your course. This implied point of view is informed by your context and affects how the learners experience the course. This point of view also impacts the way you support and mentor your learners.

Consider your response to the idea of a growth mindset for your learners and for yourself. As you read about growth mindsets, think about how your mindset might impact the success of your learners and how you might influence the mindsets of your learners.

 Exploring the Terrain:
Growth Mindset

Recent research examined the impact of faculty and learner mindsets on learner achievement and motivation. Findings suggested that learners who have a "growth mindset," a belief that intelligence can be developed, demonstrated higher achievement than those learners with a "fixed mindset," a belief that intelligence is unchangeable (Claro, Paunesku, & Dweck, 2016).

In addition, research has indicated that faculty mindset has an influence on student success. In a longitudinal study of STEM faculty, researchers found that faculty with fixed mindsets had student racial achievement gaps that were twice as large as growth-minded faculty (Canning, Muenks, Green, & Murphy, 2019). In addition, students reported that fixed-minded faculty were more likely to be demotivating and less likely to "emphasize learning and development" than growth-minded faculty. It should be noted that fixed mindset is not related to the faculty members' background (e.g., race/ethnicity, age, tenure, experience, or gender).

In this workbook, we take a growth mindset approach to learning. Engaging with the ideas and practices in this workbook can encourage the development of "learning environments where all students ... feel that they are valued and encouraged to reach their full potential" (Canning et al., 2019, p. 5).

A good starting point, as you prepare to create your course, is to reflect on your mindset about learners and their ability to grow and be successful in your course.

Your Travel Journal:
Self-Reflection

We invite you to take a few minutes to mindfully reflect on what you have just learned about your reflective practice and how it relates to and is influenced by your thoughts, feelings, and interactions with others. We also invite you to reflect on your presence in an online course and the influence that presence, including your mindset, has on learner success. Jot down your thoughts and feelings in the space provided.

Describe a specific time when you engaged in self-reflection. What was the outcome of that reflection?

What feelings did you have about participating in that reflection? If those feelings hindered your reflection, what changes could you have made to enhance your reflective experience? If those feelings enhanced your reflection, how can you continue engaging those feelings in your reflective practice?

What influences from your background helped or hindered your willingness to reflect? How might you use your knowledge of those influences to enhance your reflective experience?

Review the self-reflection questions above and identify how the cognitive, social, and emotional aspects were embedded in them. What additional questions would you ask? Which of the three aspects are most often included in your reflective questions?

What is mindful reflective practice? How does self-reflection help you prepare to create an online course?

List some ways you can create a strong positive instructor presence to convey a growth mindset to your learners.

PREPARE YOURSELF: SUMMARY

Self-reflection is something we can learn with appropriate guidance (McNiff & Whitehead, 2002). Mindfulness is a necessary part of reflection, and through mindful reflection we are more open to novelty, actively notice differences and changes in our environment and situations, and respond to others' perspectives. Mindful questioning is an essential part of self-reflection. Consider the meaning of this quotation from Langer (1997):

> *How can we know if we do not ask? Why should we ask if we are certain we know? All answers come out of the question. If we pay attention to our questions, we increase the power of mindful learning. (p. 139)*

You are now ready to learn about the foundational role of adult learning principles in creating your online course in *Chapter 3: Adult Learning Principles.*

3   Adult Learning Principles

ADULT LEARNING PRINCIPLES: INTRODUCTION

We begin this chapter by establishing the rationale for our premise that all postsecondary learners are adults. We then introduce key thought leaders on learning as well as discuss adult learning in light of recent brain research. This information provides you with a deeper understanding of how learning has been and is viewed – from Dewey's seminal works, to the application of complexity concepts, to exploring recent research on the brain and learning.

We culminate this discussion by presenting our view of learning and summarizing the key concepts that inform our view. We expand on our view of learning by including a discussion of the adult learning process that supports our view. We also introduce the adult learning assumptions and provide ideas on how to apply those assumptions in your course. In addition, we discuss the application of semiotics for inclusion of diverse adult learners.

 Travel Advisory:
Components of the Adult Learning Principles

Our view of learning, the learning process, adult learning assumptions, and semiotics for inclusion of diverse learners constitute the adult learning principles that underlie this workbook. Hereafter, these four components are referred to as *adult learning principles*.

In this chapter, we also address two critical topics that affect both your and your learners' experience: the importance of resources that support adult learning and the impact of power on adult learning. We include some potentially surprising findings on learning styles, non-verbal communication, and the learning pyramid that have become embedded in many educators' beliefs about learning. We end this chapter by addressing some common misunderstandings about the brain and learning.

When Adulthood Begins

Our focus on adult learning is important because adults differ significantly from children in their learning needs and approaches to learning (Knowles, Holton, & Swanson, 2005; Merriam &

Bierema, 2014; National Academies of Sciences, Engineering, and Medicine [NASEM], 2018). Because adult learning is our focus, we feel it is important to address the age of adulthood. Montessori (1948/1973) and Levinson (1986) provided us with an answer from the human development perspective. According to Montessori (1948/1973), the first stage of adulthood begins at age 18, while Levinson (1986) stated that the first stage of adulthood begins at age 17. Generally, by the age of 17 or 18, events occur in people's lives that indicate that they are entering adulthood. By this age, compulsory schooling has been completed and individuals generally embark on finding a job and working full-time, and/or enrolling in additional schooling (technical skills training or higher education) before pursuing full-time employment.

However, we acknowledge that the point at which adulthood begins may differ depending on the societal and cultural norms of a country. To encompass this diversity, Merriam and Brockett (2007) defined adult learners more broadly as "those whose age, social roles, or self-perceptions, define them as adults" (p. 8). For the purposes of this workbook, we will use the human development perspective that adulthood begins around the age of 17 or 18, while recognizing that there may be cultural differences.

Interestingly, we have heard many instructors in higher education refer to their adult learners as "kids." We use the term "adult learners" to remind ourselves and others that our postsecondary learners are indeed adults.

FOUNDATIONS OF OUR VIEW OF ADULT LEARNING

We begin discussing the foundations of our view of adult learning by considering key thought leaders in education and learning, including more recent research on the brain and learning. Then we illuminate the connections among the sometimes disparate and yet similar ideas.

Thought Leaders on Learning

Dewey's (1916) view of the relationship between mind and society forms the touchstone of our view of learning. As Dewey (1916, p. 314) stated,

> [e]very individual has grown up, and always must grow up, in a social medium. His responses grow intelligent, or gain meaning, simply because he lives and acts in a medium of accepted meanings and values. Through social intercourse, through sharing in the activities embodying beliefs, he gradually acquires a mind of his own. The conception of mind as a purely isolated possession of the self is at the very antipodes of the truth. The self achieves mind in the degree of which knowledge of things is incarnate in the life about him; the self is not a separate mind building up knowledge anew on its own account.

Similarly, Stacey (2001) described learning in organizations, which he referred to as "complex responsive processes." He included the use of complexity concepts as analogies to explain his ideas. Stacey proposed that the individual and social interactions were part of the same interactive pattern of relating: forming and being formed at the same time through communicative interaction between diverse people in local situations. He elaborated on the idea that within the interaction, there was no separation between the individual identity and the collective identity; neither was privileged over the other because they were both aspects of relating.

Stacey (2001) concluded that because the individual identity and collective identity were not separate, learning, and thus knowledge, was continuously constructed within the interactive process of communicating. In this way, the traditional view of knowledge as shared mental information that is stored in an individual's mind was challenged by Stacey's view of knowledge creation. Stacey's challenge has had a significant impact on how we approach learning in this workbook.

Interestingly, both Dewey's (1916) and Stacey's (2001) description of learning are supported by more recent findings linking neuroscience and educational research. Of particular interest is Immordino-Yang and Gotlieb's (2017) research-based biopsychosocial framework for affective processing. In the description of their framework, and relevant to our discussion, Immordino-Yang and Gotlieb stated: "As individuals interact with each other and work to mentally accommodate these interactions, they integrate their own actions and thoughts into the broader social context of others' actions and thoughts" (p. 362S).

Our view of learning has been informed by these and numerous other theories and concepts about learning, reflection, and complexity. Most notably, we have been influenced by the following:

- Dewey's (1916) examination of the relationship between mind and society (see the quote above) and his (Dewey, 1938) consideration of the role of experiences on learning, along with a warning that not all experiences are "equally educative" and, in fact, some can be "mis-educative."
- Mead's (1934/2015) description of the process of gesture and response in interactive communication that includes not only social but also cognitive and emotional aspects.
- Mezirow's (1991) elaboration of transformative learning as a social process and the role of reflection in learning.
- Gergen's (1994, 2009) and Gergen and Thatchenkery's (2004) views on social knowledge, social construction, language as action, generative theory, and the development of meaning through interdependent relationships.
- Weick's (1995) and Weick, Sutcliffe, and Obstfeld's (2005) description of the role of sensemaking in organizations (groups).
- Langer's (1997) discussion of mindfulness and learning.
- Stacey's (2001) description of knowledge creation in organizations from a complex responsive process perspective, and his description of learning as a transformative process that includes the social and emotional aspects.
- Knowles, Holton, and Swanson's (2005) discussion of the characteristics and needs of adult learners (androgogy).
- Immordino-Yang and Gotlieb's (2017) research on the interaction of the brain and social, emotional, and cultural influences on learning (previously discussed).
- NASEM's (2018) review of the research on the integration of the brain and learning that includes cognitive, social, and emotional aspects.

The perspectives offered by each of these authors have informed, challenged, and shaped our perspectives as we developed our view of learning.

Brain Research and Adult Learning

Based on recent research on the brain and learning, we know that learning involves the complex interplay of numerous brain structures:

> There is no learned skill that uses only one part of the brain ... Instead, the brain systems that support learning and academic skills are the same brain systems that are integral to personhood —that is, to social, cognitive, emotional, and cultural functioning ... Moreover, learners dynamically and actively construct their own brain's networks as they navigate the social, cognitive, and physical contexts. (NASEM, 2018, p. 59)

In addition, contrary to past beliefs, "the brain both shapes and is shaped by experience, including opportunities the individual has for cognitive development and social interaction" (NASEM, 2018, p. 59). In fact, evidence indicates that "individuals' brains are critically shaped by social relationships and that the information people learn through these relationships supports not only their knowledge about facts and procedures but also their emotions, motivations, and interests" (NASEM, 2018, p. 28; see also Immordino-Yang and Gotlieb, 2017).

We know that emotions are necessary for thought, as research has shown that "emotional processing steers behavior, thought, and learning [because] it is neurobiologically impossible to think deeply about or remember information about which one has had no emotion" (NASEM, 2018, p. 29). The brain doesn't waste energy remembering information that is not important to the individual. Importantly, Immordino-Yang and Gotlieb (2017) point out the social aspect of learning, stating that "individuals co-regulate and shape each other's psycho-biological selves through all kinds of interactions and relationships including those that constitute formal systems for education" (p. 360S).

So, what impact does all this information have on how you prepare and create your online course? Considering Stacey's (2001) view of knowledge creation, if online courses are created as a solitary learner experience, the learning process is incomplete. It is the instructor's responsibility to orchestrate learner dialogues within the course to foster learning. Research on the brain and learning (Immordino-Yang & Gotlieb, 2017; NASEM, 2018) and learning as an interactive process (Stacey, 2000, 2001; see also Mead, 1934/2015) points to the importance of engaging learners cognitively, socially, and emotionally within the course to encourage learning.

Notes from Our Journey:
How We Arrived at Our View of Adult Learning

The creation of our view of learning was a very chaotic process. We read, read more, read again; we gnashed our teeth during our conversations as our ideas fit together and then didn't; we agreed, disagreed, changed our ideas, went back to previous ideas; we explained, re-explained, became clear and then unclear; we questioned each other, came together, moved apart, had more conversations. Then we set "it" aside with a sigh of relief and a nagging doubt, and promised each other to return to it later.

And then one day, we came to the realization that if we were not able to articulate our view of learning, writing this workbook would be impossible (how obvious!). Soon after all that (dare we admit it?) avoidance, we decided to continue our conversation on our views of adult learning, identify similarities and differences, and explore alternative perspectives. At that point, we found that we could establish common ground, and we were able to reach consensus and articulate, hopefully clearly, "our view of adult learning."

What we learned as we reflected on our process of developing our view of learning was that our process was iterative and dialogic as we met and engaged in broad-ranging conversations about how each of us viewed learning. Our ongoing interaction shaped the changes in our individual perspectives and ultimately led us to a shared understanding. This learning process engaged our cognitive thoughts and emotional feelings through intense social engagement with each other and led to our formulation of our view of adult learning.

We hope you experience similar social interactions leading to shared understanding when you Call a Colleague. The more you engage with learning through social interactions, the more expert you will be in supporting your learners as they engage in the learning process in your online course.

OUR VIEW OF ADULT LEARNING

Our view of learning influences every aspect of this workbook. It guides how we think about learning, how we create online courses that encourage learning, how we craft learning activities, and how we approach the myriad other aspects of online courses. In other words, how we view learning provides the foundation for this workbook and the rationale for our new approach to creating online courses. As you read through the next section, think about where your view of learning and our view of learning coincide and differ, and why. You will be asked to reflect on these similarities and differences as well as the implications for creating your course.

Cognitive, Social, and Emotional Aspects of Learning

Learning involves cognitive and emotional change that occurs through social interaction. If any one of these elements is missing, learning does not occur (Immordino-Yang & Gotlieb, 2017; Mead, 1934/2015; NASEM, 2018; Stacey, 2000, 2001):

- Cognitive: Learners' thoughts about information, strategies, procedures, and/or effectiveness.
- Social: Learners' interdependent, interactive conversations/communications.
- Emotional: Learners' feelings (e.g., excitement, anxiety, frustration) and physical manifestations of emotions (e.g., tone of voice, muscle tension, facial responses) toward the interaction, another person, information, or a situation.

The learners' contexts also play an important role in our view of learning. Learning is shaped by each learner's personal history and culture (Dewey, 1938; Immordino-Yang & Gotlieb, 2017; NASEM, 2018; NRC, 2000; Schenck & Cruickshank, 2015; Stacey, 2000, 2001).

THE ADULT LEARNING PROCESS

The adult learning process is an act of social relating. Figure 3.1 illustrates the adult learning process. As a learner self-reflects on the course resources, actions, or experiences, question(s) may arise that prompt the learner to seek others' views or ideas. The catalyst for the learning process occurs when the learner publicly makes a statement or asks a question (gesture) that begins a dialogue with others. Before responding, the other person engages in *reflection-in-action*, which is a pause for private/internal monologue. During reflection-in-action, the emotional states of the other person and self are explored, a range of responses and language are practiced internally, and the possible effects of various responses on the other person are imagined – all of which is informed by the individual's history, culture, and other contextual factors. From this reflection-in-action, a response is chosen and made publicly (Mead, 1934/2015; Stacey, 2001; Weick, 1995).

The recipient(s) of the response follow(s) the same reflection-in-action process before responding. The ongoing pattern of reflection-in-action and response continues. Through this ongoing dialogue, diverse perspectives are offered and explored, generating learning as the participants begin to move toward *shared understanding* of the topic under consideration. This shared understanding continues to evolve as new information and new perspectives are introduced. Throughout this workbook, you are encouraged to engage in the learning process by *calling a colleague*.

The learner engages with resources by thinking about the information and self-reflecting on the meaning, based on the learner's past history, experience, and feeling toward the information.

Asking others a question about the information becomes a catalyst for a dialogue involving cognitive, social, and emotional aspects.

In the dialogue that ensues, everyone shares their perspectives, asks questions, and clarifies their understanding of the information. Passions arise, disagreements and misunderstandings are worked through, and slowly, shared understanding emerges.

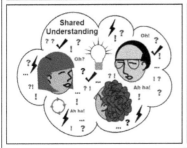

Shared understanding involving cognitive, social, and emotional aspects emerges in the dialogic space.

Figure 3.1 The adult learning process.

Travel Advisory:
Reflection-in-Action and Self-Reflection

Reflection-in-action differs from self-reflection in that reflection-in-action is an implicit part of the learning process, focuses on the immediate present, and happens quickly within a dialogic structure. It involves assessing the social and emotional impacts of potential actions that may be taken in the moment, choosing a response, and then responding publicly. After a response is chosen, the dialogue continues.

In contrast to reflection-in-action, *self-reflection* is retrospective, occurs outside of a dialogue, and explores what happened from the individual's perspective. It is an internal response to a course resource or previous experience; no feedback from others is elicited until the dialogue begins.

> **Notes from Our Journey:**
> **Calling Our Colleagues**
>
> As we delved deeper into our view of learning and the learning process, we realized that we needed to include other perspectives. It was at that point that we decided to talk with some of our colleagues within our own university and at another university. Not wanting to influence our colleagues, we asked them about their beliefs about learning and what they did to support their learners' learning. We were heartened that their comments on their view of learning and the learning process were similar to ours, but included a variety of different perspectives as well. That variety led to some interesting conversations about different perspectives on learning and encouraged us to look more closely at some of our assumptions.
>
> Each of our colleagues represented different disciplines, which also added richness to the conversation. How the learning process was applied in different disciplines – undergraduate mechanical engineering, undergraduate chemistry survey course, and an MBA capstone course – demonstrated the general applicability of our view of learning and the learning process, while reminding us of the need to include examples from multiple disciplines in the workbook and the importance of flexibility in our Change-adept Course Creation Process.
>
> When we discussed some of the challenges of working with our learners, we found that all of us faced similar challenges: how to encourage struggling students to come to us before it was too late, the issue of the imposter syndrome (I'm not good enough; I shouldn't be here), and the challenge of getting students to read/use our feedback to improve their work. A variety of solutions were discussed, some of which found their way into this workbook.
>
> In the end, we found *Call a Colleague* to be an incredibly valuable learning experience that was validating and, at the same time, cautionary (there is always another perspective to consider). Based on what we learned, we changed our approach to some of the topics. We hope our colleagues found the experience as valuable as we did.

Characteristics of the Adult Learning Process

Table 3.1 lists the characteristics of the adult learning process and the sources that informed each characteristic. Keep these characteristics of the adult learning process in mind as you prepare and create your course. They are particularly important to consider as you create your learning activities.

Table 3.1   Characteristics of the adult learning process and key sources

Characteristics	Key sources
The process is relational and interdependent in nature.	Gergen, 1994, 2009; Gergen & Thatchenkery, 2004; Mezirow, 1991; Stacey, 2000, 2001; Weick & Roberts, 1993
Verbal interaction occurs between two or more people in dialogue with each other.	Mead, 1934/2015
The process includes and is influenced by the dialogue, participants' past history, and culture.	Immordino-Yang & Gotlieb, 2017; Stacey, 2000, 2001; Weick, 1995

Table 3.1 *(cont.)*

Characteristics	Key sources
The continuous nature of dialogue and the emergence of shared understanding are iterative.	Coghlan and Brannick, 2014; Stacey, 2001
Even when shared understanding emerges, there may be different interpretations among the participants, leading to micro-diversity in the understanding of the meaning.	Stacey, 2000, 2001
Reflection-in-action is the private, internal self-dialogue that occurs before responding publicly.	Mead, 1934/2015; Stacey, 2000, 2001

Summary: Our View of Adult Learning and the Learning Process

Our view of learning incorporates three aspects: cognitive, social, and emotional. Without social interaction, learning does not occur; therefore, the learning process embodies social interaction that evokes the cognitive and emotional aspects of adult learning. The adult learning process is an act of social relating that begins when one person, based on previous self-reflection, publicly makes a statement or asks a question (gesture) in the context of a dialogue. The other person(s) engage(s) in reflection-in-action before responding. As the process of interacting continues, individuals share their perspectives. Learning occurs as the perspectives coalesce and shared understanding emerges.

 Your Travel Journal:
Our View of Adult Learning and the Learning Process

You have been presented with a lot of information, some of which may be new to you. Take a moment to consider what you have learned about our view of learning, and the learning process. Jot down your reflections to the questions in the space provided.

List the key points of our view of adult learning and the learning process and your thoughts and feelings about those points. Consider the following: What is your general feeling about our view of learning? The learning process that we described? How does our view of learning and the learning process fit with your views?

Based on what you have read, what do you think is useful and relevant based on your experience with learning and learners?

What are two or three ways you might incorporate these ideas on learning and the learning process into your course to meet the needs of your adult learners?

Call a Colleague:
Adult Learning and the Learning Process

Based on your self-reflection on what you have read in this section, call a colleague and compare your view and their view of adult learning and the learning process. Identify the similarities and differences between your own view and your colleague's view. Then compare those views with the view presented in the workbook. Share any surprises that arose during your dialogue. Explore any changes in your views as a result of your dialogue. Jot down the key points from your dialogue.

ADULT LEARNING ASSUMPTIONS AND PRACTICAL TECHNIQUES

We now switch from exploring the adult learning *process* (outlined in Table 3.1) to addressing adult learning *assumptions* by using practical techniques to meet adult learner needs (see Table 3.2). These *assumptions* are based on Knowles, Holton, and Swanson's (2005) work on *andragogy*, which is described as "the art and science of helping adults learn" (p. 61). These assumptions are generally true of adult learners; however, there are individual differences. Knowing your learners' contexts is important.

For additional resources on adult learning, see: Merriam and Bierema (2014); Merriam, Caffarella, and Baumgartner (2007), who focus on adult learning theories and practice; Mezirow (1991) on the transformative nature of reflection on adult learning; NASEM (2018) and O'Connor (2006) for general information on adult learning; Pratt (1988) on adult learning assumptions and conditions; Snyman and van den Berg (2018) on recognition of prior learning; and Taylor and Hamdy (2013) on adult learning models in medical education.

THE ROLE AND IMPORTANCE OF SEMIOTICS IN ADULT LEARNING

Adult learning assumptions indicate that adult learners want courses that are realistic, relevant, and meaningful. Semiotics facilitates meaning through the use of metaphors, stories, and images (Gannon-Cook & Ley, 2015). Semiotics may include text documents (written

Table 3.2 Adult learning assumptions and practical techniques

Adult learning assumptions	Practical techniques
Adults want to know why they need to learn something.	Provide a clear rationale for why information and learning activities are relevant.
Adults prefer to be more self-directed in their learning and responsible for their own decisions about their learning. They want control over some areas of their learning.	Provide clear milestones and instructions for learning activities and allow learners the flexibility to determine how to complete a learning activity and accomplish a milestone. For example, allow learners to choose topics that they deem relevant for papers or projects.
Adults benefit from collaboration.	Offer group and peer-to-peer learning activities that provide realistic, relevant, and meaningful practical application. Consider using collaboration techniques.
Adults prefer learning situations that include their life/work experiences as resources and build on those prior experiences.	Invite learners to share their experiences in discussions and projects. Consider using experiential learning techniques with realistic, relevant, and meaningful learning activities.
Adults are ready and motivated to learn new/more effective approaches as long as those approaches are relevant and applicable to specific, realistic life/work situations.	Offer group and peer-to-peer learning experiences that provide realistic and relevant opportunities for practical application that engage learners' past experiences and broaden their understanding. Encourage action and reflection.

words), pictures and icons (visual representations), verbal messaging (audio podcasts), and videos (words, audio, static visual representations, and active visual representations). The field of semiotics has broad implications, but for our purposes we focus on the use of semiotics for inclusion of diverse learners in online learning.

Semiotics examines the possibility of important, differing interpretations of meaning within a message; therefore, semiotics has a direct connection and impact on learning. Understanding and using semiotics will help you connect with your learners. Semiotics also helps your learners connect with each other and with the course information, thereby fostering inclusion of diverse learners.

Notes from Our Journey:
The Influence of Semiotics on Our Use of Informal Language

In this workbook, we use "you" and "we" to indicate a more informal, conversational way to address our readers and refer to ourselves as the authors. We felt that this approach better fit the focus of a workbook.

Some readers may find our informal approach to be friendly and engaging. We recognize that this informal approach may be interpreted as overly familiar by some readers who prefer a more formalized approach that refers to "the reader" and "the authors." In contrast to the informal approach, the interpretation of this more formal approach may seem respectful to some while seeming to be distancing and off-putting to others. Both views are valid and, most likely, based on differences in past experiences, professional training, and/or cultural background.

Our decision to use informal rather than formal language in this workbook is one instance of many where we considered the impact of diverse interpretations of meaning. Other semiotic considerations included our theme of a journey, the use of new terminology, the meaningfulness of the icons and illustrations, and our descriptions of new concepts. We asked others about our choices and changed our wording many times as we received feedback from others or thought more deeply about the best way to convey our meaning.

No doubt you will have similar challenges and decisions as you prepare and create an inclusive course for your diverse learners. Use *Call a Colleague* when you are unsure of a choice and need another opinion. Your goal is to be aware of potential differences that influence how your learners receive and respond to the messages you send through written words, images, audio, and video.

Semiotics, Diversity, and Inclusion

Diversity is the unique mix of individual characteristics (e.g., strengths, needs, interests, gender, age, ethnicity, culture, sexual orientation, social class, values, religion, national origin, and other aspects of diversity) that makes an individual an individual. Inclusion is the coming together of those diverse individuals in mutual respect, appreciation, belongingness, and sharing.

Establishing an inclusive course provides multiple ways for diverse learners (e.g., different backgrounds, strengths, needs, and interests) to engage in learning (Saunders & Kardia, 1997; Tobin & Behling, 2018). To create inclusive courses that serve the diverse needs of all our learners, we apply semiotics as part of the Change-adept Course Creation Process.

Diversity and inclusion apply to and benefit *all* learners. Sometimes the terms *diversity and inclusion* are read as *disabilities and accommodations*. While disabilities and accommodations are part of diversity and inclusion, diversity and inclusion have a broader scope to serve all learners' needs.

For example, providing a video script for a learner with a hearing impairment can also have a positive effect for a learner who wants to read the script and take notes during the video. Thus, the video script supports both learners' success by addressing differences in an inclusive way. This example illustrates the broad value of semiotics: providing multiple ways of accessing information benefits all learners. The Appendix contains additional suggestions for addressing learner concerns about inclusion through semiotics.

 Travel Advisory:
Accommodations for Learners with Disabilities

In addition to considering diversity and inclusion in general, supporting learners who have self-identified as having a disability that has been verified by your institution is a legal requirement in the United States. Most institutions have a person or department that is responsible for ensuring that the requirements of the Americans with Disabilities Act (ADA) (1990, amended in 2008) are followed. The ADA protects qualified individuals with disabilities from unlawful discrimination in employment, public services, and public accommodations, including institutions of higher education. If you have a learner with a disability in your course, you must provide specific accommodations for that individual based on the identified need.

Semiotics of Words

Words matter! From a semiotic perspective, the choice of words influences the learner's cognitive, social, and emotional experience in the course. In the next travel journal, we will use a disability example to illustrate our point on the importance of semiotics for inclusion of diverse learners.

 Your Travel Journal:
Semiotics of Words

Consider the following questions and jot down your reflections in the space provided.

Is there a difference in meaning if you say someone "is disabled" versus saying someone "has a disability"? If so, what is the difference?

What cognitive, social, and emotional impact might the change in wording have on the person with a disability?

What cognitive, social, and emotional impact might the change in wording have on others' view of the person with a disability?

What cognitive, social, and emotional impact might the change in wording have on your view of the person with a disability?

Using the phrase "is disabled" can restrict our focus to the learner's limitations. In contrast, "has a disability" describes one condition and allows us to broaden our focus to include other aspects of the learner's identity. When thinking about diversity, inclusion, and disabilities, consider what Langer (1997) so eloquently pointed out: "Any disability may function as an ability if we are able to view it from a new perspective" (p. 138). Langer goes on to state that "widespread failure to recognize the insights that can be found in all different perspectives may itself constitute a disability" (p.139).

Application of Semiotics to Online Courses

Now that you have had an opportunity to reflect on semiotics of words, we will explore how semiotics can be applied to online courses. Before you proceed, you may find the research on semiotics cited by Gannon-Cook and Ley (2015) of interest.

Exploring the Terrain:
Semiotics, Learner Connection, and Learner Retention

Gannon-Cook and Ley (2015) discussed the findings of two studies that compared online courses that applied semiotics (i.e., images, supporting metaphors, and stories) with online courses that did not apply semiotics. The findings of the two studies were similar. The students in the online courses that applied semiotics "felt more connected in the course … [and] there were fewer dropouts" (p. 115) compared to students in the regular online courses that did not apply semiotics. It must be noted that the findings of the two studies are indicators that cannot necessarily be generalized; however, the results are intriguing and indicate that more research is needed. The study calls attention to the potential impact of semiotics on the success of learners.

Given the role of semiotics in learner connection and learner retention, you will want to spend some time planning how you will apply semiotics. We offer some points to consider as you begin to think about semiotics in your course:

- From the moment your learners enter your course, they are taking in information you present to them. It's as if they are reading every word, image, link, and activity for the meaning of your intent as well as the information you want to impart. With this in mind, images and text in your course affect your learners' cognitive, social, and emotional responses to your course.
- By spending effort to select images and text that are realistic, relevant, and meaningful, you help your adult learners connect what they are learning to their own professional goals.
- Using semiotics enhances your learners' interaction with the course by contributing to their overall satisfaction with the course.

Semiotics is relevant for all aspects of course creation. When you think about your learners' responses to what they see in the course (i.e., the text and images), you are using semiotics. When you consider what might motivate your learners to participate in a dialogue or consider what might offend them, you are using semiotics. By applying semiotics, you will create a course that is realistic, relevant, and meaningful for diverse learners.

ADULT LEARNING PRINCIPLES APPLIED TO ONLINE COURSES: A SCENARIO

In this chapter, you have learned about adult learning principles: our view of adult learning (cognitive, social, and emotional), the adult learning process, adult learning assumptions, and semiotics for inclusion of diverse learners. In the following scenario, we will illustrate how you can apply these adult learning principles to create an online course. Imagine yourself in this scenario.

Your colleagues know that you are developing your expertise in creating online courses, and they are looking forward to receiving your guidance. To that end, one of your colleagues, Professor S. Squire, has just finished a module on writing emails for a Business Communication course and has asked you for feedback. Table 3.3 presents Professor Squire's module draft. As you look at the module draft, note your cognitive and emotional reactions.

Table 3.3   Module draft

Business Communication 101 Section 2315 Professor S. Squire
MODULE 1: Writing Emails
Objectives Assigned Reading Examples Additional Web Links Writing Resources Assignment Assignment Dropbox Discussion Forum Quiz

Before giving Professor Squire feedback, you take a moment to self-reflect.

Your Travel Journal:
Module Draft

Jot down your reflection to Professor Squire's module draft in the space provided.

What was your initial cognitive and emotional response to the module? Why?

How are self-reflection and dialogue incorporated into the module?

Do you find this module realistic, relevant, and meaningful? Why or why not?

How do you think a learner looking at this module for the first time would feel?

Is it clear what the learner should do in this module?

What feedback would you give Professor Squire?

Professor Squire was very appreciative of the feedback you gave. Based on your feedback, Professor Squire has revised the module and asked you to look at it again. Figure 3.2 shows the module revision.

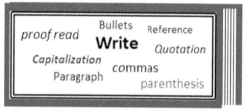

Business Communication 101
Section 2315
Professor S. Squire

Module 1: Writing Emails

What's in this module for you?

Your writing skills and your awareness of your audience can help you communicate effectively to get your job done. This module will focus on writing concise and effective emails.

Click on the link below to review the relevant skills for this module.
   Skill Checklist: Skills you'll gain

Your boss has told you to email a client. Take the actions below to produce an email that will satisfy your boss and impress the client.

R Read annotated handout on emails and self-reflect on questions provided

D Discuss what you read with partner and choose a topic for client's email

D Write first draft of your email and discuss your draft with partner

   Integrate partner feedback into final draft; submit for instructor feedback

R Reflect on instructor feedback and seek clarification as needed

Figure 3.2 Module revision.

Once again, you take a moment to self-reflect before giving feedback.

Your Travel Journal:
Module Revision

Jot down your response in the space provided.

What was your initial cognitive and emotional response to the module? Why?

How are self-reflection and dialogue incorporated into the module?

Do you find this module realistic, relevant, and meaningful? Why or why not?

How do you think a learner looking at this module for the first time would feel?

Is it clear what the learner should do in this module?

What feedback would you give Professor Squire?

Compare the use of images and the text in each example. Was there a difference between your response to the initial module and your response to the revised module? What caused the difference?

Your reputation is soaring as the "go-to" person for sound advice on creating online courses, and other colleagues have heard about your feedback to Professor Squire and the improvement that occurred in the course. They have asked you to conduct a workshop to share your knowledge of how to create an effective module. You plan to compare Professor Squire's module draft and revised module in terms of the following:

- our view of adult learning: cognitive, social, and emotional aspects
- the adult learning process
- adult learning assumptions
- semiotics for inclusion of diverse learners.

 Your Travel Journal:
Adult Learning Principles

To continue with the scenario, imagine that you are preparing for the workshop your colleagues have asked you to present. Consider the following questions and jot down your notes in the space provided.

What elements of Professor Squire's modules would you use to illustrate the adult learning principles?

Review the techniques listed in Table 3.2. Which ones have you used in your courses, and were they effective? Why or why not?

What would you say to your colleagues about semiotics for the inclusion of adult learners?

Summary of Adult Learning Principles Applied to Online Courses

The adult learning principles include our view of adult learning (cognitive, social, and emotional), the adult learning process, adult learning assumptions, and semiotics for inclusion of diverse learners. As you previously experienced, the initial contact learners have with an online course influences their willingness to engage with the learning activities, other learners, and the instructor. The adult learning principles have a major role in contributing to learners' experiences and their success.

ADDITIONAL CONSIDERATIONS IMPACTING ADULT LEARNERS

Two additional considerations that impact adult learners and that should be considered are the role of resources and the impact of power. Understanding the role of resources is particularly relevant when engaging learners with the information, and the impact of power on learning has important ramifications for instructors as well as learners.

Resources

At this point, you may be asking what role course resources (e.g., written documents, textbooks, articles, or media such as video and audio files) play in the adult learning process. We propose that these resources are tools (Stacey, 2001) that learners use to acquire information. Interacting with a resource is an individual act that leads to self-reflection on the information in the resource in an attempt to make sense of the material. Such self-reflection may focus on thoughts about the information, feelings toward the information, and/or previous experiences with the information, and most likely will include all three. In an attempt to clarify ideas or answer questions that arise from self-reflection, the learner may seek out peer(s) in the course to engage in a dialogue. Engaging with others in dialogue is necessary to complete the learning process; if the learner interacts only with the information in the resources, then the learning process is incomplete.

While the cognitive and emotional parts of learning may be evident in the learner's self-reflection on the information, social interactions are missing. Without social interaction, understanding cannot be tested, ideas cannot be challenged or supported by others, and surprise that leads to an "ah-ha" moment may never occur. More importantly, without social interaction, shared understanding can never emerge.

Power

Depending on your own personal history and culture, you may be wondering how power influences or shapes social interactions, particularly in learning situations. Power differentials occur between the instructor and the learners in several ways. Instructors have the authority to make and enforce the rules for the course and the responsibility to give grades. Additionally, an instructor may be perceived as an expert in the discipline; therefore, learners may perceive that the instructor is not to be questioned or challenged. Because of all these reasons and others, instructors have both real and perceived power over the learners. This explicit and implicit power affects the interaction between the instructor and the learners. Individual learners' past history and culture play a role in how the power differential is experienced by the learner. Your awareness and acknowledgment of this differential and how you manage it will influence how learners decide to interact with you.

In addition, learner-to-learner power dynamics also occur, even in online courses. These dynamics may be positive, such as when a member of a group steps up to lead a project and everyone agrees; or negative, such as when a project group purposely excludes one of the members through bullying comments or failing to inform that person of a group meeting. It is important to be aware of and address any negative learner-to-learner power dynamics that are occurring. Not only do those targeted learners suffer, but the entire class suffers. This type of disruption can impact the emotional well-being of everyone in the course.

Written dialogue in discussion boards and virtual meetings provides some ways for you to monitor the interactions among the learners for any potential issues. Individual self-reflection allows a space for learners to potentially reflect more deeply on their own emotions and experiences in the course and may allow you to detect concerns that are affecting an individual learner.

One way to create a meaningful learner-to-learner experience is by creating a course that is inclusive, respects diversity, and sets the expectation of collaboration at the beginning of the course. Throughout the course, you can also encourage learners to reflect on their emotional response to what is happening in the "here and now power relations (e.g., differences of gender, class, race, culture in the classroom; or broader tensions and dynamics that may have developed in the course group)" (Clancy & Vince, 2019, p. 177). Openly discussing the potential negative impact of power on learners in the course tends to minimize learner misuse of power.

Your Travel Journal:
Resources and Power

Consider the following questions on resources and power. Jot down your thoughts in the space provided.

What is your reaction to our description of resources? How is our description similar to or different from yours?

What is your feeling when the word "power" is used? Are you comfortable using your power?

List some ways you use your power as an instructor.

Have you experienced learner-to-learner power dynamics in your courses? If the dynamics were negative, how did you handle the issue? Would you do anything different the next time you identify the occurrence of a negative learner-to-learner power dynamic?

QUESTIONABLE BELIEFS ABOUT LEARNING THAT PERSIST

We believe it is important that you are aware of persistent, questionable beliefs that seemingly abound in education so that you can avoid them as you create your course. The puzzling aspect of questionable beliefs is that even when research has shown certain beliefs to be questionable or even false, they persist. To counter some of these beliefs, we have included two *Exploring the Terrains*. The first addresses questionable beliefs about learning; the second addresses questionable beliefs about the brain and learning. You be the judge!

Exploring the Terrain:
Learning Styles, Non-verbal Communication, and the Learning Pyramid

We have identified three pervasive, persistent beliefs that are deeply entrenched in instructional practice and perpetuated in the literature of education, workforce development, and business, as well as other disciplines. These three beliefs are:

- An individual's learning style should dictate the type of instruction they receive.
- Ninety-three percent of our communication is non-verbal, also known as the 7-38-55 rule.
- We remember 10 percent of what we read, 20 percent of what we hear, 30 percent of what we see, 50 percent of what we see and hear, 70 percent of what we say and write, and 90 percent of what we do.

All three of these persistent beliefs have been called into question, yet they continue to be repeated in current literature, touted by professional development consultants, and practiced in teaching. So, let's set the record straight.

Learning styles. "There is widespread belief that learners have specific learning styles and that education should be individualized ... to the preferred style of the learner" (Kirschner & van Merrienboer, 2013, p. 169). Several major limitations undermine this belief. While a large number of studies on learning styles exist, only a small percentage of these studies have examined matching instruction to learning style. Furthermore, among the studies of learning style-based instruction, only a small number are methodologically sound. Based on the findings of the methodologically sound studies, there is no reason to tie instructional techniques to learning styles (Rohrer & Pashler, 2012).

Adding to the confusion about learning styles, there is no agreed-upon measure of learning styles, and in fact, there is not even agreement on the number of different learning styles, which range from 3 to 71 (de Bruyckere, Kirschner, & Hulshof, 2015). Furthermore, while learners profess a bias toward a particular learning style, learners are in reality "ambidextrous," meaning that they can easily change the way they process information depending on the task at hand or the instructional approach used, all while experiencing equal success in learning.

While learning styles, *prima facie*, seem to make sense as a way to differentiate instruction for learners, research is mixed at best. In fact, learners in Allcock and Hulme's (2010) study stated that they preferred a variety of instructional approaches. In fact, varying the modality to suit the information, not the individual's perceived learning style, may challenge the learner to engage and develop deeper understanding (Whitman & Kelleher, 2016).

One other pertinent piece of information on learning styles relates to how the brain works. Learning styles assume that the brain processes information gained from one sensory modality independently from information gained through another sensory modality. In fact, research shows the opposite: "Input modalities in the brain are interlinked: visual with auditory; visual with motor; motor with auditory; visual with taste; and so on" (Geake, 2008, p. 130).

In summary, changing a teaching approach to mirror the learning style of a student does not improve the learning outcome (Allcock & Hulme, 2010; Coffield, Moseley, Hall, & Ecclestone, 2004). Although learners may indeed have preferences about how they learn and even regularly adhere to specific learning strategies, there is no strong evidence to support that adapting instruction to learning styles benefits learning (Allcock & Hulme, 2010; de Bruyckere et al., 2015; Rohrer & Pashler, 2012; Willingham, 2018).

Ninety-three percent of meaning is communicated non-verbally.   The oft-stated rule about communication is that 7 percent of meaning is conveyed through words, 38 percent of meaning is conveyed through tone of voice, and 55 percent of meaning is conveyed through body language; thus, 93 percent of meaning is communicated non-verbally. This statement is a misinterpretation of Mehrabian and Ferris' (1967) original findings. In their study, 37 female students in an undergraduate psychology course at the University of California participated in a laboratory experiment. Only one word, "maybe," was used to convey positive, neutral, and negative facial expressions and tone of voice. The researchers were investigating "the way people communicate their emotions. He [Mehrabian] never intended his findings should be applied to all forms of communication between people" (de Bruyckere et al., 2015, p. 83). Mehrabian stated numerous times over the years that his findings were "misquoted" and "clearly, it is absurd to imply or suggest that a verbal portion of all communication constitutes only 7% of the message" (as cited in Lapakko, 1997, p. 65).

Unfortunately, this misinterpretation that 93 percent of communication is non-verbal continues to be widely disseminated (de Bruyckere et al., 2015; Lapakko, 2007). While we recognize that non-verbal communication is part of the learning process, overstating its importance diminishes the need to focus on the multiplicity of ways we interact with each other to create meaning together.

Learning pyramid (originally Dale's Cone of Experience).   The learning pyramid depicts the percentage of information that people remember based on the type of learning activity. Although these numbers change depending on who reports them, a typical example follows. People remember 10 percent of what they read; 20 percent of what they hear; 30 percent of what they see; 50 percent of what they see and hear; 70 percent of what they say and write; and 90 percent of what they do (de Bruyckere et al., 2015). While Dale (1969) created a visual pyramid-shaped cone to illustrate audiovisual media from the most concrete to the most abstract, no pedagogical labels or percentages were included in the original model. In fact, Dale (1969) stated that the categories were flexible divisions.

Interestingly, no research has been found to validate the "learning pyramid" percentages or indicate the origins of the percentages. At one point, the National Training Laboratories (NTL) was credited with the creation of the learning pyramid percentages. But no evidence has been found to support this claim. It has been suggested that the percentages came from military research during World War II; however, the quest continues to find the original research. In their investigation, Subramony, Molenda, Betrus, and Thalheimer (2014) found evidence that the percentages may trace back to 1912 or earlier.

In addition, Lalley and Miller (2007) listed multiple issues with the learning pyramid, including lack of rigorous research. de Bruyckere et al. (2015) pointed out that "no significant differences between the efficacy of the different approaches could be established" (p. 33).

Summary: a cautionary note.   These examples illustrate how ideas are spread and over time become accepted as fact even when the "fact" may be questionable at best. Rather than taking an assertion at face value, even if it has been around for a long time – maybe *especially* when it has been around for a long time – it is best to examine how the idea originated and decide whether rigorous research supports the interpretation.

Exploring the Terrain:
Assumptions about the Brain and Learning

We will explore the following assumptions about the brain and learning:

- We use only 10 percent of our brain.
- Our left brain is analytical and our right brain is creative.

As you think about the information presented about these assumptions, consider the potentially harmful effects that false beliefs about learning can have on learners over time. These types of assumptions can undermine learners' beliefs in their own potential to learn. These assumptions can also influence how instructors view their learners' abilities and influence the approach instructors take with specific learners.

We use only 10 percent of our brain.   This belief has been attributed to various individuals: an Italian neurosurgeon around 1890, William James, Albert Einstein, and even US advertisers during World War II who, in order to sell home health guides, wanted to convince consumers that they were not very smart (Geake, 2008).

Positron emission tomography (PET) and functional magnetic resonance imaging (fMRI) allow us to see the detailed activity of our brains. "These scans make it clear that there is neural activity throughout the whole brain, even when we are sleeping" (de Bruyckere et al., 2015, p. 101). In addition, because our brains consume a great deal of energy, there is little chance they would have evolved with unused capacity (de Bruyckere et al., 2015; NASEM, 2018).

Our left brain is analytical and our right brain is creative.   Studies of patients with life-threatening epilepsy (abnormal brains) who had the connection between the two hemispheres of their brains severed were conducted in the 1970s (Geake, 2008). Once the connection was severed, each hemisphere could process different types of information, leading to the misinterpretation of right- and left-brain thinking. While the researchers were careful to point out that the patients' brains were abnormal, that caveat was ignored by the general public, and the findings were applied to all.

According to Singh and O'Boyle (2004), research shows that

> the brain does not consist of two hemispheres operating in isolation ... Thus, hemispheric specialization cannot be conceptualized as the static difference in the processing capacity of two independent and isolated hemispheres, but rather consists of a dynamic interactive partnership between the two. (p. 371)

Brain scans confirm the dynamic interaction between the right and left hemispheres in normal brains, thereby disconfirming the belief of right brain–left brain dichotomy.

Summary.   New brain imaging technologies "have provided neuroscientists with real-time visual representations of the functioning, living brain that had not been previously possible" (Clement & Lovat, 2012, p. 535). Based on the evidence, it is clear that our brains do not have a large percentage of unused brain capacity, thereby debunking the belief that we use only 10 percent of our brain. Similarly, based on evidence from brain scans, it appears that our brains are usually engaged in a dynamic interaction between the right and left hemispheres of the brain, thereby disconfirming the belief that the left brain is analytical and the right brain is creative.

Your Travel Journal:
Questionable Beliefs

Jot down your thoughts about questionable beliefs using the questions below to guide your reflection.

What is your reaction to the information presented on learning styles? Non-verbal communication? The learning pyramid?

Why do you think these beliefs continue to persist and what, if anything, are you willing to do to "set the record straight" about these beliefs?

What is your reaction to the assumptions about our brains and learning?

ADULT LEARNING PRINCIPLES: SUMMARY

You examined our view of adult learning and the adult learning process and explored your views of learning through self-reflection and dialogue with others. You reviewed important assumptions about how adults learn and identified techniques you could incorporate in your course to meet adult learning needs. You also explored semiotics for inclusion of diverse learners. You considered the importance of resources and the influence of power on adult learning. Finally, you investigated some common misconceptions about learning.

You are now ready to begin *Chapter 4: Course Destination*.

4   Course Destination

COURSE DESTINATION: INTRODUCTION

A destination is the end point of a journey. In the same way, the course destination is the end point of the course. In our approach, the course destination specifies what learners can do with the knowledge they have gained in the course. Choosing the course destination occurs at the beginning of the Change-adept Course Creation Process because you have to know where you want your learners to go in order to decide how to help them get there!

That said, in order to determine your course destination, there are several actions that must occur first. In this chapter, you will complete the following actions:

- Choose the course you will work on and state a rationale for your choice.
- Identify your adult learners' contexts and implications for your course.
- Choose topics.
- Choose skill areas.
- Choose a course destination that concisely conveys the topics and skill areas involved in the course.
- Identify possible course themes connected to the destination.

YOUR COURSE

The need to create a new online course usually stems from one of two situations: The academic curriculum committee approves your request to create a new course in an online format, or you have been asked to take an existing face-to-face course and put it online. Regardless of your situation, online courses markedly differ in the ways you present information, structure the course, create inclusiveness, appreciate diversity, engage learners, and communicate with learners.

Throughout this chapter and the next several chapters, we will present an example of an instructor creating a Theories of Personality online course to illustrate the elements of the Change-adept Course Creation Process. Each time we present an element of the process, we include the instructor's self-reflection and actions taken. Then you will apply what you learned from the example to your own course.

Travel Advisory:
Using a Course Log

We recommend that you set up an electronic folder that will contain preparatory work and items for your course. This organizational feature will likely save you countless hours of hunting for the location of a file that has information that you have already created and want to use. We will refer to this storage location for your work as your *course log*. You will use the *course log* as part of your Application as you progressively create your course.

Let's begin with the first element of the process: choosing a course and stating a rationale. By stating a rationale, you remind yourself of your purpose in creating the course you have chosen.

In our example, the instructor first chooses a course and provides a rationale for this choice.

Theories of Personality Example:
Course Choice and Rationale

I have chosen to work on the Theories of Personality course. This is a half-semester course (seven weeks) that learners typically take in their first year or sophomore year. The course is required for the psychology major but can also be taken by non-majors.

My rationale for choosing this course is that I have had success with this course in a face-to-face format, but I have never taught it online. I'm curious to see how I can adapt it for online learning. In addition, I have just enough time to work on it right now, whereas I wouldn't have enough time to work on one of my full-semester upper-level courses.

Now choose your course and state why you chose that course.

Application:
Choose Your Course and Provide a Rationale

Choose a course to work on. In your *course log*, write the following information:

- course title
- course number
- course level (undergraduate: first year, sophomore, junior, senior, or mixed levels; graduate to master's, doctoral)
- course type (required for major or minor, elective, etc.).

Briefly state your rationale for choosing to work on this course.

Now that you have chosen a course and stated your rationale for choosing this course, you are ready to think about the learners who will take this course.

YOUR ADULT LEARNERS' CONTEXTS

Although we view the learning process as universal, each learner's experience will be unique. Adult learners are not a monolithic group. As NASEM (2018) stated:

> *Each learner develops a unique array of knowledge and cognitive resources in the course of life that are molded by the interplay of that learner's cultural, social, cognitive, and biological contexts. Understanding the developmental, cultural, contextual, and historical diversity of learners is central to understanding how people learn. (p. 33)*

You need to know who your learners are before you define the course destination. Consider our metaphor of a journey again: A good tour guide will assess travelers' needs, preferences, and experiences when planning a tour. Although you cannot perfectly customize your course to your learners' contexts, awareness of your learners' contexts (past and present) is critical to creating an inclusive online course that supports your learners' success.

Review the instructor's identification of learners' contexts in our example.

Theories of Personality Example:
Learners' Possible Contexts

At my institution, learners are generally traditional-aged college students (18–21 years old), and most have full- or part-time jobs. There is a high percentage of first-generation learners in our student population, and many learners are bilingual.

Now identify your learners' possible contexts. If you have taught your course or a similar course at your institution, you will have some idea of your learners' contexts – past and present. If you haven't, you may want to check with a colleague.

Application:
Identify Your Learners' Possible Contexts

Review the following list of possible contexts and circle those items you think best describe the learners in your course. Remember to consider your learners as a whole, not as specific individuals. You are looking for patterns of similarity and diversity in your learners' contexts.

First-generation college	English is a second language	Low or high income
Military experience	Have siblings	Parents completed high school or have some college education
Entered college immediately after high school	Transferred from a community college	Live on campus
Live at home with parents	Live off campus	Homeless
Work part-time while in school	Work full-time while in school	Entered as an undergraduate after working for some time
Married	Have children	Full-time student

Part-time student	Scholarship or student loan	Working professional
Experience with/knowledge of the course topic	Age	Comes from a different country
Have different cultural experience	Other: list	Other: list

Additional sources for developing a better understanding of your learners may be found in the demographic data your institution gathers on the student population in general. Some schools provide analysis of student data (e.g., by academic department). If you are new to your institution, it is important for you to review this information.

Notes from Our Journey:
Our Readers' Contexts

To understand our readers' contexts, we focused on collecting data and reflecting on the characteristics of you, our readers, and how your characteristics might affect your experience of the workbook.

In an attempt to explore your context, we interviewed instructors from different institutions and instructional designers who support instructors. We included the characteristics of these individuals to extrapolate to our potential readers. In addition, we used our varied experiences in creating and teaching online courses and our professional instructional design experience in assisting instructors in a variety of subjects to help us identify key areas to address in the workbook. In addition, we applied our knowledge of adult learning, inclusion, and semiotic theory to meet the diverse needs of our readers.

As we wrote this workbook, we continuously reflected on and discussed the range of our readers' experiences with and knowledge about teaching online courses and teaching in general. We considered what information to include in the workbook and how to structure this information.

By examining our readers' possible contexts and characteristics, we made the following assumptions:

- You want to create effective online courses. Otherwise, you would not have picked up the book.
- You are busy. So we created a workbook that provides you with a "just enough, just in time" approach to theory and research by presenting *Exploring the Terrain* quick-reads that you can apply right away.
- You most likely are task- and action-oriented. Otherwise, you probably would not have picked a workbook. We provide you with focused learning activities to move you forward quickly in your course creation.
- You want to make your own informed decisions, so we give you the tools and quick explanations or examples and provide options on ways to build your course.
- Space is provided in the workbook to capture your thoughts and ideas. This process provides you with an opportunity to personalize your workbook so that it is uniquely yours and reminds you of what you learned as you went through the process of creating your online course.

Additional Aspects of Learners' Contexts: Technology Skills and Readiness

There are two additional areas to explore about your learners that may affect their ability to be successful in an online course. The first area is technology – learners' access to and ability to use it. Even if your learners are considered "digital natives" (35 and younger), not all of them will have the technology skills needed to successfully participate in an online course (de Bruyckere, Kirschner, & Hulshof, 2015). It follows that the same is true for learners of all ages. You can consider your learners' previous experience with online learning, their access to technology, and their proficiency with the technology skills your course will require. Depending on your learners' contexts, you may need to direct learners to supports for accessing and using the technology in your course.

The second area is learners' readiness to engage in the course. The readiness of your learners will determine what topics you will choose, how much information you will be able to cover, types of resources you will use, and how you will approach and structure your learning activities. Also consider learners' possible emotional responses to the course. What do they enjoy? What concerns them? Your learners' responses can inform how you present certain topics.

In our Theories of Personality example, the instructor has given some thought to how these additional aspects of learners' context (technology and readiness) apply to the learners in this course. Review the instructor's summary.

Theories of Personality Example:
Technology Skills and Readiness

At my institution, online learning is relatively new. Although most of my learners have plenty of experience with being online, they have not had much experience with learning online. Learners' writing challenges come up frequently in faculty conversations, and I have observed that my learners often struggle with writing.

This course is offered to all levels (first year through senior), but most of the learners who take it are first years or sophomores. I usually have a mix of psychology majors and non-majors, but all learners have taken Introduction to Psychology as a prerequisite for this course. In the past, my learners tended to respond with particular enthusiasm when I presented information about personality assessment.

Now identify your learners' technology skills and readiness for the course.

 Application:
Identify Your Learners' Technology Skills and Readiness

Identify your learners' technology skills and access, and your learners' readiness for your course. If you have not taught this course before, call a colleague to discuss these aspects of your learners' context. Summarize key points in your *course log*.

Implications of Adult Learners' Contexts for Online Learning

Learners' contexts have an impact on their experience in an online course. At this point, it is helpful to start thinking about the implications of learners' contexts for some of your initial course creation decisions.

Review the implications of learners' contexts for the instructor's initial decisions about the Theories of Personality course.

Theories of Personality Example:
Implications of Learners' Contexts

Based on my summary of my learners' contexts, I identify the following implications for my course creation process:

- Although my learners are technologically savvy, their relative lack of experience with online learning suggests that I will need to orient them to the technology in this course.
- Because my learners are generally 18–21 years old, they are unlikely to have in-depth work experience in my discipline (psychology). However, they do have some work experience that I can draw upon.
- Because most of my learners work, I need to keep time constraints in mind.
- Learners' struggles with writing suggest that some direct instruction in writing will be needed.
- My learners probably have a basic understanding of foundational psychological concepts; however, I will need to check their depth of understanding.

Now identify the implications of your learners' contexts for your course.

Application:
Identify Implications of Your Learners' Contexts

Review the aspects of your adult learners' contexts that you have identified in the previous applications (learners' possible contexts; technology and readiness). Identify the implications of your adult learners' contexts for creating your online course. At this point, you can focus on implications for initial decisions about your course. Summarize these implications in your *course log*.

TOPICS

Now that you have given some thought to your adult learners' contexts and their implications, you can choose topics for your course. Topics are the broad areas of knowledge that are relevant for your course. We start with topics because this is an area of expertise for most instructors and because topics are an organizing factor in the Change-adept Course Creation Process.

As an expert on your course, you are in a good position to know what the main topics are. Sometimes these topics are dictated by institutional standards; other times, these topics are dictated by the textbook associated with a course. Regardless of how much flexibility you have in selecting the topics, it is a good idea to identify the topics in terms of the general areas of knowledge that a professional in your discipline would know.

Notes from Our Journey:
Calling a Colleague about Choosing Topics

To gain an additional perspective on how to choose topics for a course, we called a colleague, Dr. Laura Schaefer of Rice University. Dr. Schaefer shared her process of choosing topics for an engineering class:

> I first consider the major topics that the students need to learn in the class, from both a technical and [a] broader point of view. I then do a web search on syllabi prepared by faculty at other institutions to get an idea of how other schools might approach some of these topics.

I also read through existing textbooks to see if any of them effectively cover any (or all, but that is rare indeed) of the topics that are important. Looking at the syllabi and textbooks also alerts me to other related topics that I might not have initially considered, and I will revise my general course outline at that point.

This description illustrates the value of seeking a broad perspective on the course's topics before narrowing the list of topics to those that are most important.

Let's return to our example. Review the instructor's process for choosing topics for the Theories of Personality course.

Theories of Personality Example:
Topics

I reviewed my institution's course description for this course. I also perused the textbook that I have used in this course when teaching it face-to-face. In addition, I considered my knowledge of the field and what theories are most important for understanding personality. I have particular expertise in personality assessment, so I want to share some of that knowledge with my learners. Based on these factors, I narrow my list to the following broad topics:

- psychoanalytic theories
- behavioral theories
- social-cognitive theories
- trait theories
- humanistic theories
- personality assessment.

Now choose your topics.

Application:
Choose Your Topics

Consider the various broad topics you may include in your course. You may want to review your institution's course description, other institutions' syllabi for the course, textbooks, and other sources of ideas. You can brainstorm many topics before narrowing them down to a list of the topics you will include in your course. Include your list in your *course log*.

SKILL AREAS

We have found that the majority of online courses we have reviewed focus heavily on acquisition of topic knowledge, with only secondary (if any) explicit focus on skill development such as writing, critical thinking, or inquiry and analysis. This situation is regrettable: Learners' skills are evaluated in various assignments (e.g., a written research paper, a source analysis that requires critical thinking), but actual instruction on these skills – including opportunities for learners to practice and receive feedback – is absent.

Instructors may assume that adult learners enter higher education with these skills fully formed, only to be shocked when learners do not show evidence of excellent writing skills in a final paper, for example. To help remedy this situation, we have included skill areas as an explicit focus in the course creation process.

What are skill areas? *Cambridge Dictionary* defines a skill as "an ability to do an activity [task] or job well, especially because you practiced it." We conceptualize skill areas as broad categories of skills that learners will develop and strengthen throughout a course and beyond. Most skill areas are applicable across topics and disciplines, though some (e.g., quantitative reasoning) are particularly relevant for certain disciplines.

Skill areas determine how learners will show their learning. By including an explicit focus on a few key skill areas in your course, you set expectations for your learners that these underlying skill areas are central to their learning in your course.

Examples of Skill Areas

Here are some examples of broad skill areas from the Association of American Colleges and Universities (AAC&U) VALUE project on essential learning outcomes (Rhodes, 2010):

- critical thinking
- creative thinking
- ethical reasoning
- information literacy
- inquiry and analysis
- intercultural knowledge and competence
- oral communication
- problem-solving
- quantitative reasoning
- teamwork
- written communication.

Although this list is not comprehensive, it provides some ideas for general skill areas that you might include in your course.

Review the instructor's decision process to select skill areas for the Theories of Personality course. Note in particular the rationale for selecting certain skill areas, based on the instructor's understanding of professional standards (i.e., what skills a professional in the discipline requires) and of learners' contexts.

Theories of Personality Example:
Skill Areas

Although I don't expect all of my learners to become psychologists, I want to help learners develop some of the skills that are important in the field of psychology. I also remember that I have identified writing as an area where my learners tend to struggle, so I want to be sure to include writing as a focus. I identify these skill areas as most important and as most relevant for my learners:

- critical thinking
- teamwork
- writing.

Now choose the skill areas you will include in your course.

Application:
Choose Your Skill Areas

Identify the main skill areas that are important in your discipline. In other words, what skills are needed to be successful in your discipline? Think in terms of the practical applications of skills.

Identify a few (two or three) skill areas in which you will evaluate learners' progress over time. Keep your learners' contexts in mind as you choose the skill areas: Too many skills can become unwieldy and possibly detrimental to learning. Write the skill areas in your *course log*.

YOUR COURSE DESTINATION

You have chosen your course, identified your learners' context and implications, chosen topics, and chosen skill areas. Now it is time to choose a course destination that concisely conveys what learners can do with the knowledge they gain in the course.

If you have a course goal or description that your institution requires you to use, you may include that information in your course. Nevertheless, we encourage you to create a course destination as well. A course destination is usually more succinct than the course description and connects the topics of the course to the skill areas learners will develop in the course.

The general format of a course destination includes a phrase that captures the main topics of the course and a description of how learners will apply the skill areas to the topics. Two examples of formats include:

- Through _____ (skill areas), learners can _____ (verbs) (about/on/etc.) _____ (topics).
- Learners can _____ (skill areas) (about/on/etc.) _____ (topics).

Travel Advisory:
Course Goal versus Course Destination

Conceptualizing the course destination in terms of skill areas requires a subtle but important shift in thinking that we will reinforce several times in this book: When it comes to learning, spending more time on developing cognitive, social, and emotional skills within the context of a limited amount of information is wise (DiCarlo, 2009; Monahan, 2015). If your institution's course goal already includes the skills you will emphasize in your course, you can adopt your institution's course goal as your course destination. Otherwise, you can choose to supplement the course goal with a statement of your skill-focused course destination.

Review the instructor's process for choosing a course destination for Theories of Personality.

Theories of Personality Example:
Course Destination

In choosing a course destination, I start with my course's description in the university catalog:

Course Description: Consists of the study and evaluation of theories of personality. Psychoanalytic, behavioral, social-cognitive, trait, and humanistic theories will be studied. Emphasis is placed on the structure and dynamics of human behavior and empirically supported personality assessment strategies.

The description contains all of the topics in my course, but it seems too wordy. I decided to sum up all of the topics of the course in just a few words: major theories and assessment of personality.

I also decided to describe the skill areas (critical thinking, teamwork, and writing) in terms of behaviors that my learners will show in my course. I decided that "collaborate, think critically, and communicate" would be clear and concrete.

Finally, I bring together the topics and the skill areas in a single, succinct statement about what I want learners to be able to do with the knowledge they gain in the course:

Course Destination: Learners can collaborate, think critically, and communicate about major theories and assessment of personality.

Notice how the destination is more focused. It includes what learners are going to learn to do with the topics they learn, namely collaborate, think critically, and communicate, which are directly related to the skill areas of this course (team work, critical thinking, and writing).

Now choose your course destination.

Application:
Choose Your Course Destination

Considering the topics and skill areas you have chosen for your course, choose your course destination. You can use one of the following formats.

- Through _____ (skill areas), learners can _____ (verbs) (about/on/etc.) _____ (topics).
- Learners can _____ (skill areas) (about/on/etc.) _____ (topics).

Write your course destination in your *course log*.

Now that you have chosen your course destination, it's time for dialogue.

Call a Colleague:
Your Course Destination

It's never too early to discuss your work with a colleague! Discuss whether your course destination is a good fit for the course. Jot down your dialogue notes in the space provided.

COURSE THEME

A course theme can emerge from your course destination. A course theme is a unifying idea, meaningful metaphor, or storyline that engages learners and helps them create connections to the topics. A theme also helps to organize the various elements into a coherent whole. A theme can be emphasized through the use of meaningful images and choice of words. Above all, themes can help offer the adult learner the chance to transfer learning to realistic situations while practicing skill areas.

One type of theme is a scenario-based theme, which presents a realistic, relevant, and meaningful context for learners' participation in the course. Examples of scenario-based themes appear in Table 4.1.

Table 4.1   Examples of scenario-based themes

Discipline	Scenario-based themes
Business	The theme for the Business Ethics course is the purchasing department of a fictional company, Business, Inc. In the scenario, the learners buy materials for a project at Business, Inc. Acting as team employees, learners discuss their proposed purchases using business reasoning that demonstrates ethical decision-making as well as cost savings. Images include a conference room, diagrams, and charts. A dollar sign is used as an icon that represents the discussion boards.
Biology	The theme for the biology course is a hospital lab setting. The learners are interns at the lab. In the scenario, the learners review the lab results for various patients and suggest possible issues indicated by the various results. Images and role-play contribute to the feel of a realistic setting. Images include lab photos and pictures of relevant hospital areas. A label at the bottom of every module shows the numerical formulas that the learners will need to commit to memory as they apply the formulas to the scenario for that module. A beaker icon represents discussion boards and is used to denote the learners' mixing of ideas to solve a problem in the discussion board.

Table 4.1   *(cont.)*

Discipline	Scenario-based themes
Computer science	The theme for the computer science course is a software company. The learners are part of a team working for the software company to develop a new software product. In discussions, the team members (i.e., your learners) mentor and advise each other. Weekly project team meetings mirror the connection of course topics and are presented to the team members in a realistic report. Images include a company conference room where project management meetings (i.e., team discussions) are held. An icon of a conference room represents the discussion boards.
Math	The theme for the math course is the broad use of applied math. In a math course, you could offer a choice of scenarios so learners choose the one that has the most meaning. All choices should have realistic situations that require applied math, but the scenario can be real or fantasy. For example, one scenario may be a company that wants to send passengers to the Moon and needs to figure out the math that calculates how to get the space craft from Earth to the Moon and back. Another example may be applying math to finance the roll-out of a new product. Yet another example could be a manufacturing company finding that its primary widget is no longer priced competitively and must be re-engineered to reduce the manufacturing cost. When using various scenarios, the images should reflect the theme of the broad use of applied math. The same holds true for icons and word choice.

When you select a theme for your course, consider your diverse learners. As you consider different themes, reflect on the potential multicultural meanings (semiotics) and goodness-of-fit with course topics. Be mindful of your choices.

Notes from Our Journey:
Our Workbook Theme

After one false start using a weaving metaphor, we quickly discovered that the metaphor of a journey was more appropriate. Our frustration with the weaving metaphor was replaced with emotional satisfaction in coming up with a theme that worked: a journey.

A journey is multiculturally meaningful. We felt certain that you were familiar with undertaking journeys both metaphorically and physically. Therefore, we agreed that using a journey as a theme would best suit the needs of the workbook and your needs. Once we selected our journey metaphor, we found ways to use it in textual references (terms, titles, labels) and icons.

And a cautionary note ...

An external reviewer commented that our theme of "a journey" was not consistently used throughout the book proposal. Upon review and reflection, we agreed that the reviewer was correct. To remedy the situation, we individually reviewed the workbook to identify any inconsistencies or deviations from our theme. To reinforce our theme and remind readers that this is a journey, we made some changes. Our reflections became *Notes from Our Journey* and quick-reads became *Exploring the Terrain*. We also used terms such as "map" and "itinerary" to describe course creation elements. These changes and others are consistent with our theme of a learning journey.

Selection of a scenario-based theme can be informed by your awareness of situations and settings in which professionals in your discipline would use the knowledge of the topics in your course. Keeping this in mind, review the instructor's ideas for a theme for the Theories of Personality course.

Theories of Personality Example:
Theme Ideas

Based on my awareness of where psychologists might use their knowledge of personality, I identify a theme that involves my learners working as interns in one of three possible settings:

- personality research lab
- university counseling center
- psychotherapy clinic.

Now identify possible themes for your course.

 Application:
Identify Possible Course Themes

Choose a possible theme for your course. Consider themes that are related to the course destination and that are meaningful to your learners. Write your possible themes in the spaces provided. Include the rationale for your choices (i.e., why you think the themes you chose are appropriate and relevant to your topics). You may want to ask your colleagues for feedback while you are deciding on your theme.

Theme Idea:	Rationale:
Theme Idea:	Rationale:
Theme Idea:	Rationale:

COURSE DESTINATION: SUMMARY

In this chapter, you chose the course you will be working on throughout this workbook. You considered your unique learners and their contexts, with an eye to understanding how these contexts influence learners' experience in your course. You also chose course topics and skill areas related to your discipline. Finally, you chose a course destination and began to think about a course theme.

You are now ready to begin *Chapter 5: Course Map*.

5   Course Map

COURSE MAP: INTRODUCTION

At this point, you have selected a course to create, developed an understanding of your learners' contexts, chosen your course destination, and identified one or two (or more) possible themes. Now you are ready to begin the process of developing a course map, which involves creating a visual mind map of what learners will learn in your course.

Anyone taking a journey to a new destination needs a map (whether paper or electronic) to guide the way. Similarly, by showing the topics and essential information in your course – and most importantly the connections among topics – a course map guides your development of the course. You have seen the roadmap for our workbook in *Chapter 1: Start Here*. Your course map will be similar.

In this chapter, you will complete several actions:

- map topics
- identify essential information within each topic
- identify connections among topics
- cluster topics in light of commonalities
- choose a course theme that ties the topic clusters together.

BENEFITS OF COURSE MAPS

We include a course map for two reasons. First, a course map allows you to see the connections among your topics. Such connections (as we will discuss momentarily) are key for learners' understanding of the topics. Second, an online course is a visual environment for many learners. Although you could create an outline of the topics, an outline doesn't have the same visual impact as a map, nor does it easily show connections among topics. You may decide to create an outline at some point, but the map is a solid starting point. Our hope is that your course map will also become a resource for your dialogue with colleagues. You may even decide to share a simplified version of your map with learners.

In this chapter, we ask you to work with your course in a deep, involved, and iterative way to help you create a course that meets your adult learners' needs. By spending extra time on this preparatory piece, you will find that the Change-adept Course Creation Process goes more smoothly.

**Travel Advisory:
Preparing Your Course Map**

You have options in the process of preparing your course map. The process we present here involves a series of actions. You can follow the sequence we have provided in this chapter, completing the actions step-by-step, or you can read the entire chapter and then go back and complete the actions. Giving you a choice of how to prepare your map is consistent with adult learning assumptions and with the Change-adept Course Creation Process. The process is flexible and iterative; your choices will be based on your own preferences.

As a point of interest, note that one of the first books on mind mapping was published by Buzan and Buzan (1993). The use of mind maps has expanded over the years, and mind maps are applied in multiple ways in business and education.

As our book title suggests, we developed a mind map that we called a "roadmap" of our book's topics. Compare our workbook roadmap with an earlier version (Figure 5.1). As you compare these two maps, you can see how a mind map is structured as well as a clear picture of the changes that occurred over the course of creating our workbook. Comparing the two roadmaps provides a perfect example of how creating a course (or in this case, a workbook) is an iterative, non-linear process that results in changes over time.

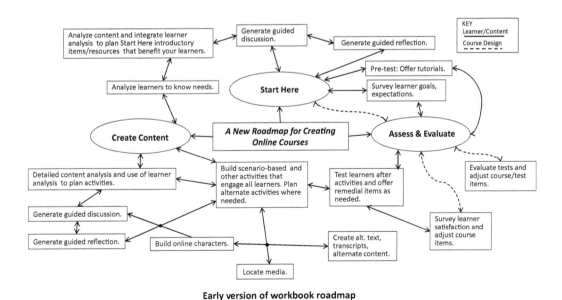

Early version of workbook roadmap

Figure 5.1 Comparison of workbook roadmap with an earlier version. *(continued on p. 64)*

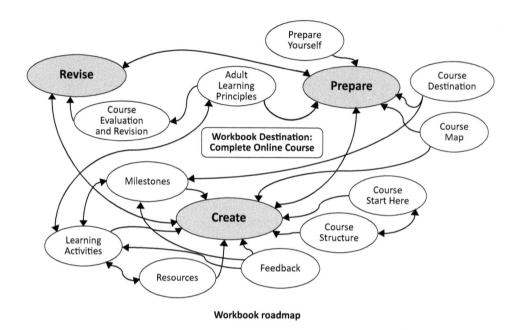

Workbook roadmap

(*cont.*)

We continue our example of the Theories of Personality course. Review the instructor's first step in preparing a course map.

**Theories of Personality Example:
Begin Course Map with Topics**

I have six topics: psychoanalytic theories, behavioral theories, social-cognitive theories, trait theories, humanistic theories, and personality assessment. I put my course destination in the middle of my course map. My topics are in large circles surrounding the destination (Figure 5.2).

Now begin your course map with topics.

**Application:
Begin Your Course Map with Topics**

You are ready to begin preparing your course map in your *course log*. You can review our workbook roadmaps (Figure 5.1) to help you visualize how your course map might look.

- Begin by writing your course destination at the center of the page.
- Next, write the main topics you have chosen to include in your course on the outer edge of the page, encircling the course destination.

The wording of each topic should be minimal. The overall look of the course map should be clean and easy to read. The structure is non-linear and provides an intuitive way to organize the main elements of your course. Using colors, shapes (e.g., circles with text inside), and pictures can enhance your mind map but is not essential to the meaning.

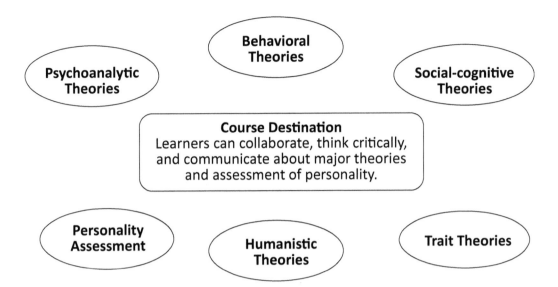

Figure 5.2 Theories of Personality course map with topics.

ESSENTIAL INFORMATION

All topics contain information. Depending on the nature of the course, you may have a lot of information to cover (e.g., first year survey courses). Similarly, your institution may expect you to cover a long list of information due to program, government, and/or professional standards in your discipline. In other situations, you may have more liberty to determine what information you want learners to learn. Regardless of your situation, you can designate some information as essential.

Essential information is information that all learners in your course need to know to succeed personally and/or professionally. Even if you must expose learners to a large amount of information (e.g., so that your learners will remember the information long enough to pass a certification test), you can spend more time emphasizing the essential information. If you have more leeway in choosing what information to cover, we recommend covering essential information in more depth.

Notes from Our Journey:
Broadening and Narrowing of Information

As we began to develop our workbook, we each researched a variety of topics and shared all we learned during our exploration. This exploration resulted in a very broad scope of information. We discussed what we thought was important to include based on our respective backgrounds. We then reviewed our workbook destination, which narrowed the scope of our information. When we took into account the expertise of our readers (context), we decided that our readers would likely include both new and experienced online instructors and instructional designers. Because of the diversity of reader expertise, the challenge was to decide how broad the scope of the information should be. We needed to include the essential information as well as supplementary information that was relevant to the creation of online courses and that addressed the various levels of expertise of our readers (broaden).

We decided to include *Exploring the Terrain* to provide quick-reads on theory and ideas, history, and interesting, relevant information (narrow). The more passionate we became about our workbook, the more difficult it was to maintain focus on our workbook destination. We also realized that intriguing details, while interesting to us, did not necessarily serve to enhance our readers' understanding. Our process of choosing essential information was iterative, non-linear, and socially constructed, always keeping our readers' needs in mind. New information was proposed and discussed. Some information was changed, some information was dismissed, and some of the dismissed information was reintroduced later as our knowledge and intent became clearer. In the end, our choice of information was guided by our workbook destination and tied to our readers' contexts.

Throughout the Change-adept Course Creation Process, you will experience broadening (brainstorming many options) and narrowing (determining which options work best).

In our example, the instructor goes through a similar process of broadening and narrowing to choose essential information. Review the instructor's thought process.

Theories of Personality Example:
Essential Information Chosen and Added to the Course Map

Each topic in this course includes a huge amount of possible information for learners to learn. I keep in mind the brief length of my course (seven weeks) and my desire for learners to gain deeper knowledge of a smaller number of key concepts rather than superficial knowledge of a larger number of concepts. After brainstorming, I choose the essential information that a professional in my discipline would need to know. My choice is based on my professional knowledge of the discipline and my knowledge of my learners' contexts.

Psychoanalytic Theories	**Trait Theories**
Developmental stages and complexes	Central and cardinal traits
Id, ego, superego	Personality factors
Conscious, preconscious, unconscious	
Archetypes	**Humanistic Theories**
Self-concept, internal object relations	Hierarchy of needs
	Person-centered approach
Behavioral Theories	
Classical and operant conditioning	**Personality Assessment**
Stimulus and response	Psychoanalytic: Rorschach, TAT
Reinforcement and punishment	Trait: Big 5, MMPI
	Humanistic: Q-sort
Social-Cognitive Theories	
Expectancy	
Locus of control	
Observational learning	

Figure 5.3 illustrates the essential information that I have placed within each topic circle on my map.

Behavioral Theories
- Classical and operant conditioning
- Stimulus and response
- Reinforcement and punishment

Psychoanalytic Theories
- Developmental stages and complexes
- Id, ego, superego
- Conscious, preconscious, unconscious
- Archetypes

Social-Cognitive Theories
- Expectancy
- Locus of control
- Observational learning

Course Destination
Learners can collaborate, think critically, and communicate about major theories and assessment of personality.

Trait Theories
- Central and cardinal traits
- Personality factors

Personality Assessment
- Psychoanalytic: Rorschach, TAT
- Trait: Big 5, MMPI
- Humanistic: Q-sort

Humanistic Theories
- Hierarchy of needs
- Person-centered approach

Figure 5.3 Theories of Personality course map with essential information.

Now choose your essential information and add it to your map.

Application:
Choose Essential Information and Add It to the Course Map

Brainstorm possible topic-related information in your *course log*. Then narrow this information to the essentials. Here are some questions to help you choose essential information:

- What information is necessary for learners to understand the course topics?
- What information is required for learners to meet ethical and professional standards, including passing relevant certification/licensure/other exams (e.g., teacher certification, nursing licensure, counselor licensure)?

You can circle, highlight, or otherwise designate certain information as essential in your *course log*. If other information on your list is not required by your institution, consider deleting this information.

Add the essential information to your course map by including the information inside or close to the relevant topic.

CONNECTIONS AMONG TOPICS

A disconcerting feature of many online courses (and, indeed, of many educational programs) is the lack of connection among the various topics that learners are expected to learn. Hussey and Smith (2002), the NRC (2000), and Shireman (2016) have critiqued the popular use of long lists of learning objectives and outcomes in the absence of emphasizing the connections among these objectives, outcomes, and the work that learners do in a course. The NRC (2000) has stated that *it is the network, the connections among objectives, that is important ... Stress on isolated parts can train students in a series of routines without educating them to understand an overall picture that will ensure the development of integrated knowledge structures and information about conditions of applicability.* (p. 139)

In contrast to an isolated approach, we provide an approach that helps adult learners make the needed connections: connections among course topics, connections between course topics and relevant skills, and connections between the course and learners' personal and professional goals. You will see connections featured in the examples we present, and we will encourage you to make connections explicit to learners.

To use our journey metaphor again, imagine taking a guided tour of a country over the course of several weeks. A good tour guide highlights recurring historical and cultural elements that appear in the various locations and points of interest that you visit. The tour guide also reminds you of things you have already experienced in that country and points out how new experiences are similar or different. As a result, you feel that you have a better understanding of the country's history and culture rather than a set of random, unconnected facts and experiences.

If each topic is presented in an isolated way, with no continuity across the course (other than a cumulative final, paper, and/or project), then it is harder for learners to organize all of the information and make sense of it. In contrast, when topics are presented together, learners see meaningful connections and better understand how various pieces of information fit together (Kember, 2004; Kember & Leung, 2006).

Guidelines for Finding Connections among Topics

Your determination of how topics are connected is based on your own expertise in your discipline. This may include professional experience (if applicable) or other experience. Experts can quickly see connections among topics in their discipline; however, novices need guidance to see those connections (NRC, 2000). To identify connections among topics in your course, ask yourself these questions:

- How are topics related in your profession/discipline/realistic scenario?
- What topics can be compared/contrasted?
- What topics offer two perspectives on the same issue?
- If topics show historical/chronological development, what is the common thread across periods/eras?
- If topics develop from simple to complex, what is the common thread across topics?

Finding connections among topics also helps learners to develop and synthesize multiple perspectives on a topic, which Bartunek, Gordon, and Weathersby (1983) call *complicated understanding*.

 Exploring the Terrain: Complicated Understanding

According to Bartunek et al. (1983), complicated understanding includes two key concepts.

- Cognitive complexity: the ability to differentiate among several characteristics and integrate the interrelationships among the differentiated characteristics.

- Complementarity: the ability to apply multiple perspectives to a situation/issue.

Complicated understanding results in important cognitive, social, and emotional outcomes:

- empathy for conflicting views and social understanding
- tolerance for diversity and ambiguity
- more accurate perceptions
- ability to take others' perspectives
- thinking in more complex and abstract ways while paradoxically thinking in more precise and specific ways
- action of mutual interdependence
- more complete synthesis of viewpoints.

To apply complicated understanding to your course, you may want to emphasize some of the following approaches:

- Begin with more structured topics with fewer perspectives and move learners toward more complex topics requiring greater depth of understanding. This process helps learners develop more complex cognitive, social, and emotional understanding as they engage with information.
- Encourage learners to include different perspectives.
- Move from "either–or" and "both–and" thinking to "many together" thinking.
- Integrate various approaches/perspectives that are interdependent and synthesize.
- Challenge learners to explore areas outside their comfort zones.
- Include thinking, feeling, acting, and reflecting for self and group.
- Include multiple teaching approaches.

Complicated understanding challenges your learners to develop a deeper shared understanding (i.e., the ability to take in and synthesize multiple viewpoints rather than an endorsement of a single viewpoint). By connecting topics, you help learners to develop complicated understanding.

Let's return to the example. Review how the instructor looks for connections among the topics.

Theories of Personality Example:
Finding Connections among Topics – Part 1

During the stage when I was looking for inspiration for topics in my course, I came across a syllabus for an online Theories of Personality course (see Table 5.1). I was intrigued because it seemed to match all of the topics I wanted to include! However, I was concerned because the course appears to make no connections among topics. Each week, there is a single topic, and learners' knowledge of the topic is evaluated with a quiz and a discussion board. The research paper focuses on a single topic. The cumulative exam evaluates knowledge of all of the topics, but learners do not make any connections among the topics in the exam or elsewhere.

Table 5.1   Theories of Personality course with no connections among topics

Week	Topics	Activities
1	Psychoanalytic theories	Discussion board on psychoanalytic theories Multiple-choice quiz on psychoanalytic theories
2	Behavioral theories	Discussion board on behavioral theories Multiple-choice quiz on behavioral theories
3	Social-cognitive theories	Discussion board on social-cognitive theories Multiple-choice quiz on social-cognitive theories
4	Trait theories	Discussion board on trait theories Multiple-choice quiz on trait theories
5	Humanistic theories	Discussion board on humanistic theories Multiple-choice quiz on humanistic theories
6	Personality assessment	Research paper on personality assessment
7	Exam	Cumulative multiple-choice exam

We return to the instructor's decision process.

Theories of Personality Example:
Finding Connections among Topics – Part 2

In contrast to the course syllabus I reviewed (Table 5.1), I want to emphasize connections among topics. Psychoanalytic theories and behavioral theories are often seen as being in conflict, so those topics are connected by virtue of their differences. I draw a line between these two topics and include short double lines to indicate connection through contrast.

Social-cognitive theories emerged from behavioral theories, so those topics are also connected. I draw an arrow from behavioral to social-cognitive.

The facets of personality assessment I have included are instruments that are connected to psychoanalytic, trait, and humanistic theories, so I connect those topics to the personality assessment topic with arrows.

My course map now shows the topics, essential information, and their connections (Figure 5.4).

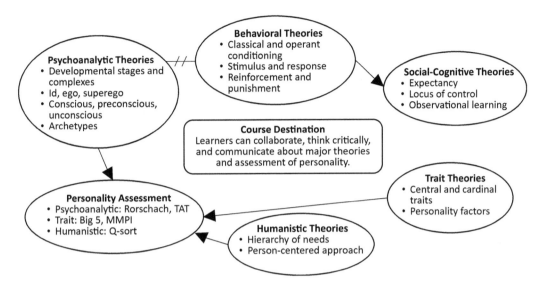

Figure 5.4 Theories of Personality course map with connections among topics

Now, in your course log, connect the topics on your course map.

Application:
Connect Topics on Your Course Map

To connect topics on your course map:

- Draw connecting branches between topics that are connected. At a minimum, find a connection between two topics in your course.
- If you find that all topics are connected to all other topics, consider which connections are the strongest and indicate those with bold lines.
- On the other hand, if you have one or more topics that are isolated, consider whether these topics are really needed and, if so, whether they can be connected to any other topics.

TOPIC CLUSTERS

You have identified connections among your topics. Now you need to determine how topics cluster together based on these connections. What do the connected topics have in common? You can use your professional experience and/or knowledge of your discipline to make this determination. The number of topic clusters determines the number of learning activities you will include in your course.

Review the instructor's clustering of topics.

Theories of Personality Example:
Topic Clusters

As I look at the connections I have drawn, two clusters emerge. One cluster includes psychoanalytic, behavioral, and social-cognitive theories. A common thread across topics in this cluster is that these theories are the basis for different therapeutic approaches. I will have a learning activity for that cluster.

The other cluster includes psychoanalytic, trait, humanistic, and personality assessment. The common thread for this cluster is personality assessment approaches. I need a learning activity for that cluster, too.

Based on my map, I have two learning activities in my seven-week course (Figure 5.5). Two activities seem reasonable for the amount of time available.

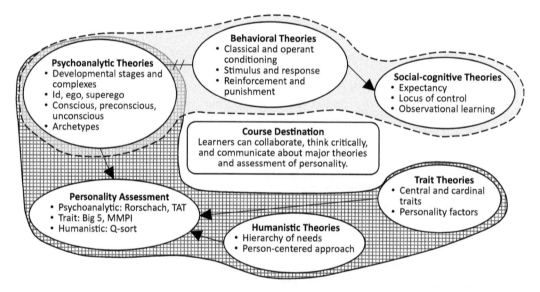

Figure 5.5 Theories of Personality course map with topic clusters.

Now, identify topic clusters on your course map.

Application:
Identify Topic Clusters on Your Course Map

To identify topic clusters:

- Look at the connections on your map. Which connected topics can form a meaningful cluster?
- Draw a shape around the connected topics that will form a topic cluster.
- In your *course log*, write the commonality among the topics in each cluster.
- If you have a topic that is not connected to other topics, you either find a connection or else plan to create a brief learning activity for that topic.

Milestone:
Your Course Map

Congratulations! You have reached your first milestone: a map of your course topics, how these topics are connected to each other, and the topic clusters that will be the basis of the learning activities you create.

Call a Colleague:
Your Course Map

It's time for dialogue! Contact one of the people on your *Call a Colleague* list and share your course map. Ask for and be open to feedback. Check for clarity and completeness, and seek feedback on the connections you have drawn among topics as well as your clustering of connected topics. Remember: the Change-adept Course Creation Process is iterative and involves change.

Jot your discussion notes in the space provided below.

COURSE THEME

Now that you have topic clusters, it's time to revisit the possible themes you considered in *Chapter 4: Course Description*. The clusters of topics may suggest a theme that can tie the course together.

Review the instructor's decision about a course theme, based on the clusters of topics.

Theories of Personality Example:
Course Theme

I have one cluster that is about theories that inform treatments and another cluster about personality assessment approaches. Both clusters would be a good fit with the university counseling center or psychotherapy clinic theme. Based on my own past experience working in a clinic, a psychotherapy clinic is the best theme for my course. If I didn't have this experience, I might choose a different theme.

Course theme: I choose the theme of a psychotherapy clinic in which learners work as interns.

Note that in this example, the theme will be woven throughout the course as a scenario. Even if you do not have professional experience outside of academia, your theme can include a professional scenario that is engaging to your learners. Examples of themes (and related disciplines) include learners working as curators at a museum (art history, history), researchers (natural and social sciences), professional apprentices or interns (business, counseling, education, journalism, nursing, technical courses), artists (art, drama, music), and so forth.

Now choose your course theme.

Application:
Choose Your Course Theme

Based on the topic clusters you have identified, choose a course theme that fits your clusters. The course theme can be a scenario and/or a unifying set of images and text that are related to your discipline and to the clusters you have created. Write your course theme in your *course log*.

FREQUENTLY ASKED QUESTIONS

In this chapter, we have introduced some ideas that may be different from your usual approach to creating a course. These ideas include:

* choosing essential information to emphasize in your course
* making connections among topics explicit to learners
* using a course theme to unify the course.

The following frequently asked questions (FAQs) attempt to address some questions you may have about these ideas and the work you have done so far. We begin with an *Exploring the Terrain* about the first FAQ:

FAQ: Where do learning objectives fit in this process?

Exploring the Terrain:
Learning Objectives

Many programs require instructors to formulate or adopt learning objectives (what learners will know and be able to do by the end of the course).

Along with other writers (e.g., Hussey & Smith, 2002; Shireman, 2016), we have observed several phenomena that have given us pause about incorporating the typical use of objectives into the Change-adept Course Creation Process:

* Instructors often define the objectives in linear, finite terms, such as, "by the end of this course, you will be able to...," rather than acknowledging that learning is a complex, ongoing process that continues beyond the course.
* Instructors may create a long list of learning objectives that are probably impossible for most learners to truly achieve.
* Instructors provide a list of objectives but do not indicate how the objectives are connected.

If you recognize yourself in our description, you are not alone; we first observed these behaviors in ourselves!

To avoid the baggage of the term "objectives," as well as the linear and finite view of learning that this term may imply, we chose to use the course map approach rather than to list objectives. The course map illustrates essential information, shows connections, is growth-oriented, provides a visual representation of the complexity of the learning process (semiotics), and better meets the needs of diverse adult learners.

FAQ: My institution has provided me with a list of mandated end-of-course learning objectives. Are you telling me to ignore this mandate and just use a course map instead?

Indeed, we are not! You should certainly include whatever your institution requires. Just as we have noted that you can supplement your institution's required course goal (if applicable) with a course destination, you can supplement a required list of objectives with your course map. Treat objectives as essential information and proceed with the process accordingly, grouping your essential information (objectives) into topics, making connections, and identifying clusters.

Including a course map is not incompatible with using learning objectives; you can take a "both–and" approach rather than an "either–or" approach to this issue.

FAQ: When will I choose assessments?

You have anticipated the next step in the process! However, as you will see, we conceptualize assessments as *Milestones* to avoid challenges with the term "assessment" and to include a specific emphasis on skill areas.

SUMMARY: COURSE MAP

In this chapter, you mapped your course topics. You identified essential information within each topic and then drew connections among topics. You developed topic clusters and chose a course theme based on the clusters as well as your knowledge of your discipline. This work resulted in your first milestone: a course map.

This chapter ends the **Prepare** section of the workbook. You are now ready to begin the **Create** section with *Chapter 6: Milestones*.

CREATE

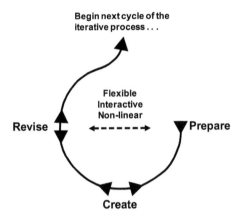

Change-adept Course Creation Process. © 2020

In the *Prepare* section of this workbook, you prepared yourself through self-reflection, explored adult learning principles (our view of learning – cognitive, social, and emotional aspects; the adult learning process; adult learning assumptions; and semiotics for inclusion of diverse learners), chose your course destination, prepared a course map illustrating connections among topics, and chose a course theme.

In the *Create* section of this workbook, you will create all of the items you need for your online course. By the end of the *Create* section, you will have a complete online course that is ready for your online learners.

Chapter 6 focuses on creating *milestones*, which provide evidence of learning.

Chapter 7 focuses on creating a *learning activity* for a specific milestone.

Chapter 8 focuses on selecting *resources* for the learning activity.

Chapter 9 focuses on opportunities for learners to receive *feedback* throughout the learning activity.

Chapter 10 focuses on *course structure*, including an *itinerary* of learning activities and *modules* for your online course.

Chapter 11 ends the *Create* section with your *Course Start Here*, which is your learners' entry point into your course.

Throughout this section, you will continue to see the Theories of Personality course used to illustrate the steps of the process. However, you will also find ideas and examples from other disciplines.

6   Milestones

MILESTONES: INTRODUCTION

You have mapped the topics for your course and shown the connections among them. The course map represents the basic knowledge learners will gain on their way to the course destination. The next step is to identify milestones, which integrate topics and skill areas into tangible evidence of learners' progress toward the course destination.

Consider our journey metaphor again. On a journey, travelers often stop at various points on the way to their destination. They may take pictures, purchase souvenirs, or engage in other actions to commemorate that they have reached a milestone in their journey. The milestone is not the destination itself, but rather is a sign of progress toward the destination.

Similarly, learners may write papers, create projects, do presentations, solve problems, and produce other tangible evidence of their learning throughout a course. These products demonstrate learners' topic knowledge and skill at key points. We decided that *milestone* nicely captured the main evidence of learners' progress toward the course destination.

 Travel Advisory:
Milestones versus Assessments

We conceptualize assessments (or what some instructors call outcomes) as milestones. We do this for two reasons:

- Milestones emphasize progress toward the destination, rather than finite outcomes.
- Learners often view work labeled "assessment" as the most important part of the course. In our view, what learners do prior to the assessment is just as important. We use the term "milestone" to avoid the baggage of "assessment" and to signal that these are progress points along the way.

Summative and Formative Milestones

In the previous chapter, you created topic clusters that grouped topics together based on connections. We noted that each topic cluster will be the basis of a learning activity. Similarly, each topic cluster will have at least one *summative milestone* that occurs at the end of the learning activity for that cluster. Summative refers to the fact that the milestone "sums up" learners' achievement of topic knowledge and skill. Summative milestones require instructors' summative feedback.

In addition, learning activities may also include earlier evidence of progress. Such evidence constitutes *formative milestones*, as these can help "form" learners' future work through formative feedback. At this point, your work on milestones will focus on summative milestones; you will choose formative milestones in *Chapter 7: Learning Activities*.

In this chapter, you will complete the following actions:

- identify possible summative milestones related to skill areas
- choose a summative milestone for each topic cluster.

MILESTONES AND SKILL AREAS

There are countless types of milestones, ranging from written work to oral presentations to tangible creations. Your choice of milestones should be determined by the skill areas that you want your learners to develop. For example, if writing is one of the skill areas you have chosen, then you will need a milestone that involves written work. If teamwork is a skill area, then you need a milestone that involves a group product. If critical thinking is a skill area, then the milestone should involve a product that shows learners' abilities to think critically. The key is to choose milestones that are a good match with the skill areas you have chosen for your course.

Examples of milestones and some relevant skill areas include:

- a lab report on a simulated science experiment (skill areas: inquiry and analysis, writing)
- a primary source analysis of a historical document (skill areas: critical thinking, writing)
- a group research project video presentation (skill areas: inquiry and analysis, teamwork)
- a product redesign project report (skill areas: technical skill, writing)
- a statistical problem set (skill areas: problem-solving, quantitative reasoning).

The process of choosing a milestone starts with the question, "In what ways would professionals in my discipline demonstrate their knowledge of the topics, using one or more of the skill areas identified in this course?"

Table 6.1 presents examples of skill areas and relevant summative milestones. Think about which of these are relevant for your profession/discipline.

Table 6.1   Examples of skill areas and summative milestones

Skill areas	Summative milestones
Communication	Essay, oral presentation, podcast, blog/vlog, article, report
Creative abilities	Work of art, performance, model
Critical thinking and problem-solving	Text analysis, evaluation of sources, critical literature review
Inquiry and analysis	Research summary, lab findings
Quantitative reasoning	Problem set, data presentation, data analysis
Teamwork	Team educational campaign, written dialogue, peer review form, team report on a simulation experience
Technical skill	Design project, prototype, algorithm

We now continue with the example of the Theories of Personality course. Review the instructor's process of identifying possible summative milestones based on skill areas.

Theories of Personality Example:
Skill Areas and Possible Summative Milestones

I previously identified three skill areas that are important for psychologists: critical thinking, teamwork, and writing. Looking at Table 6.1, I come up with some initial ideas. I also consider how professionals in my discipline (i.e., psychologists) might demonstrate these skills. I develop the following list of possible summative milestones for my course:

Critical thinking
    Case analysis and interpretation
    Critical literature review
    Interpretation and synthesis of assessment data
    Interpretation and synthesis of research findings

Teamwork
    Team discussion about clients
    Team research presentation
    Team educational presentation

Writing
    Journal article
    Magazine article
    Therapy notes
    Assessment report
    Informational brochure

Now identify possible summative milestones related to your skill areas.

Application:
Identify Possible Summative Milestones Related to Skill Areas

Consider the examples in Table 6.1 and your own knowledge of how professionals in your discipline use the skill areas you have chosen. List possible summative milestones in your *course log*.

You might have noticed that we have not used Bloom's taxonomy in our process. Although Bloom's taxonomy is often used to develop learning objectives and outcomes, in our view using Bloom's taxonomy to create milestones is not effective. We explain why in the next *Exploring the Terrain*.

Exploring the Terrain:
Bloom's Taxonomy

Bloom's taxonomy enjoys widespread recognition and use throughout the field of education. However, today there is mounting concern about the efficacy of the taxonomy.

History. In 1948, a committee formed to develop a way to classify educational goals so that faculty in higher education could better assess their students' performance. Bloom, Engelhart, Furst, Hill, and Krathwold's (1956) original taxonomy was based on a highly structured hierarchy of six cognitive categories. The categories were arranged from the lowest (basic knowledge) to the highest level of complexity (evaluation). The use of the cognitive domain hierarchy has expanded beyond its original intent for use in higher education and been adopted worldwide, most predominately in K–12 settings, and continues to be used to guide the development of learning objectives, activities, and outcomes.

Bloom's cognitive domain taxonomy was revised by Anderson and Krathwold (2001). The six cognitive categories were renamed and, in some cases, reordered. A knowledge dimension consisting of four types of knowledge was added that created a matrix of the relationship between the cognitive processes and the type of knowledge. More recently, higher education has conceded, sometimes with angst, to the use of the taxonomy in writing objectives.

Bloom's other domains. There are two additional domains that are mentioned in connection with Bloom's taxonomy – affective and psychomotor. In 1964, Krathwold, Bloom, and Masia added the affective domain to Bloom's taxonomy. The affective domain has been largely ignored and has not been revised. While Bloom et al. (1956) recognized the existence of the psychomotor domain, they felt that there was little need for it in education; therefore, it was never part of Bloom's taxonomy. However, several versions of psychomotor domain taxonomies have been published over the years (e.g., Harrow, 1972).

Concerns about Bloom's cognitive domain. There is concern that the basic premise of Bloom's taxonomy, that higher-level cognition is built on lower-level cognition, has led to a diminished appreciation of those "lower-level" skills, which in reality can be quite complex. According to Kagan (2005), our brains do not process information hierarchically from lower to higher level of complexity. In fact, we each have "unique patterns" of thinking that are not arranged hierarchically. In addition, *any* cognitive skill, whether designated as lower or higher by Bloom's taxonomy, can in actuality be more or less complex depending on the depth of thinking in which one engages. Even seemingly simple cognitive tasks can in fact be complex.

For example, although "remembering" is considered the lowest level of cognition in Bloom's taxonomy, consider the complexity of memorizing a soliloquy from one of Shakespeare's plays. Such memorization will be challenging without an understanding of the piece and the circumstances within the play when it is performed, an examination of the emotional state of mind of the character, and so forth. In other words, understanding and remembering are intertwined, rather than occurring in a hierarchical way (Weinstein, 2019).

The bottom line is that "there are many types of thinking and each type of thinking develops and functions relatively independently from the others" (Kagan, 2005, "Beyond Bloom," para. 1). Perhaps a more mindful, integrative approach to learning that connects differing cognitive processes with the social and emotional aspects would be a more effective approach than using Bloom's taxonomy. In addition, the exclusive focus on the cognitive aspect of learning does not reflect the overall learning process that also includes the social and emotional aspects of learning. As we know from brain research, there is a strong emotional aspect of learning (NASEM, 2018).

And one final note. Admittedly, Bloom's cognitive taxonomy provides us with a handy list of verbs to use to describe what learners will do in our course. However, we must be mindful that Bloom's words represent a simple-to-complex hierarchy. As Kagan (2005) discussed, "recall" – considered lower-level thinking in Bloom's taxonomy – can in actuality represent either simple or complex thinking depending on the task. The same can be said for "evaluation," considered higher-level thinking. If your institution requires you to create learning objectives and outcomes based on Bloom's hierarchy, it may be best to provide additional information to the learner (e.g., a description of the skill areas being developed in the course) so that the intent of the learning outcome is understood. In our experience, the chief value of Bloom's taxonomy is the impressive array of learning-related verbs that can serve as a reminder of the many things learners might do in a course.

Now that you have some initial ideas for summative milestones, it's time to narrow them down. Consider your learners' contexts, professional applications, theme, and topic clusters. Note that one milestone does not have to involve all of the skill areas. Collectively, however, the milestones should involve all skill areas.

Review the instructor's process for choosing a milestone for each topic cluster.

Theories of Personality Example:
Summative Milestone for Each Topic Cluster

The topics in my first cluster (Figure 5.5) are all theories that have therapeutic implications. Thus, I might want my learners to show their knowledge of the topics in the context of working with clients (which also fits my theme of a psychotherapy clinic). As I look at my list of possible milestones, I decide that therapy notes, an assessment report, and interpretation and synthesis of assessment data are not suitable because my learners won't actually be working with clients. A journal article, critical literature review, and interpretation and synthesis of research findings require more knowledge and experience than my learners have.

However, a case analysis and interpretation might be a good fit. Even though learners are not actually working with clients, I could develop some "cases" of clients that learners could analyze and interpret individually or in teams. If I add writing to the milestone, then my milestone for this cluster is "written case analysis and interpretation."

In my experience, written work that learners complete as a team does not necessarily demonstrate an individual learner's knowledge of the information. Thus, I am going to choose an individual format for this milestone. Teamwork may be involved in the activity, but the final milestone will reflect learners' individual performance in two skill areas: critical thinking and writing.

For my second cluster, I return to my list of possible milestones that I brainstormed earlier. The common thread for this cluster is assessment, but I know that my learners are not qualified to do assessments. However, they could learn more about assessments and explore why different theories take different approaches to assessment.

So far, I have one written assignment. It's a short course, so I want to use a different format for the other milestone. Many learners like making and watching videos, so I decide that the other milestone will be a video presentation. I'll add a team element to this milestone so that learners show their teamwork in the summative milestone. The addition of teamwork to this milestone suggests that a team educational presentation (by video) would be a good fit. Thus, my milestone format for this cluster is a team educational video presentation. The skill areas for this milestone are critical thinking and teamwork.

Together, my summative milestones cover all three skill areas: critical thinking, teamwork, and writing.

Now choose a summative milestone for each of your topic clusters.

Application:
Choose a Summative Milestone for Each Topic Cluster

- Choose a topic cluster from your course map. You can start with any cluster.
- Look at the essential information in that cluster.
- Ask yourself: "In what ways would professionals in my discipline show their knowledge of the essential information in the topic cluster, using one or more of the skill areas I have chosen for my course?" List as many possibilities as you can identify.
- Once you have an initial list of possible milestones for your topic cluster, you can begin to narrow the list. Use your knowledge of your learners' contexts, the nature of the essential information in the topic cluster, professional applications of the essential information, and the course theme to rule certain formats in or out. Note your final milestone for the topic cluster in your *course log*.
- Repeat this process with the other topic clusters on your course map. Keep in mind the amount of time available for your course and the expected workload for you and your learners.

Each topic cluster will have at least one summative milestone. Although you may decide that a topic cluster needs more than one summative milestone, we recommend that you stick with one summative milestone per cluster for now to keep things simple. You may also want to think about the total time available in your course, as this may inform the milestones you include. For example, a seven-week course may not be long enough for learners to complete a full literature review, but it may be long enough for learners to complete an annotated bibliography. Use your knowledge of your course length and your learners' contexts to make your decisions.

MILESTONES AND ADULT LEARNING PRINCIPLES

Two aspects of adult learning principles that clearly relate to milestones are the importance of making learning realistic, relevant, and meaningful, and the possibility of providing choices for learners.

Realistic, Relevant, and Meaningful Milestones

Because you have created your milestones with realistic applications in mind, your milestones will be meaningful and relevant to learners. In contrast, multiple-choice tests tend to be less realistic, thereby making it difficult for learners to see the connection between the milestone and their personal and professional goals.

We acknowledge that multiple-choice tests and quizzes provide a convenient way to measure learners' recall of large amounts of information. These tests and quizzes are also popular for large classes and in disciplines that have mandated testing for professional certification or licensure. If your situation or discipline requires you to include a multiple-choice test or quiz, we recommend the following guidelines:

- Provide frequent practice with the types of items that will be on tests/quizzes.
- Provide learners with suggestions for study skills that aid in memorization.
- Ensure that tests/quizzes adequately measure the essential information.
- Incorporate several shorter tests/quizzes, rather than one or two long exams.
- Use low-stakes, formative self-quizzes to help learners gauge their current recall of information. (See *Chapter 7: Learning Activities* for more details on formative milestones.)
- Create tests/quizzes that go beyond memorization by requiring application of skills (e.g., in critical thinking or problem-solving) to the information.
- Include at least one short-answer self-reflection item in the measure. This item can be evaluated for participation only, rather than being graded. However, including a reflection item in a test/quiz reinforces the importance of self-reflection in the learning process. It can also give you qualitative information about your learners' learning.
- Check test/quiz quality by ensuring you are testing what you mean to test (validity) and by conducting an item analysis to ensure that your questions are accurate and effective (reliability).
- Include an additional summative milestone that involves realistic, relevant, and meaningful application of the skill areas you have chosen for your course.

In summary, tests and quizzes often fall short of being the realistic, relevant, and meaningful milestones we want to include in a course. However, you can incorporate tests and quizzes in ways that may be helpful to learners and supplement tests and quizzes with another type of summative milestone.

Choice in Milestones

Instructors are often glibly told to provide choices in their courses but are not given guidance on what that means. One place where choice may be appropriate is in milestones.

When considering providing choices in a milestone, make sure that the choices are equivalent (i.e., provide equal opportunities for learners to show their progress on the relevant skill areas and their knowledge of the essential information for that milestone). For example, if one of the skills you are evaluating is writing, then both milestone types must provide equivalent opportunities for learners to demonstrate their writing skills. Table 6.2 presents three examples of choice within a milestone.

Table 6.2 Examples of choice within a milestone

Milestone	Type of choice and considerations
A written description or diagram of how the scientific process applies to a biology experiment	In this milestone, learners have a choice of whether to present their knowledge verbally or visually.
Skill area: critical thinking	This type of choice is appropriate when a skill (e.g., critical thinking) can be demonstrated in various ways (e.g., verbal or visual).

Table 6.2   (*cont.*)

Milestone	Type of choice and considerations
A paper on the causes and effects of immigration within the United States, with a focus on one of these topics: • History and impact of Irish immigration to the United States • History and impact of Mexican and South/Central American immigration to the United States Skill area: writing	In this milestone, learners have a choice of paper topics. This type of choice is appropriate when essential information (in this example, causes and effects of immigration) is included in both choices. Additional information that learners can choose to write about (in this example, history of specific immigrant groups) is equivalent across choices. In addition, the skill area of written communication is equivalent across choices because both choices involve a written paper.
Newspaper editorial or blog on educational inequity in schools Skill area: writing	In this milestone, learners have a choice of format within the same skill area (writing). This type of choice is appropriate when the skill area (in this case, written communication) can be demonstrated in a variety of equivalent formats.

Consider whether you can include learner choice in one or more milestones. Be sure to look at the choices that you provide in terms of the skill areas and essential information in that milestone to ensure that choices are equitable.

Milestone Review

Review the instructor's determination of how well the milestones reflect adult learning principles.

Theories of Personality Example:
Milestones and Adult Learning Principles

I have two summative milestones: a written case analysis and interpretation and a team educational video presentation. Both milestones seem manageable within a seven-week period, and both are suitable for my learners' contexts. All skill areas are covered: Writing appears in the written case analysis and interpretation, teamwork in the team educational video presentation, and critical thinking in both milestone formats. In addition, I will give learners a choice of what information to cover in their educational video presentation. Both milestones fit my course theme, which is a psychotherapy clinic. Both milestones also offer realistic, relevant, and meaningful applications of course information.

Now apply adult learning principles to your milestones.

Application:
Your Milestones and Adult Learning Principles

Review your milestones in your *course log* to ensure alignment with topics, length of time available in the course, theme, and learners' contexts. Make sure that all skill areas are covered. Apply adult learning principles (our view of learning – cognitive, social, and emotional aspects; adult learning process; adult learning assumptions; and semiotics for inclusion of diverse learners) to your milestones.

Call a Colleague:
Summative Milestones

Discuss with your colleague the summative milestones you have chosen. Seek feedback on the extent to which your milestones reflect adult learning principles. Jot down your notes in the space provided.

MILESTONES: SUMMARY

You have now chosen a summative milestone for each topic cluster. These milestones are connected to the skill areas you have chosen for your course.

You are now ready for *Chapter 7: Learning Activities.*

7   Learning Activities

LEARNING ACTIVITIES: INTRODUCTION

Now that you have your course map, you may be thinking about how learners will achieve each milestone and progress toward the destination. A learning activity is the vehicle through which learners learn essential information, strengthen their skills, and achieve the summative milestone. Table 7.1 presents the elements of a learning activity.

Table 7.1   Elements of a learning activity

Elements	Descriptions
Milestone (summative)	Tangible result of a learning activity that represents learners' progress toward the course destination
Purpose statement	Succinct statement of how the learning activity will help learners apply the topics/essential information to produce the summative milestone in the context of the theme
Actions	Self-reflection, dialogue, and application
Resources	Items that contain information needed to complete the activity.
Feedback	Information provided to learners about their progress (formative feedback) or final result (summative feedback)

We begin the chapter by discussing experiential learning and collaboration, which together provide a framework for developing learning activities consistent with adult learning principles (our view of learning: cognitive, social, and emotional; the learning process; adult learning assumptions; and semiotics for inclusion of diverse learners). Experiential learning and collaboration contribute to meaningful learner connections (Liu, Magjuka, Bonk, & Lee, 2007). Therefore, we include both experiential learning and collaboration in every learning activity.

We will show you several examples of learning activities. You will then choose a topic cluster and complete the following actions to create one learning activity:

- Develop your learning activity purpose statement.
- Choose actions (self-reflection, dialogue, and application) for your learning activity.
- Integrate the course theme into your learning activity.
- Create formative milestones.
- Review your learning activity in terms of adult learning principles.

Travel Advisory:
Creating Learning Activities

Consistent with the iterative nature of this workbook, we will walk you through the entire process of creating a single learning activity in Chapters 7–9. In this chapter, you will focus on the learning activity purpose statement and actions learners take within the learning activity. In Chapters 8 and 9, you will focus on resources and feedback, respectively. In Chapter 10, you will repeat the process to create additional learning activities as needed.

EXPERIENTIAL LEARNING

Experiential learning involves learning within the context of a relevant, realistic, meaningful activity. Case studies, simulations, lab experiments, and research projects are examples of experiential learning methods that require learners to work individually and/or in collaboration with others to gain direct experience with the course topics, to apply information to real situations, and to self-reflect and engage in dialogue about their experience. In addition, experiential learning allows you to immerse learners in the course theme, which makes the course more exciting and realistic.

Travel Advisory:
Terminology in Experiential Learning

Note that many terms in experiential learning are often used synonymously in the literature (e.g., case study, simulation, scenario, role-play, situation-based learning). Rather than quibble over definitional differences, we present these experiential learning activities as a group because they have similar characteristics.

Tips for Experiential Learning

Table 7.2 presents tips for integrating experiential learning into your course. You can keep these tips in mind as you create learning activities.

If you have not had work experience outside academia, you can still use scenarios. One suggestion is to have learners create their own scenarios; another option might be to work with professionals in your discipline outside of academia to create a realistic scenario. Keep in

Table 7.2 Tips for experiential learning

Tips	Explanations
Provide a realistic context for learners' work by including a scenario.	Scenarios make learning activities more realistic, relevant, and meaningful to learners. For example, when you create a workplace scenario that demands knowledge and skill applications, learners experience the real needs of a workplace in a memorable way.
Keep the purpose of the learning activity in mind.	Experiential learning should not simply be a gimmick or include "bells and whistles" that don't actually contribute to learning. Only include experiential learning if it makes a learning activity more realistic, relevant, and meaningful.
Create opportunities for learners to interact with each other in realistic ways.	Simulations, role-plays, and case studies, all of which involve learners immersing themselves in a realistic situation, require learners to collaborate and make decisions and solve problems together based on information they receive.
Engage learners' curiosity through activities that involve hands-on projects that are related to skill areas.	Experiments, research, and projects provide direct experience with the kinds of skills learners will need in their future professions (e.g., communication, problem-solving, critical thinking, teamwork, analysis and interpretation).
Incorporate learners' personal or professional environment into the learning activity.	Field-based activities, service learning, and interaction with one's community resources (local library, museum, government office, etc.) can provide a more immersive experience that is realistic, relevant, and meaningful.

mind that work is constantly changing, so you will need to review your scenario with professionals in the workforce regularly.

COLLABORATION

How many times have you given a group a project to complete only to observe that their group process is to work individually to complete the project in pieces rather than collaborate? Scheuermann (2018) has distinguished collaboration from group work in terms of accountability, noting that group work involves a "divide and conquer mentality" (para. 5), whereas collaboration requires a group to work together and be accountable to each other.

Collaboration also requires ongoing, meaningful interaction among learners who perceive themselves to be part of the group. According to Shedroff (2001) and Wilson, Ludwig-Hardman, Thornam, and Dunlap (2004), successful online groups exhibit the following characteristics:

- Create collective identity among learners (sense of belonging), which fosters continued participation.
- Establish respectful inclusion around diverse perspectives.
- Create a sense of ownership among learners.
- Provide appropriate ways of communicating among learners (asynchronously and synchronously).
- Promote interaction and collaboration with others to create and expand the group's shared understanding through dialogue (e.g., projects, peer reviews, and other mutually beneficial learning activities) and reflection.

Such collaboration requires the establishment of trust early in the course.

 Exploring the Terrain:
Swift Trust

"Trust formation is a dynamic process that takes different forms at different stages of a relationship" (Robert, Dennis, & Hung, 2009, p. 268). *Swift trust* refers to the initial trust formed when individuals who are unknown to each other first meet as a group. Swift trust is applied to groups that come together for a short period of time to interdependently accomplish a "relatively clear goal or purpose" (Meyerson, Weick, & Kramer, 1996, p. 167).

For you, as an instructor, the question becomes how to create a learning activity that encourages learners' development of swift trust with course peers. Swift trust can be promoted in several important ways. Most notably, swift trust is fostered by providing learners with a basic level of relevant knowledge about each other so that they can establish a group identity.

In addition, the following techniques foster swift trust and engage adult learners.

- When creating project groups, allow learners to choose their group members based on the orientation discussion posts and times available for synchronous, virtual communication.
- Give detailed instructions on rules for group projects, simulations, case studies, and other interactive tasks. Provide detailed guidance, and establish a timeline on what is due and when. A clear structure helps foster the formation of swift trust.
- Asking group members to post a description of group member roles and responsibilities, task lists, timelines, project purpose, agreed-upon meeting times, and alternate contact information, helps learners to stay on track and reduce the perceived risk of participating together while establishing group member interdependency.

Swift trust influences learners' performance in the near term and the development of deeper trust among members of cohorts in the longer term. Therefore, swift trust deserves mindful attention as you consider the importance of collaboration for adult learners. The presence or absence of swift trust impacts learners' feelings of inclusion or belongingness in the course, thereby affecting the group's ability to work together.

In our experience, collaboration is one of the most challenging aspects of online courses for both instructors and learners. It is not that groups are inherently difficult; rather, the logistics of collaboration can create frustrations, and too often learners view dialogue as "busy work" rather than as a meaningful part of a learning activity. We provide tips on how to anticipate and manage these challenges in the following group FAQs (frequently asked questions).

Group FAQs and Possible Solutions

Learners (and thus instructors) are often wary of activities that require collaboration. Table 7.3 presents instructors' FAQs about groups and provides possible solutions to learners' and instructors' concerns.

Table 7.3   FAQs about groups and possible solutions

FAQs	Possible Solutions
Should groups be instructor-created or learner-created?	There is no clear evidence that instructor-created vs. learner-created groups are more effective. Instructor-created groups may be beneficial when groups need to be formed early in a course and when the instructor wants learners to work with peers they don't know already. Learner-created groups may be beneficial when learners have had a chance to get to know each other and when collaboration benefits from shared interests. However, as a rule of thumb, remember that adult learners like choice. Allowing learners to choose their own groups increases their ownership of the group process and commitment to each other.
What tools can my learners or I use to form groups?	Instructor-created groups can be formed randomly or intentionally based on information obtained in the course. Your learning management system (LMS) may have a group tool that allows you to randomly assign group members or manually assign group members. If your LMS has the capability, you can set up groups that learners can join by signing up for a group. You will need to let the learners know how many members can be in each group. For example, you can use a discussion tool to let groups self-form with ground rules, such as "no more than four people in a group."

Table 7.3 *(cont.)*

FAQs	Possible Solutions
When should groups be formed?	We recommend that you orient learners to the importance of collaboration and that groups be established as early as possible.
My course groups are formed. Now what?	Once groups are formed, it is helpful for group members to discuss their expectations and roles. This discussion may involve the use of a group/team agreement that includes their shared goals, expectations, and responsibilities. Group members should share a variety of ways for their group members to contact them.
My learners say they hate group work. Should I just avoid it altogether?	Learners often dislike group work because of negative past group experiences and/or because they prefer to be accountable only to themselves and the instructor. Learners may also resist group work because they feel that they don't have time to talk to their peers or because the logistics of scheduling are complex. You can help learners identify what they need from other team members in a collaborative activity. This activity can involve setting a team agreement and a process for giving and receiving feedback on the group process.
I'm hesitant to include a group activity because I'm worried it will be inconvenient for my learners or result in chaos.	It is important to set expectations at the beginning of a course when group work communication is involved. You can provide learners with a variety of flexible communication options (e.g., phone, video conferencing, live chat room) and encourage them to find the right option for their group. At the same time, take into account learners' contexts. For example, if you have learners in different time zones/countries, be sensitive to learners' needs while also pointing out that many work contexts require conferencing across time zones.

Table 7.3   *(cont.)*

FAQs	Possible Solutions
In my discussion board instructions, I usually tell my learners to post and reply to two other learners' posts. However, learners don't sustain the dialogue; they just fulfill the requirements and then drop the conversation.	Finding the right dialogue prompt is also key. Avoid using prompts that have only one answer (e.g., exclusively factual knowledge) and/or that elicit closed-ended responses. Instead, use prompts that are exciting or controversial (if appropriate), and/or that involve personal opinion blended with topic knowledge. In addition, the number of people involved in a dialogue may be too large for a meaningful dialogue. It can be helpful to have dialogue occur within smaller groups or pairs rather than as part of the whole class. Finally, establish clear guidelines on what is expected, including the quality of a response in addition to the quantity of a response. Providing examples of successful dialogue posts and replies can be effective, though caution is needed to avoid learners simply mimicking the example.
Should I participate in my learners' discussions or be present for other group interactions?	Learners may rely too heavily on the instructor when the instructor is a dominant force in the discussion. We have found that meaningful discussion among learners happens when the instructor either "pops in" to the discussion for a short time, is present but mostly observes during the discussion, or responds to the discussion at the end by summarizing and asking additional questions. For example, an instructor may want to be present for each group's initial brainstorming discussion for a group project. However, the instructor can inform the group that the instructor's role is to observe and be available for group questions at the end of the brainstorm. By observing, the instructor gains insight into the group's dynamics and how group members might work together; at the same time, the group benefits from access to the instructor for guidance. If you are quiet and learners are engaged in the conversation or task, they quickly forget you are there!

Travel Advisory:
The Use of FAQs

Do you enjoy the FAQ format of information and find it useful? If so, you might want to consider providing information in this format in your Start Here (see *Chapter 11: Course Start Here*) and throughout your course.

Your Travel Journal:
Experiential Learning and Collaboration

Think about the role of experiential learning and collaboration in your course, then answer the following questions. Jot down your responses in the space provided.

What are your learners' typical reactions to experiential learning?

What are your learners' typical reactions to collaboration?

How do you manage groups in your course?

Based on your experience, what aspects of your learners' contexts might make collaboration especially helpful? Especially challenging?

Now that we have established the importance of experiential learning and collaboration, let's take a look at some examples of learning activities.

LEARNING ACTIVITY EXAMPLES

The following examples are learning activities that incorporate experiential learning, collaboration, and adult learning principles. We begin with an example of a research paper. Look for cognitive, social, and emotional elements; the role of self-reflection and dialogue; how the example makes learning realistic, relevant, and meaningful; and semiotics for inclusion of diverse learners.

Research Paper Learning Activity

NN	**Research synthesis paper for All the News network**	
Purpose: The purpose of this activity is for you to gain experience with the scholarly research process in the context of a realistic professional situation. In completing this activity, you will also gain in-depth knowledge of a course topic of your choice.	*Milestones*: • Research topic map, paper outline, and reference list (formative) • Final draft of paper (summative) • Self-reflection on writing process (summative)	
Setting: You work as a research assistant for News Network, an international news network that publishes syntheses of scholarly research with implications and recommendations for a general audience. Your job is to choose a topic from a list of topics approved by the network, research the topic, and write a research synthesis paper on this topic to support a recommendation for your readers. Your instructor is your editor.	*Skill areas*: • Finding, evaluating, and using resources • Writing • MLA-style citations and references	
Overview of actions and feedback: • Duration: eight weeks • You will choose a topic and create a map of sub-topics. You will then research the topic and find scholarly sources to support your recommendations. • You will create an outline and MLA-style reference list for your editor's feedback. • You will then draft your research synthesis paper and share it with a fellow assistant (classmate) for feedback in a virtual meeting. • Your final research synthesis paper will be submitted to your editor for final feedback. • You will self-reflect on the writing process and submit your self-reflection for editor feedback.	*Resources*: • Document on the writing process, with self-reflection questions • Illustrated handout on topic maps • Illustrated handout on outlining • MLA handbook and handout • Video on finding sources, with transcript • Video on research synthesis, with transcript • Guidelines for the research synthesis paper • Primary source material that you select (five sources)	

Here are a few notes about the research paper learning activity:

- Cognitive, social, and emotional aspects of learning are evident: The activity incorporates cognitive information (the writing and research process), social interaction (peer feedback), and an emotionally appealing context for the activity (news scenario).
- Self-reflection occurs in a self-reflection milestone, and dialogue occurs in a virtual peer meeting.
- The purpose of the activity is clearly stated.
- The scenario makes the activity realistic, relevant, and meaningful.
- Learners apply their learning about the writing and research processes in a practical way. They develop recommendations for a "real" audience based on what they read.
- Learners choose the topics they want to research.
- Diverse learners are included through the use of a theme with broad appeal and the provision of resources in multimodal formats (e.g., illustrated handouts and videos with transcripts).
- The actions occur in a logical order and are completely aligned with the purpose of the learning activity.
- The activity allows learners to experience the connection between the course topics (writing process and research process) and a topic of their choice.
- Learners have the chance to practice and receive feedback on skill areas before the summative milestone (final paper).
- Eight weeks appears to be a reasonable amount of time for learners' completion of the activity and for the instructor to give ample feedback.
- We anticipate that learners' responses to this activity would include interest and engagement.

Questions for Applying Adult Learning Principles

The next two examples present learning activities that involve experiential learning and collaboration. As you review each learning activity, ask yourself these questions to apply adult learning principles:

- How are the cognitive, social, and emotional aspects of learning being fostered?
- Where do self-reflection and dialogue occur?
- Is the purpose of the activity clear?
- What makes the activity realistic, relevant, and meaningful?
- What practical applications of the information does the learning activity involve?
- In what ways is learner choice involved?
- How are diverse learners included?
- Do the actions occur in a logical order and fully serve the purpose of the activity?
- What connections are learners making among topics?
- Do learners have the chance to practice skills before the summative milestone?
- Is the time allotted for the activity sufficient?
- What might be learners' response to the activity?

Mechanical Engineering Group Project Learning Activity

This example is based on a learning activity created by Dr. Laura Schaefer of Rice University. We first present an overview of the activity, followed by a description of teams' weekly actions.

QE	**Quality engineering project for Build Construction Management, Inc.**

Purpose:	*Milestones:*
The purpose of this activity is for you to work as a team to design and analyze interrelated mechanical and electrical systems that will meet client needs for lighting, climate control and ventilation, hot water, and appliances in an "optimal" fashion.	• Client progress review summary of non-HVAC energy needs for the building (formative) • Client progress review summary of total energy needs for the building (formative) • List of metrics (formative) • Oral presentation and Q&A with client (summative) • Team written report (summative)
Setting:	*Skill areas:*
You work for Quality Engineers, an engineering firm. Your firm has been contracted to design a set of interconnected building systems for business and residential units being constructed by your client (i.e., your instructor).	• Problem-solving • Oral communication • Teamwork
Overview of actions and feedback:	*Resources:*
• Duration: eight weeks • Conduct your preliminary investigation and submit the first client progress summary. • Conduct investigation of total energy needs, and submit the second client progress summary. • Design your system, integrating alternative technologies for two input sources, and analyze the energy and economic performance of that system. • Use multiple metrics to assess the proposed building and energy systems and submit the list • Prepare oral presentation (<10 min) on the system. • Reflect on your work as a team, and prepare the final report for feedback.	• Textbook: chapters 15–20, with self-reflection questions • Video: control systems overview, with transcript and self-reflection questions • List of approved building types • Cost assumptions • Web resources (maps, seasonal data) • Climate and solar insulation data resource • Note: you can choose any location for your building, as long as your location experiences (at least) three distinct seasons.

Learning Activity Weekly Team Actions and Milestones for Quality Engineering Project

Week 1
Review the resources and respond to the self-reflection questions to prepare for the activity. As a team, choose both a general location for your building and then a potential actual site using Google maps, specifying the orientation of your building and the shading from natural and man-made surroundings. Acquire seasonally averaged climate and hourly solar insolation data for that location from publicly available databases or the provided resources.

Week 2
Conduct an inventory of expected appliance and lighting electrical needs, which will vary depending on whether your chosen structure is for commercial or residential use.

Milestone: Client progress review summary of non-HVAC energy needs for the building (week 2)

Week 3
Acquire the heat transfer characteristics of your building envelope materials, and analyze the heat gain or loss by season for a given operating set point.

Week 4
Using conventional HVAC technologies and their corresponding efficiencies, calculate the required energy consumption to offset that heat gain or loss, and resulting economic and environmental cost (CO_2 emissions, based on fuel stock). Identify which alternative input sources (wind, sun, hydro, etc.) will be used as replacement systems, and tabulate their efficiencies, costs, and range of operating conditions.

Milestone: Client progress review summary of total energy needs for the building (week 4)

Week 5
Specify the required control strategies that will be used for the integration of the alternative systems. Using the seasonal data, calculate the energy, economic, and emissions offsets that can be gained from those systems (if any) over a set lifetime.

Week 6
For the economic analysis, include projected changes in utility costs and the effect of the time value of money. If savings are generated, calculate the return on investment (ROI); if the alternative systems lead to greater expenses, convert those expenses to a cost-per-ton-of-CO_2 saved for the environmental impact.

Milestone: Use of multiple metrics to assess proposed building and energy systems (week 6)

Week 7
Prepare an oral report discussing your findings. Include charts documenting the clear comparison between baseline and alternative systems using all of the relevant metrics, and present preliminary conclusions on the best choice of systems.

Week 8
Prepare a written report with full documentation of all of the selected building energy systems. Discuss additional considerations, such as regulatory concerns and building standards that would also need to be applied. Analyze in qualitative terms whether a different location for your building would lead to different outcomes, and also if the operation of the building is price-sensitive to a high or low degree. End the report with reflection on your team.

Milestones: Oral presentation and Q&A with client (week 7) and team written report (week 8)

Business Simulation Learning Activity

CC	**District managers' group project for Corporation Corp, Inc.**

Purpose:

The purpose of this learning activity is for you to work together as a managers' group to apply what you learned about organization change and organizational culture to a business situation using actual data collected from a company, and to individually reflect on your experience.

Milestones:

• Written cross-functional managers' group recommendation report (summative)
• Written individual self-reflection paper (summative)

Setting:

You work for a district office that is part of Corporation Corp. Your team includes the district manager, plus managers from five functional departments that will be represented: dispatch, customer service, maintenance, drivers, and accounts payable/accounts receivable.

Skill areas:

• Data interpretation
• Teamwork
• Writing

Resources:

• Challenge from the COO.
• Employee survey data summaries by functional department and district-wide (used with permission of the company).
• Employee listening session data summaries by functional department and district-wide (used with company permission).
• General description of the situation in each functional department and district-wide.
• Cameron, K. S., & Quinn, R. E. (2006). *Diagnosing and changing organizational culture: Based on the competing values framework* (rev. ed.). San Francisco, CA: Jossey-Bass.
• Organizational Culture Assessment Instrument (Cameron & Quinn, 2006).
• Other summaries and reports generated by individual group members and the group as a whole.

Actions and feedback:

• Duration: six weeks
• Your instructor will assign you one of the six managers' roles. Depending on the number of learners in the class, some functional departments may not be included. This decision will be up to the instructor.
• You will represent your functional department in two synchronous virtual meetings to review the data, discuss the district culture, and write a report to recommend changes to address employee concerns and meet the COO's challenge to the district.
• You will review and comment on other manager groups' recommendations.
• You will self-reflect on your experience throughout the process and write a final self-reflection paper.
• Your instructor will provide summative feedback on the two milestones.

Additional details for this learning activity, plus an additional learning activity for a human growth and development course, can be found in the Appendix.

LEARNING ACTIVITY PURPOSE STATEMENTS

You have seen a few examples of learning activities. Now you are ready to create your own! At this point in the process, you will work with a single topic cluster from your course map and create a learning activity for that cluster. We recommend that you choose the cluster that is the most important. Use your knowledge of your discipline and your learners to decide which cluster is most important.

Do you remember identifying a rationale for your course choice in *Chapter 4: Course Destination*? The rationale provided you with a sense of purpose. Adult learners want to know why they are doing an activity! Therefore, creating a learning activity starts with writing a learning activity purpose statement. The learning activity purpose statement acts as a compass to guide your creation of the learning activity. If an action is unrelated to the purpose, it should **not** be included in the learning activity.

The purpose statement begins with the phrase "The purpose of this activity is. . ." and summarizes the topics and summative milestone for that activity and incorporates the theme, if applicable. For example, you can use this format:

The purpose of this learning activity is for you to apply _____ (the topics) to produce _____ (the summative milestone) in the context of _____ (the theme).

Note that this is just one format. The key is for you to emphasize the topics, the summative milestone (which, you may recall, is based on skill areas), and the theme. You can keep your purpose broad enough to cover any actions learners take as part of the activity, yet make it succinct to avoid confusing learners.

Let's return to our example of Theories of Personality. Review the instructor's purpose statement for the first learning activity, focusing on the theories cluster.

Theories of Personality Examples:
Learning Activity Purpose Statement for Theories Cluster

I have chosen to work with the theories/therapies cluster first because it contains the most important and foundational information that my learners will learn in the course. The milestone is a written case analysis and interpretation, and my theme is a psychotherapy clinic. My purpose statement for this learning activity follows:

The purpose of this learning activity is for you to apply theories of personality to a written case analysis and interpretation within a psychotherapy clinic setting.

Additional examples of learning activity purpose statements for other disciplines can be found in the Appendix.

Now write your learning activity purpose statement.

Application:
Write Your Learning Activity Purpose Statement

Choose the most important topic cluster and the summative milestone associated with it. In your *course log*, write a purpose statement that summarizes the topics, milestone, and theme for that cluster. If you are not using a scenario for your theme, you can focus on the topics and milestone.

 Call a Colleague:
Learning Activity Purpose Statement

Talk with a colleague about your purpose statement to get feedback on clarity and scope. If your colleague is not following the approach presented in this workbook, you might find that "objectives" and "assessments" come into the conversation. Be prepared to discuss how the Change-adept Course Creation Process concepts (topics, skill areas, course map, course destination, milestones, and theme) complement concepts from traditional instructional design.

ACTIONS WITHIN LEARNING ACTIVITIES

Now that you have written your learning activity purpose statement, you are ready to choose the actions that make up the learning activity. Learning activities include three types of actions that engage the cognitive, social, and emotional aspects of learning:

- self-reflection
- dialogue
- application.

Actions can be interwoven in a learning activity, and there is no set order in which actions must occur. Indeed, although most actions occur before summative milestones, at times one or two actions (e.g., self-reflection on feedback) may occur after the summative milestone. However, we have found that the following pattern of actions is quite effective:

- self-reflection on information
- dialogue sparked by self-reflection
- application of the information in a way that produces the milestone.

In this section, we will continue our Theories of Personality example to show how you can use this pattern to create a learning activity. You will create your own learning activity in steps, modeling the example. Once you have gained practice with creating a learning activity that follows the pattern of self-reflection–dialogue–application, you can branch out and explore other patterns of actions for additional learning activities.

Self-reflection

We begin with self-reflection because it is the catalyst for the learning process. Self-reflection is not expressing a superficial opinion, simply agreeing or disagreeing with another's perspective, or stating a brief thought or feeling. Rather, self-reflection is an active process that involves grappling with what one has read/heard/seen/experienced and attempting to make sense of it, in reference to one's own thoughts and feelings. Self-reflection can also involve thinking about how skills and topic knowledge can be applied in a realistic setting. Examples of actions that involve self-reflection include responding to reflection questions, keeping a reflection journal, and writing a reflection essay.

Exploring the Terrain:
Guidelines for Self-Reflection

Eyler and Giles (1999) identified five aspects of effective reflection activities:

- Foster connections (particularly among the cognitive, social, and emotional aspects of an experience).
- Occur continuously, not just once or twice in a learning experience
- require application within a specific context.
- Challenge the person doing the reflecting to contemplate new ideas, experiences, and information.
- Provide coaching to support successful reflection.

In addition, self-reflection is more meaningful when learners understand the purpose of self-reflection and have a clear understanding of participation expectations.

Travel Advisory:
Emotional Aspects of Self-Reflection

Some learners are uncomfortable with sharing their reactions. You can help learners manage their discomfort by explaining why you are asking challenging questions and by reassuring learners that uncomfortable feelings are common when reflecting on difficult and/or personal issues. At the same time, you must respect that some learners might not feel ready to share more personal experiences or emotions. In addition, you must be respectful of learners' privacy by not requiring them to share private information. Structuring reflection questions to give learners the option of how much they share of themselves is an important part of inclusion (Kisfalvi & Oliver, 2015; Taylor, 2018).

Effective self-reflection requires carefully crafted questions or prompts that help learners to think about information and about their responses to information. Take some time to think about self-reflection in your learning activity.

Travel Journal:
Self-Reflection in Your Learning Activity

How will self-reflection help learners to achieve the milestone for this learning activity?

What will the focus of self-reflection be (e.g., learners' prior experiences with the topic, learners' emotional responses to the information, learners' questions about the information)?

How will learners self-reflect (e.g., internal monologue, taking notes, writing in a journal, writing an essay, recording a podcast)?

Review the instructor's thought process in deciding how self-reflection will be present in a learning activity.

Theories of Personality Examples:
Self-Reflection in the Learning Activity

For my learning activity on psychoanalytic, behavioral, and social-cognitive theories, self-reflection will help learners understand the information and think critically about what they are learning.

I decide that the first purpose of self-reflection is to help learners activate their prior knowledge and experience with the topics. Activating prior knowledge will help prepare learners to learn the new information about the theories. These self-reflection prompts will need to be presented *before* the information in a resource.

I also want learners to self-reflect on their emotional responses to the theories so that they are aware of their own assumptions and possible biases as they get ready to apply the theories to a case. In addition, learners need to identify aspects of the theories that they don't understand or that they have questions about. These self-reflection prompts will need to be presented *after* the information in a resource.

For both instances of self-reflection (before and after learners see the new information), I want learners to respond to the questions informally, by thinking and taking notes.

Having decided on the purpose, focus, and format of self-reflection, I am ready to create some prompts for self-reflection! However, I realize that I don't know exactly what information learners will be reflecting on yet, as I haven't chosen resources. I will make a mental note to revise my self-reflection prompts when I choose my resources (see *Chapter 8: Resources*).

For now, I create the following prompts for self-reflection:

(Before the resource) You are going to read/view some information about three of the most important theories of personality: psychoanalytic, behavioral, and social-cognitive. Before you start, reflect on what you already know about these three theories. Take some notes on your reflection, then read/view the information.

(After the resource) What is your reaction to the main concepts of each theory? Which theory makes the most sense to you, and why? How might your own reactions to each theory influence the way you view cases? What will make it easier or more challenging for you to interpret a case from the perspective of each theory? Briefly write down your thoughts and feelings about each theory as you prepare for the next part of the learning activity.

Now begin to create your learning activity with self-reflection.

Application:
Start Your Learning Activity with Self-Reflection

Identify how self-reflection will be present in your learning activity and write the details in your *course log*. If you already know what information you want learners to reflect on, you can create self-reflection prompts now. If not, spend some time thinking about this aspect, write down some ideas, and complete this part later (e.g., in *Chapter 8: Resources*).

Dialogue

Through dialogue, learners share their thoughts, feelings, and experiences through social interaction, thereby allowing for the emergence of shared understanding. Without dialogue, shared understanding does not occur. Therefore, the quality of learning will be heavily influenced by the way you create dialogue as a central part of the learning activity. Examples of actions that involve dialogue include engaging in written dialogue (e.g., through online discussion boards), having conversations in real time, and talking with people outside the course about course topics.

Exploring the Terrain:
Guidelines for Dialogue

Learners have a variety of feelings about engaging in dialogue and other collaborative actions (Kisfalvi & Oliver, 2015). Because dialogue sometimes elicits negative emotions in some learners, it can be tempting to avoid it altogether or to make all "dialogue" brief written exchanges that are universally neutral (Clancy & Vince, 2019). However, the flip-side of this coin is that online learners often feel isolated and report that they lack a sense of community with their peers (Wilson et al., 2004). In addition, omitting dialogue neglects the essence of the learning process. We believe that true learning happens in interactions among learners; thus, points of learner-to-learner connection are essential for adult learning.

Research (e.g., Rovai, 2007; Simon, 2018) offers tips for creating effective online dialogue:

- Create clear expectations regarding dialogue participation.
- Give learners time to get used to the dialogue format.
- Explain the role of the instructor in dialogue.

- Give feedback and coach learners to respond to dialogue in a meaningful way.
- Provide alternate formats for dialogue.
- Make dialogue questions/prompts meaningful and interesting, with enough depth to allow for diverse opinions and ideas.
- Incorporate learner leadership of dialogue and rotate the leader role.

In addition, you can help your learners get the most out of dialogue by anticipating points at which learners might have emotional reactions to a dialogue and reassuring learners ahead of time that such emotions are a natural and useful part of the learning process. It can be helpful to have learners share their reactions to dialogue with you and with their peers, if they are comfortable doing so. Furthermore, you can structure dialogue to maximize the social benefit by limiting the number of participants in a dialogue and posing questions that engage learners in lively conversation rather than eliciting closed-ended responses.

Travel Advisory:
Asynchronous and Synchronous Dialogue Formats

Dialogue in online courses is often asynchronous, meaning that the dialogue usually involves a time lag between learners' posts on a discussion board and learners' responses to each other's posts. Asynchronous formats are particularly useful for:

- shorter dialogues
- conversations that you need to monitor closely
- less complex ideas
- potentially controversial ideas where space between responses may promote more thoughtful responses rather than "off the cuff" reactions.

Online dialogue can also be synchronous, meaning that it involves real-time conversations (either oral or written) among learners. Synchronous formats may be appropriate for:

- longer dialogues
- small groups
- conversations that learners can engage in with minimal oversight
- more complex ideas
- scenario-based role-plays (see the Appendix for examples).

As with self-reflection, effective dialogue also requires carefully crafted questions or prompts that help learners to share their thoughts, feelings, and experiences with each other. Take some time to think about dialogue in your learning activity.

Travel Journal:
Dialogue in Your Learning Activity

How will dialogue help learners to achieve the milestone for this learning activity?

What will be the focus of dialogue (e.g., learners' self-reflections; information that is new, controversial, or challenging; learners' questions about information)?

How will learners engage in dialogue (e.g., written dialogue, virtual meeting; whole class, small groups, or partners; with or without the instructor present)?

Now review the instructor's thought process in deciding how dialogue will be added to the learning activity.

Theories of Personality Example:
Ideas for Dialogue

Dialogue is the heart of the learning process. Therefore, I want learners to have ample opportunity to dialogue with each other about the information and their self-reflection on that information. Such dialogue will help them understand the information and take multiple perspectives.

My first thought is that I could create small groups of learners and have them share their self-reflections on each theory. However, it might be more interesting and lively if learners have to share their understanding of information from two different theories, with some learners "advocating" for one theory and others "advocating" for the other. Looking at the topics in my cluster, I notice that the psychoanalytic vs. behavioral theories comparison is a natural focus for such a dialogue.

But what do I want learners to get out of the dialogue? The purpose of dialogue should be connected to the milestone. Given that learners are going to write a case analysis and interpretation, it would be helpful for them to start getting some practice with analyzing and interpreting cases. A group dialogue is a good way to do this, particularly because case analysis and interpretation involves exploring multiple perspectives on a case and providing a solid rationale for the final interpretation.

However, given that there are just two theories involved, I decide that learners will work in pairs (rather than small groups). The dialogue will focus on competing interpretations of a case, with each learner advocating for one of the two contrasting theories (psychoanalytic vs. behavioral). I make a mental note that I am going to need to create a case that has elements of both theories so that the interpretation is ambiguous.

Next, I review my cluster – I've covered psychoanalytic and behavioral theories, but I also included social-cognitive theories in this cluster. Social-cognitive theories emerged from behavioral theories, so it might be a good idea for learners to have another dialogue. The learner in each pair who previously "advocated" for behavioral theories will now "advocate" for social-cognitive theories in the case interpretation; the learner who previously "advocated" for psychoanalytic theories will now "advocate" for behavioral theories. Again, I make a mental note that I will need an additional case that includes elements of these two theories.

I know that I will need to create some dialogue prompts so that partners engage in a meaningful dialogue about the two cases. Looking at my milestone again and at the skill areas involved, I see that the final milestone involves writing. It's a good idea to have learners practice this skill during the learning activity, so I decide that learners' dialogue will be in written form using an asynchronous discussion board.

Based on the initial brainstorm, the instructor narrows and integrates the actions into an initial learning activity.

Theories of Personality Example:
Initial Learning Activity with Self-Reflection and Dialogue

Case 1: Psychoanalytic vs. Behavioral Theories

(Before the resource) You are going to read/view some information about two of the most important theories of personality: psychoanalytic and behavioral. Before you start, reflect on what you already know about these two theories. Take some notes on your reflection, then read/view the information.

(After the resource) What is your reaction to the main concepts of each theory? Which theory makes the most sense to you, and why? How might your own reactions to each theory influence the way you view cases? What will make it easier or more challenging for you to interpret a case from the perspective of each theory? Briefly write down your thoughts and feelings about each theory as you prepare for the first dialogue.

(Dialogue) Review your self-reflection notes, then participate in a written dialogue about the two theories (psychoanalytic and behavioral). You and your partner will each choose one of these theories, interpret the case from the perspective of your chosen theory, and provide a written explanation. You will ask your partner questions about his or her theory and interpretation and then respond to your partner's questions.

Case 2: Behavioral vs. Social-Cognitive Theories

(Before the resource) You are going to read/view some information about an offshoot of behavioral theories: social-cognitive theories. Before you start, reflect on what you already know about this theory. Take some notes on your reflection, then read/view the information.

(After the resource) What is your reaction to the main concepts of the theory? Does this theory make sense to you, and why or why not? How might your own reactions to each theory influence the way you view cases? What will make it easier or more challenging for you to interpret a case from the perspective of this theory? Briefly write down your thoughts and feelings about the theory as you prepare for the next dialogue.

(Dialogue) Review your self-reflection notes, then participate in a written dialogue about the two theories (behavioral and social-cognitive). If you chose psychoanalytic theories last time, choose behavioral theories this time; if you chose behavioral theories last time, choose social-cognitive theories this time. You and your partner will each interpret the case from the perspective of your chosen theory and provide a written explanation. You will ask your partner questions about his or her theory and interpretation and then respond to your partner's questions.

Now you can add dialogue to your learning activity.

Application:
Add Dialogue to Your Learning

Identify how dialogue will be present in your learning activity and write the details in your *course log*. If you already know what information you want learners to discuss, you can create dialogue prompts now. If not, spend some time thinking about this aspect, write down some ideas, and complete this part later (e.g., in *Chapter 8: Resources*).

Notes from Our Journey:
Timing of Self-Reflection and Dialogue

In writing this workbook, we knew we wanted to make self-reflection and dialogue a key part of your (our readers') experience. We identified points in the workbook through *Your Travel Journal* and *Call a Colleague* where these actions would help you identify existing ideas and assumptions, explore new ways of thinking, and evaluate your learning activities. These opportunities mirror the purpose of self-reflection and dialogue in your course.

Note that we have sometimes included opportunities for self-reflection and dialogue before presenting information and sometimes after, depending on the purpose of the action. Our choice illustrates that the timing of self-reflection and dialogue depends on what you want learners to accomplish through these actions.

Application

Application involves using information in the context of realistic, relevant, and meaningful experiences while practicing the skill areas associated with the milestone. Examples of applications include writing a paper, conducting an experiment, and engaging in a role-play as part of a scenario. Applications can directly prepare learners for a milestone. For example, if the milestone is a research paper, then applications might include creating a research topic mind map, writing an outline of the paper, writing a first draft, checking the paper with a revision and editing checklist, and writing the final paper. If the milestone is an algebraic problem set, applications might include completing practice equations in the context of a realistic scenario and then checking one's work against the answers in the textbook.

Travel Advisory:
Application of Resources

You may be tempted to include an action in which learners simply read or view the resources but not use the information in those resources in some way. In contrast, we recommend pairing resources with other actions. For example, rather than stating, "Read the chapter," we would state, "Read the chapter and complete the following self-reflection questions" or "Refer to the chapter as you complete the case study dialogue." In each case, the resource is connected to an action.

Table 7.4 presents sample milestones and relevant applications. There is quite a bit of overlap among these categories, but we have simplified the information to give examples of applications that are a good fit with specific milestones.

Table 7.4 Milestones and relevant applications

Milestones	Relevant applications
Research paper	Find sources, outline, draft, edit and revise, write
Text analysis	Compare and contrast text, analyze source, interpret meaning
Work of art	Sketch, plan, rehearse, create
Lab report	Conduct an experiment, graph findings, analyze data
Case study discussion	Research multiple viewpoints, explore hypotheses
Design project	Build, design, create a program, write code
Simulation report	Role-play, interview, practice
Educational campaign	Conduct interviews, survey target audience

Take some time to think about application in your learning activity. You can also begin to think about the time needed for learners to apply what they are learning.

Your Travel Journal:
Application in Your Learning Activity

In addition to self-reflection and dialogue, what do learners need to do in the learning activity to achieve the milestone? How much time will learners need to practice the skills involved in the milestone? Jot down your notes in the space provided.

Review the instructor's decisions about how to integrate application into the learning activity and how much time the activity will require.

Theories of Personality Example:
Ideas for Applications and Time Requirements

The milestone requires that learners analyze and interpret a case with reference to the three theories in this cluster. Learners will already be engaging in analysis and interpretation of cases in the form of a dialogue, so I could just stop there. However, something seems missing: I realize that

I don't have a way to determine whether learners understand the key points of each theory well enough to apply the information to the final case. In addition, I remember reading about *complicated understanding* and decide that I want learners to be able to synthesize multiple perspectives on a case. I need additional applications to help with both of these purposes.

To make sure that learners are understanding the key points of each theory prior to the milestone, I could give them a quiz. However, a quiz wouldn't really capture their ability to communicate about the theories. Instead, I decide to require each partner to briefly explain the key concepts of the other partner's theory. This step has the added benefit of preventing learners from getting locked into a single viewpoint. For example, if one partner identifies the presence of the unconscious in the case (from a psychoanalytic perspective), the other partner must briefly explain the concept "unconscious" in his or her reply. In addition, I note that the dialogue will need to be viewable only by the partners involved so that learners are not distracted by other partners' dialogues.

To give learners practice with synthesizing multiple perspectives on a case, I decide to modify the dialogue format further. Instead of simply responding to each other's interpretations by summarizing key points and asking questions, learners could also compare and contrast their perspectives on the case and then reach consensus about which parts of each theory best fit the case. I also decide that I need to be more specific with what I want learners to do in their interpretation of each case, to mirror the final milestone.

Finally, I need to see what each learner can do individually, so I decide to add a third case (combining all three theories) that learners analyze and interpret individually. Working independently, learners will identify elements of each theory that apply to the case, give specific examples, and synthesize the three theoretical perspectives for the final interpretation of the case. Each learner's response to the third case is the summative milestone: a written case analysis and interpretation.

In all, the learning activity involves three parts: the first two case dialogues and then a final case analysis and interpretation for the milestone. Three weeks (one week per case) should be enough time for these three parts.

Theories of Personality Example:
Revised Learning Activity and Time Requirements

My revised learning activity (with applications built in) looks like this.

Case 1: Psychoanalytic vs. Behavioral Theories (One Week)

(Before the resource) You are going to read/view some information about two of the most important theories of personality: psychoanalytic and behavioral. Before you start, reflect on what you already know about these two theories. Take some notes on your reflection, then read/view the information.

(After the resource) What is your reaction to the main concepts of each theory? Which theory makes the most sense to you, and why? How might your own reactions to each theory influence the way you view cases? What will make it easier or more challenging for you to interpret a case from the perspective of each theory? Briefly write down your thoughts and feelings about each theory as you prepare for the first dialogue.

(Dialogue) Review your self-reflection notes, then participate in a written dialogue about the two theories (psychoanalytic or behavioral). You and your partner will each choose one of these theories. Once you have chosen a theory, create a post in your team discussion board that includes the following:

- Identify three theoretical concepts that are present in the case.
- Give a specific example of each concept as illustrated in the case.

You will then respond to your partner's post with the following:

- Summarize and briefly explain (in your own words) the three concepts your partner identified.
- Ask your partner questions about his or her theory and interpretation.
- Respond to your partner's questions and continue the discussion, comparing the two interpretations.
- Together, reach a consensus about how both theories apply to the case.

Case 2: Behavioral vs. Social-Cognitive Theories (One Week)

(Before the resource) You are going to read/view some information about an offshoot of behavioral theories: social-cognitive theories. Before you start, reflect on what you already know about this theory. Take some notes on your reflection, then read/view the information.

   (After the resource) What is your reaction to the main concepts of the theory? Does this theory make sense to you, and why or why not? How might your own reactions to each theory influence the way you view cases? What will make it easier or more challenging for you to interpret a case from the perspective of this theory? Briefly write down your thoughts and feelings about the theory as you prepare for the next dialogue.

   (Dialogue) Review your self-reflection notes, then participate in a written dialogue about the two theories (behavioral and social-cognitive). If you chose psychoanalytic theories last time, choose behavioral theories this time; if you chose behavioral theories last time, choose social-cognitive theories this time. Once you have chosen a theory, create a post in your team discussion board that includes the following:

- Identify three theoretical concepts that are present in the case.
- Give a specific example of each concept as illustrated in the case.

You will then respond to your partner's post with the following:

- Summarize and briefly explain (in your own words) the three concepts your partner identified.
- Ask your partner questions about his or her theory and interpretation.
- Respond to your partner's questions and continue the discussion, comparing the two interpretations.
- Together, reach a consensus about how both theories apply to the case.

Case 3: Integration of Psychoanalytic, Behavioral, and Social-Cognitive Theories (One Week)

For the final case, reflect on your self-reflection notes, your written dialogues, and the feedback you have received. Then identify elements of each theory that apply to the current case, give specific examples, and synthesize the three theoretical perspectives for the final interpretation of the case. Your final case analysis and interpretation (completed individually) is your milestone for this activity.
   Total amount of time: three weeks

This example illustrates connections among the actions of a learning activity. Learners experience actions as a whole activity, not as a series of unrelated actions. In addition, in this example the final application results in the summative milestone for the learning activity.
   Now you can identify possible applications for your learning activity.

Application:
Add Applications to Your Learning Activity and Review Time Requirements

Identify how applications will be present in your learning activity and write the details in your *course log*. Consider which applications will be completed by groups (if applicable) and which will be completed individually. Be sure to include the application that produces the summative milestone for the learning activity. Finally, indicate the approximate time requirements for each part of your learning activity and the total amount of time the activity will take.

Actions: Summary

You have reflected on how your learners will self-reflect, engage in dialogue, and apply their learning through applications. You have also connected these actions within a learning activity. Now you are ready to make your learning activity realistic, relevant, and meaningful by integrating your course theme.

LEARNING ACTIVITIES AND THE COURSE THEME

A learning activity involves a series of connected actions. However, these connections become clearer and more cohesive when you use the course theme to provide a realistic, relevant, and meaningful context for the learning activity.

Review how the Theories of Personality instructor integrates the course theme into the learning activity.

Theories of Personality Example:
Course Theme in the Learning Activity

As I review my notes, I am pleased by how well the actions flow together. Learners will self-reflect and then engage in dialogue and application, resulting in the summative milestone of a written case analysis and interpretation. However, I sense that something is lacking. I need a common thread that will pull everything together. I remember my theme: a psychotherapy clinic. Can this theme draw the actions together in a way that makes the learning activity more realistic, relevant, and meaningful? Yes! I weave the theme into my description of the learning activity with the following introduction:

Welcome to the Integrative Psychotherapy Clinic! In this activity, you and a partner are interns who are rotating through three departments led by three theorists: Dr. Freud's Psychoanalytic Department, Dr. Skinner's Behavioral Department, and Dr. Bandura's Social-Cognitive Department. In each theorist's department, you will learn about key theoretical concepts. Your job is to self-reflect on what you learn, discuss with your partner how theories apply to cases presented in the clinic, and use your learning to analyze and interpret a case from all three theoretical perspectives in the Integration Department. You will be working on developing your critical thinking and writing skills as well.

In this example, the addition of a scenario ties everything together and gives a rich context for learners' engagement in the activity.

 Application:
Integrate the Course Theme into Your Learning Activity

In your *course log*, write your ideas about how to integrate your course theme into your learning activity.

FORMATIVE MILESTONES

At this point, you have organized self-reflection, dialogue, and application into a learning activity that ends with a summative milestone. The next step is to determine whether you want to give feedback on any actions prior to the summative milestone. If you decide that such feedback is necessary, you can designate certain points as formative milestones.

Travel Advisory:
Self-Check Quizzes as Formative Milestones

Some courses require an objective measure of learners' acquisition of information. If this is the case for your course, consider incorporating a self-check quiz as an application in your learning activity. Self-check quizzes are formative measures of learning. Although they typically do not integrate skill areas (particularly when the quiz format is multiple-choice), self-check quizzes can be useful for learners' self-evaluation of topic knowledge. You might want to integrate a low-stakes, self-check quiz as a formative milestone to help learners determine whether they are ready for the other actions in the learning activity or whether they need to review the resources again before continuing on to other actions. Another option is to encourage learners to take a self-check quiz until all answers are correct.

Review the instructor's decision about formative milestones.

Theories of Personality Example:
Formative Milestones

In my learning activity, I definitely want to give feedback on learners' work on the second case, as it is the closest match to the summative milestone. I also realize that if I don't correct misunderstandings on the first case, learners won't necessarily self-correct. Thus, I decide to give feedback on their work on the first case, too.

Based on these decisions, my learning activity now has three milestones: the two dialogues (formative) and the final case analysis and interpretation (summative). This is manageable for me, because this class tends to have about 25 learners. However, if I have a larger class, I might keep all formative feedback brief and/or just give formative feedback on the second case.

Now decide which actions require your feedback and create formative milestones for these actions.

Application:
Create Formative Milestones

Looking at the actions in your learning activity, decide whether feedback is necessary. If so, create formative milestones for these actions. A formative milestone will be a tangible product that will receive your formative feedback. Note formative milestones in your *course log*.

ADULT LEARNING PRINCIPLES IN A LEARNING ACTIVITY

Now that you have the initial elements of your learning activity – purpose statement, actions, milestones (formative and summative), and theme – you can review your learning activity in terms of the adult learning principles. It helps to first put your learning activity into a format where the key information is in one place. Keep in mind that the details are in your *course log*.

Review the learning activity for the Theories of Personality course.

Theories of Personality team educational video on assessment	
Purpose: The purpose of this learning activity is for you to apply theories of personality to a written case analysis and interpretation within a psychotherapy clinic setting.	*Milestones:* • Dialogue posts and responses (formative) • Final individual case analysis and interpretation (summative)
Setting: Welcome to the Integrative Psychotherapy Clinic! In this activity, you and a partner are interns who are rotating through three departments led by three theorists: Dr. Freud's Psychoanalytic Department, Dr. Skinner's Behavioral Department, and Dr. Bandura's Social-Cognitive Department. In each theorist's department, you will learn to apply key theoretical concepts to clinical cases. Your job is to self-reflect on what you learn, discuss with your partner how theories apply to cases presented in the clinic, and use your learning to analyze and interpret a case from all three theoretical perspectives in the Integration Department.	*Skill areas:* • Critical thinking • Writing
Actions and feedback: • Duration: three weeks • Case 1: Psychoanalytic vs. behavioral theories – self-reflection and written dialogue • Case 2: Behavioral vs. social-cognitive theories – self-reflection and written dialogue • Case 3: Integration of theories – final case analysis and interpretation • Your instructor will provide feedback on each dialogue and on your final case analysis and interpretation	*Resources:* • To be determined

Your Travel Journal:
Review of Adult Learning Principles

As you look at the learning activity for the Theories of Personality course, consider how you might answer the following questions:

- How are the cognitive, social, and emotional aspects of learning being fostered?
- Where do self-reflection and dialogue occur?
- Is the purpose of the activity clear?
- What makes the activity realistic, relevant, and meaningful?
- How does the activity involve practical applications of the information?
- In what ways is learner choice involved?
- How are diverse learners included?
- Do the actions occur in a logical order and fully serve the purpose of the activity?
- What connections are learners making among topics?
- Do learners have the chance to practice skills before the summative milestone?
- Is the time allotted for the activity sufficient?
- What might be learners' response to the activity?

Now review your learning activity in terms of adult learning principles.

Application:
Review Your Learning Activity in Terms of Adult Learning Principles

In your *course log*, put your learning activity into a format that includes key information in one place. You don't need to write all of the instructions for learners yet; just include the overview (as shown in the full learning activity examples in this chapter). Then review your learning activity in terms of the following adult learning principles:

- How are the cognitive, social, and emotional aspects of learning being fostered?
- Where do self-reflection and dialogue occur?
- Is the purpose of the activity clear?
- What makes the activity realistic, relevant, and meaningful?
- How does the activity involve practical applications of the information?
- In what ways is learner choice involved?
- How are diverse learners included?
- Do the actions occur in a logical order and fully serve the purpose of the activity?
- What connections are learners making among topics?
- Do learners have the chance to practice skills before the summative milestone?
- Is the time allotted for the activity sufficient?
- What might be learners' response to the activity?

Call a Colleague:
Your Learning Activity

You have created your learning activity. Now it is time to call a colleague for dialogue. Be open to feedback, and jot down your notes in the space provided.

LEARNING ACTIVITIES: SUMMARY

In this chapter, you began to create a learning activity by developing a learning activity purpose statement, choosing actions (self-reflection, dialogue, and application), integrating the course theme into your learning activity, creating formative milestones, and reviewing your learning activity in terms of adult learning principles.

You are now ready for *Chapter 8: Resources.*

8 Resources

RESOURCES: INTRODUCTION

Resources are sources of information that support learning (Stacey, 2001). Resources can include books, articles, online text, videos, audio recordings, slideshow presentations, figures, tables, images, handouts, sample papers, and other formats. Resources are needed for a learning activity and help learners achieve their milestones.

Your resources can be created or adapted from existing resources. Since online resources are abundant, one of your biggest challenges will be not to select too many resources but instead include just those resources that are needed for the learning activity.

In this chapter, you will continue developing the learning activity you created in the previous chapter by completing the following actions:

- explore resources
- review resources in terms of adult learning principles
- select resources
- consider characters to enhance course theme
- organize resources.

RESOURCE EXPLORATION

To begin exploring possible resources for your learning activity, ask yourself one question: *What resources do learners need for this learning activity?* Resources should provide both topic-related information as well as information that learners need to develop their skills in the skill areas you have identified.

Review how the Theories of Personality instructor answers this question.

Theories of Personality Example:
Resource Exploration

Looking at my learning activity on the three theories of personality, I know I need to provide learners information about the three theories, so I will need one or more resources that contain this information. I also want to give learners some guidance on writing and critical thinking, so I will need resources for these skill areas as well.

Some possible resources I might use include:

Topic-related resources	Skill-related resources
A textbook on theories of personality	APA style manual and website
Videos on personality theories	Annotated handout on APA style
Journal articles on personality	Slide presentation on critical thinking
Annotated handouts on personality concepts	Website on critical thinking
Cases for analysis and interpretation	

Now explore what resources you might use in your learning activity.

 Application:
Explore Resources

Consider the topics (including essential information) and skill areas involved in your learning activity. Explore possible resources that contain this information, and list possibilities in your *course log*. Also include any resources that you might need to create.

RESOURCE REVIEW

For a moment, think of a resource as a one-way source of information. Unlike in a face-to-face class, where the instructor is available to ask and answer questions on the spot, most online learners read/view/listen to the resources on their own time, in the absence of the instructor.

If learners perceive a resource to be confusing, irrelevant, or unengaging, learners will be less likely to use and benefit from the resource. Thus, potential resources need to be reviewed in terms of the adult learning principles. Similarly, if you are considering creating a resource, the same principles can guide your resource creation.

Let's look at the instructor's review of resources.

Theories of Personality Example:
Resource Review

In previous versions of this course, I have used a textbook on theories of personality. However, the textbook is expensive and contains much more than the essential information. It could be a good resource for learners who plan to go on to graduate school, but it is more than my learners need for the learning activities in the course.

I know that learners are drawn to videos, so I might look for a video on each of the three theories. I will check with the library to see if there are any relevant videos in our databases; if not, I will search for open educational use videos. I can create summary documents containing each theory's essential information. I might add a brief case example for each theory in the relevant resource, to pique learners' interest and to help learners prepare for the work of the learning activity. I will need to create some self-reflection questions for each resource as well.

With regard to skill areas, my learners do not need the entire APA style manual for improving their writing. I'm tempted to provide a link to the APA style website (a professional website for my discipline), but I know that my learners need more specific information on writing. I will create an annotated handout on APA style and writing tips, including the APA site's URL.

A slide presentation might be an option for the critical thinking skills involved in case analysis and interpretation.

Finally, I need to create three intriguing and realistic cases with key features of the theories.

Now narrow your list of possible resources by considering how adult learning principles are evident in each resource.

Application:
Review Resources in Terms of Adult Learning Principles

Review each resource in terms of the following aspects of adult learning principles:

- How are cognitive, social, and emotional aspects of learning addressed by the resource?
  - Cognitive: Is the information in the resource clear, correct, and appropriate for the learners' contexts (e.g., level of prior knowledge of the topics)?
  - Social: Is the resource socially respected (e.g., written by an expert in the field, peer reviewed, produced by a professional organization)?
  - Emotional: Is the resource approachable and appealing?
- What aspects of the resource will learners self-reflect on and/or discuss?
- Is the resource realistic, relevant, and meaningful, with practical applications?
- Can diverse learners access and use the resource? What are the semiotic meanings of the text and images in the resource?

Jot down your notes on each resource in your *course log*. Based on your review, narrow down your list of resources to a short list of resources that best demonstrate adult learning principles. Keep this short list in your *course log*.

RESOURCE SELECTION

Once you have narrowed down your list of resources, it is time to make your final selection. You may discover that your short list includes more than one resource for the same information. Or you may notice that you need to create one or more resources for certain information. In either case, you will need to select a resource format that works best for the information you want to present. You may consider documents, slide presentations, videos, websites, and other formats. Regardless of the format you choose to present information, we suggest that you use multimodality to address inclusion and diversity.

Exploring the Terrain:
Resource Multimodality for Inclusion and Diversity

Presenting information in a multimodal format (i.e., verbal and visual) has significant implications for accessibility and fosters an inclusive learning environment. Hull and Nelson (2005) defined multimodality as

[T]he integration of words with images, sound, music, and movement to create digital artifacts [resources] that do not necessarily privilege linguistic forms of signification but rather draw on a variety of modalities—speech, writing, image, gesture, and sound—to create different forms of meaning. (pp. 224–225)

Including multimodal resources gives learners a choice of how to approach their learning, while challenging them to experience other approaches (Sankey, Birch, & Gardiner, 2011).

For example, video is a medium that uses multimodality to express an idea or topic through the use of several of the following: images, movement, written word, spoken words, and/or music. Online discussions may be structured to include a mix of written text, visual images, and/or audio files. Presenting the same information in a variety of formats enhances the ability of learners to access and better understand information. However, caution must be taken when considering how the information will be offered through the differing modalities. As Koc-Januchta, Hoffler, Thoma, Prechtl, and Leutner (2017) pointed out,

[S]imply combining text and pictures does not always lead to improvement in learning results. The effectiveness of the combination is highly dependent on such aspects as the form of visualization, the type of learning task, the number of referential connections between text and pictures, and personal characteristics of the learner. (p. 171)

Sankey et al. (2011) found that while learners did not necessarily perform better in a multimodal environment, they felt that having multiple representations of information helped their "comprehension, understanding, and retention of [information]" and were "more interesting and enjoyable to use" (p. 31).

Travel Advisory:
Resources and Copyright Laws

We can't leave this section without a word about copyright laws. Not all government works are copyright-free. State and local government material might not be copyright-free, so you need to check. Organizations might not have free materials either. The long and the short of it is to check each and every time you use resources.

Let's return to the Theories of Personality example to see how the instructor selects the final set of resources.

Theories of Personality Example:
Resource Selection

I decided to include videos on the three theories of personality. The videos should be up-to-date, and ideally they should show psychologists in action. Once I identify some videos, I view them to make sure that they are appropriate and inclusive. I make sure that the videos include closed captioning or a transcript. I also write more detailed self-reflection questions based on the information presented in the videos.

I also decided to include summary documents (with a mini-case) for each theory. I will need to create these. I check the Appendix of this workbook for tips on creating documents and see that images can enhance text. I create the summary documents to include realistic, relevant, and meaningful applications of the information.

For writing, I decided to create an annotated handout on APA style and writing tips, supplemented by the website's URL. Once again, I add images to the text.

I thought that a slide presentation would be a good idea, but then I find a great online resource about case analysis and interpretation that perfectly fits the learning activity and that meets adult learning principles. The website is described as an open educational resource and is available for linking to online courses, so I substitute the website for the slide presentation.

Now select your final set of resources for the learning activity.

Application:
Select Resources

Select your final set of resources for the learning activity and list them in your *course log*. If needed, revise existing resources and/or create new multimodal resources that fulfill adult learning principles. The Appendix includes additional guidance for creating resources. Now is also a good time to create more specific prompts for self-reflection and/or dialogue related to the resources you have selected. Check all resources for copyright restrictions.

COURSE THEME AND CHARACTERS AS RESOURCES

There is another resource we want to show you that is easier than you think and can greatly enhance your learning activity. Characters are a theme-related resource. The use of characters has been found to relieve the feeling of isolation that learners may have in online courses (Reeves, 2004). According to Reeves, learners grant authority to online characters. This granting of authority means that you can use a character as an assistant to offer information, guide learners through the actions, or offer advice on study skills. The character can enrich another resource by acting as a CEO, a board member giving advice, a nurse, a head accountant, or other person that can help the learners transfer learning to real scenarios.

Figure 8.1 is a simple photo of different poses of a person with captions. You may choose to take photos of yourself or someone who has given you written permission to use their photos in your course. We suggest not using your learners. There are web and software options that supply animated characters with audio, in which case you will need a transcript. You can build your own characters using shapes to create a head and eyes. See Table 8.1 for ideas and cautions. Some adult learners will not care for the use of a character, so include other formats to provide learners with the same information.

I really like this next
chapter! Read it and
self-reflect.

Now wasn't that
interesting? Let's discuss
it in the forum.

Figure 8.1 Example of a character.

Your own creativity and your theme can assist you in creating an engaging character to help your learners identify with the resources. The examples in Table 8.1 were inspired by actual courses that were the result of an instructional designer partnering with faculty.

Table 8.1 Character roles and examples

Character roles	Examples
Provide information in a realistic manner	In an art history course, an online character could be a guide in the Smithsonian or a tour guide of Greece and Italy that travels back through time.
Provide information in story form that is memorable and short	A mouse appears at the top of each module or topic and guides the learner through a history course. This mouse has been everywhere and can recount a short human interest story that previews each topic. Give this mouse a name to make it a character. If you can sketch the mouse, you can use different poses and add objects from the time period. (Watch out for copyright laws – don't use a protected mouse image.) This mouse works for a literature or a philosophy course as well. However, keep semiotics in mind when choosing a character. For example, for some of your learners a mouse may be frightening or represent something "unclean." Other characters may have similar negative connotations.

Table 8.1 (*cont.*)

Character roles	Examples
Method to present factual information	A course on films can have a character as a famous (fictitious) actor from another era who gives advice and facts on acting, costumes, theater makeup, stage directions, and lighting. Watch out for copyright issues and avoid using real actors' names or photos.
Provide information in Start Here	A character can give information about the course that is more memorable and easier to access than it is in the syllabus. A character continues in the course to present information at useful intervals.
Theme resource to activate learning	A married couple (one from the United States and the other from England) have different ideas about the American Revolution in a history course. Throughout the course, this couple opens each module with an argument over the cause of the war using the same facts to be learned in the module. In a business course, business partners can argue good business practices as an introduction to each topic or module.
Method to offer online resources that include enrichment, leveling, or remedial resources	A teaching assistant (TA) character can guide the learners to try different study strategies and point out helpful websites for the library, writing, grammar, and online tutoring. What might your TA say to your learners before taking the exam or afterward? If you have a remedial link, your character can explain that the skill is complex and takes persistence, while being empathic to learner frustrations (Reeves, 2004).
Feedback delivery resources	You can inform learners that you will play a character who is a professional authority in a scenario. As the character, you can give feedback to the learner. You are able to express what a CEO might say when reading a learner's paper. As the character, you can offer strategies in ways that suit the character's professional persona. Include the character's picture in your feedback, and tell your learners that you are sending along his or her message.

Let's look at the use of characters in the Theories of Personality course.

Theories of Personality Example: Characters

I want to include two characters who can "mentor" learners and give them guidance. A good fit for the theme would be senior interns. I decide to include a male senior intern and a female senior intern who will model some of the analysis and interpretation skills I want learners to acquire.

Because I have already decided to include mini-cases in my summary document for each theory, I think that these documents would be a good place to show the characters modeling the skills. I choose names for the characters based on the names of other personality theorists whom learners will learn about, Carl and Karen, which enhances my theme.

Now determine whether you want to include a character in your course.

Application:
Consider Using a Character

Based on your course theme and the specifics of your learning activity, consider whether a character could enhance your learning activity. Jot down your ideas in your *course log* and consult your IT team for technical assistance with creating characters.

RESOURCE ORGANIZATION

The final consideration is how to organize your resources. You will want to keep track of all resources, as well as any other items you create for your course (e.g., instructions for a learning activity). Table 8.2 presents a sample organizational system for resources that we call a file locator. You can create a file locator as a spreadsheet or document table that includes this information for all of your resources, and then save this file organizer in your *course log*.

This information allows you to more easily locate a resource. The file locator also reminds you of any copyright issues that might occur over time. A few weeks into a course, you might not remember the location details when you need to access and edit a resource. If you generate a file locator and keep it in your *course log*, you will stay organized.

Table 8.2 File locator

Title of file	Type of file	Location(s) in course	Embedding code used in course	Source information URL link
Date accessed	Copyright information and dates used		Accessibility notes (alt tags, transcript, descriptions, timing)	

Review a sample entry in the instructor's file locator for the Theories of Personality Course.

Title of file	Type of file	Location(s) in course	Embedding code used in course	Source information URL link
Psychoanalytic Theories handout	Document (doc)	TBD	N/A	N/A
Date accessed	Copyright information		Accessibility notes (alt tags, transcript, descriptions, timing)	
N/A	N/A – self-created		Images in document include alternative text tag.	

Now organize your resources.

Application:
Organize Your Resources

Using the file locator, organize your resources. Keep track of each resource in a spreadsheet, and organize related files (e.g., all resources needed for a learning activity) in electronic folders.

RESOURCES: SUMMARY

In this chapter, you explored resources, reviewed your resources in terms of adult learning principles, selected resources, considered using a character, and organized your resources.

You are now ready for *Chapter 9: Feedback*.

9   Feedback

FEEDBACK: INTRODUCTION

As you have found in our description of the learning process and in our conceptualization of learning activities, learning occurs through dialogue. A dialogue is a specific form of discussion that involves the interactive exchange of learners' thoughts, experiences, and emotions. Through this interaction, learners receive feedback from others and explore others' perspectives. Cambridge Dictionary defines feedback as a "reaction to a process or activity, or the information obtained from such a reaction"; the same source also defines feedback as "information about something such as . . . someone's work, that provides an idea of whether people like it or whether it is good."

In both of these definitions, feedback involves interaction. Thus, feedback is different from simply providing neutral information in response to a question, such as one's name or one's favorite novel. Rather, feedback requires responding to a person's work, ideas, or opinions, in a way that communicates what we think or feel about what we have seen and/or heard.

In this chapter, you will complete the following actions:

- choose the focus and timing of your formative and summative feedback
- determine how peer feedback will be incorporated
- determine how learners will use feedback
- create or revise a feedback tool
- update your learning activity and write learning activity instructions.

INSTRUCTOR FEEDBACK

Instructor feedback can be formative or summative. Summative feedback is provided on summative milestones. Summative feedback is always evaluative with reference to the knowledge and skill areas the milestone demonstrates. Although summative feedback usually includes a grade, some authors (e.g., Brookhart, 2019) have argued that grades are not essential for learning. A full discussion of the pros and cons of grades is beyond the scope of this book, but we refer you to Schinske and Tanner (2014) for additional information on alternative grading practices.

Formative feedback is provided on formative milestones. Formative feedback informs learners of their progress toward accomplishing the summative milestone. We strongly encourage you to include formative feedback throughout a course in addition to your summative feedback. The following *Exploring the Terrain* examines benefits of and suggestions for using formative feedback.

**Exploring the Terrain:
Formative Feedback**

According to Nicol and Macfarlane-Dick (2006), "Students interact with subject content, transforming and discussing it with others, in order to internalize meaning and make connections with what is already known" (p. 200). The question is how to expand the learning process to include formative feedback. Nicol and Macfarlane-Dick maintain that in higher education, feedback is still generally viewed as a "transmission process" about what is right or wrong with students' work and to point out their strengths and weaknesses. Students are expected to take this feedback and make corrections or demonstrate improvement on subsequent assignments. As part of this process, instructors assume that the feedback they provide is easy for the students to understand and incorporate. Another key assumption is that feedback involves only a cognitive transfer of information, rather than involving not only cognition but also motivation and beliefs (in our terms, social and emotional aspects; Schoenfield, 2016/1992) that have been shown to influence how students feel about themselves.

To address these assumptions about feedback, Nicol and Macfarlane-Dick (2006) proposed a conceptual model of self-regulated learning and feedback that includes external feedback from the instructor and peers as well as self-reflective feedback. They defined good feedback as "anything that might strengthen the students' capacity to self-regulate their own performance" (p. 205).

Nicol and Macfarlane-Dick (2006) provide some ways to make formative feedback relevant to learners. Formative feedback addresses cognitive, social, and emotional aspects of learning. Most importantly, as the authors sum up:

> If students are to be prepared for learning throughout life, they must be provided with opportunities to develop the capacity to regulate their own learning as they progress through higher education . . . [F]ormative assessment and feedback might be organized so as to support this development. (p. 215)

A summary of Nicol and Macfarlane-Dick's seven principles of formative feedback (pp. 205–215) is presented in Table 9.1. As you consider the principles of good formative feedback, think about how adult learning assumptions are reflected in these principles.

Table 9.1   Principles of formative feedback, purposes, and practices

Principles	Purposes and practices
Clarify good performance (goals, criteria, and standards)	Ensure learners' understanding of goals, criteria, and standards for the activity and milestone. Provide examples that explicitly show what is required and the standards that will be used so that students can compare their work to the example. Include definitions, discussion, reflection, and peer review about the goals, criteria and standards.

Table 9.1   *(cont.)*

Principles	Purposes and practices
Develop self-reflection of learning	Provide learners with opportunities to reflect on their emotional responses to learning activities. Provide self-reflection prompts on learning strategies and the results of these strategies once the milestone is complete. Include metacognitive awareness as part of this reflection (included as part of the cognitive aspect in our view of learning).
Provide high-quality information about learning.	Provide timely feedback that offers constructive corrective feedback as well as appropriate praise. Feedback should be directly tied to goals, standards, or criteria. Note that a large number of criteria can lead to learners checking off boxes rather than actual learning. Feedback should be prioritized according to needed improvement and limited to encourage use.
Encourage instructor and peer dialogue about learning	Engaging in dialogue between learners and instructor or among peers ensures an active role that promotes the emergence of shared understanding (the learning process). Dialogue with the instructor helps students immediately clarify any misunderstandings. Small-group sessions to review common errors among learners are another way to provide feedback in a group. Peer feedback exposes learners to alternative perspectives on learning strategies and can aid in the construction of new knowledge. In addition, peer dialogue may promote learner persistence.
Promote positive beliefs about self and learning	Be aware that high stakes summative assessment tends to make learners focus on passing the test and obtaining good grades rather than to focus on learning and mastering the course topics. When grades are given with feedback, feedback is largely ignored and comments are not used to improve. Feedback that provides information about progress is more motivating and results in higher self-esteem. Be aware of the impact of a growth mindset (Claro, Paunesku, & Dweck, 2016), which encourages learners to increase effort to meet a challenge, versus a fixed mindset, which leads learners to believe that their ability to learn is limited.
Close the gap between current and desired performance	Closing the performance gap can be achieved by providing feedback on sections of the work as it is created, providing feedback on one milestone that will allow improvement on the next milestone, and/or asking learners, based on feedback given, to identify actions that they can take to improve.

Table 9.1   *(cont.)*

Principles	Purposes and practices
Provide information to the instructor to adapt teaching strategies	Reviewing the feedback you give your learners helps you understand how your learners progress and what challenges they face during the course. This information enables you to refine your course to better meet your learners' needs. Some methods you might consider using to gather this type of information from your learners include asking your students to request specific feedback when they submit a milestone, or asking them to identify areas that they found difficult as they completed the milestone. Asking groups of learners to post "a question worth asking" to a discussion board is another way to gather the same information.

Travel Advisory:
Automated Formative Feedback

Online tests and quizzes typically provide automated feedback about which items learners respond to correctly and incorrectly. We recommend that you enhance automated feedback by including formative feedback with each incorrect item. For example, you can build suggestions and self-reflection questions into automated feedback. By prompting learners to think about why they responded incorrectly, you can help learners to self-evaluate their learning strategies.

Exploring the Terrain:
Timeliness of Instructor Feedback

Feedback can immediately follow the milestone or it can follow at a later point. Immediate feedback includes automatic feedback on objective quiz or test items, oral feedback provided to learners immediately after a live-streamed discussion, feedback conferences that occur in real time, and feedback provided during a synchronous dialogue. Goodwin and Miller (2012) suggest that immediate feedback is helpful when learners are acquiring new concepts and skills and need to check their understanding, whereas briefly delayed feedback is better for application tasks, as a brief delay gives learners an opportunity to self-correct without relying on the instructor's feedback. However, regardless of the milestone, timely feedback is essential (Wiggins, 2012). Feedback should be given quickly enough that learners can make use of the feedback while they are still in the course.

We return to the Theories of Personality course example. Review the instructor's decisions about formative and summative feedback.

**Theories of Personality Example:
Formative and Summative Feedback**

In my learning activity on theories, I identified three milestones: two formative milestones (the two written dialogues between partners) and one summative milestone (the final written case analysis and interpretation, completed individually).

The two formative milestones require formative feedback. My feedback will be in the form of qualitative comments and will focus on the following areas relevant for the milestone:

- Learners' factual knowledge of the theories: correct explanation of theoretical concepts
- Critical thinking: correct application of theoretical concepts to the case
- Writing skills: grammar, organization, and APA style.

In each case, I will point out what learners did well and what areas need improvement for all three skill areas.

The summative milestone requires summative feedback. My feedback will focus on the same areas, but instead of qualitative comments, I will identify (e.g., with a rubric or checklist) learners' accomplishment of the milestone and assign a grade according to my established criteria.

Now choose the focus and timing of your formative and summative feedback.

 **Application:
Choose Focus and Timing of Formative and Summative Feedback**

- Look at the milestones for your learning activity.
- Describe the type of feedback (formative or summative) each milestone requires.
- Choose the focus of the feedback for each milestone (topic knowledge and skill areas).
- Decide when you will give the feedback. This decision helps with your overall planning for the learning activity. For example, if you have a large class, you will need more time to give feedback to all learners. Note the type, focus, and timing of your feedback for each milestone in your *course log*.

Peer Feedback

Although the instructor's feedback is often what learners are most familiar with and desire because of the instructor's power to give grades (see *Chapter 3: Adult Learning Principles*), the feedback received during learner-to-learner dialogue can be some of the most powerful feedback learners actually receive. Peer feedback involves learners sharing and responding to each other's work. Peer feedback strategies include peer review of written work, peer observation of group participation, and peers giving each other feedback after a role-play or simulation.

Exploring the Terrain:
Peer Feedback

The benefits of peer feedback are numerous (e.g., Brill & Hodges, 2011; Nicol, Thomson, & Breslin, 2014). Receiving peer feedback can reinforce and complement feedback provided by the instructor. Peer feedback also provides a unique perspective on learners' work. In fact, sometimes peers notice things that the instructor has missed! Knowing that peers will give feedback also prompts learners to broaden their perception of their audience. Peer feedback, especially when used in the early stages of a learning activity, helps learners clarify their thinking.

Learners also benefit from giving feedback. Giving feedback can prompt learners to think about an activity differently – not just from their own perspective but also from their peers' perspective. Seeing peers' work can also challenge learners' assumptions and help them think about course information in new ways. Furthermore, giving feedback requires that learners use social-emotional skills, such as empathy. We have observed that peer feedback has the added advantage of increasing learners' engagement and connection with each other. It can help build trust and provide support among the learners in the course.

Boud (1991) suggests that helpful peer feedback should be realistic, specific, sensitive to the receiver's goals, timely, descriptive, non-judgmental, direct, and positive. We emphasize that peer feedback should be non-evaluative; it should be useful information, rather than a critique or formal assessment of a peer's performance.

To elicit high-quality peer feedback, Nilson (2003) suggests that you ask learners to "identify or to personally react to defined parts of the paper, speech, or project" (p. 37) rather than asking them to evaluate each other's work. This guideline promotes peer feedback that is appropriate to the developmental level of learners and that requires learners to pay mindful (rather than superficial) attention to each other's work.

Learners often need specific guidance about how to give and receive feedback, particularly if this is a new experience or if learners have had negative experiences with peer feedback in past learning situations. It helps to coach learners on the feedback process by providing clear expectations of what feedback is and isn't, how to reconcile contradictory feedback (i.e., a peer says one thing and the instructor says something else), and by modeling feedback. We recommend that the benefits of giving feedback be explained, particularly to avoid learners' impressions that they are "doing the instructor's work" by giving peer feedback (which can lead to understandably negative reactions). In addition, creating a course culture that values respect for various perspectives can contribute to effective peer feedback processes.

Making peer feedback formative, with an opportunity for the instructor to address any errors in the feedback, can help to alleviate learners' fears that receiving negative feedback will hurt their grades. We encourage you to consider how to integrate peer feedback into your overall feedback plan.

Review the instructor's decisions about peer feedback.

Theories of Personality Example:
Peer Feedback

Learners will be engaged in written dialogue about the first two cases. In this activity, I don't want my learners to give each other feedback on writing or critical thinking skills, but I do want them to point out any conceptual areas that were incorrect or unclear in each other's posts. I will add this element to the instructions for the dialogue in my learning activity.

Now determine how peer feedback will be incorporated into your learning activity.

Application:
Determine How to Incorporate Peer Feedback

Some degree of peer feedback is already built into the learning activity by virtue of the fact that learners are interacting with each other through dialogue. You can decide whether and how additional peer feedback will be incorporated into your learning activity. Keep in mind that peer feedback should be formative and should not be used to evaluate learners' performance. Note points of peer feedback within the learning activity in your *course log*.

LEARNERS' USE OF FEEDBACK

Feedback is information. As with any information, learners need to self-reflect on feedback and engage in dialogue to clarify any questions they have about the feedback they receive. However, this doesn't always happen.

Notes from Our Journey:
Learners' Use of Feedback

We have had countless experiences with giving extensive written comments on learners' paper drafts (even to the point of practically editing the document), only to find that learners had not integrated the feedback into their revisions. More importantly, we discovered that learners often could not apply our feedback on one paper to improve their next paper.

We initially hypothesized that perhaps learners weren't reading the feedback. Although some learners may not have read the feedback, other learners may not have had a strong enough foundation to understand and apply the feedback. The extensive information we were providing (grammatical corrections, wording suggestions, sentence structure improvements, etc.) did not translate to learning these writing conventions because our learners rarely sought clarification and dialogue about the feedback. To address this situation, we started requiring them to self-reflect on the feedback and seek clarification as needed.

By requiring learners to self-reflect on milestone feedback and seek dialogue as needed, you help learners develop their own reflective practice (Cantillon & Sargeant, 2008). We describe two strategies: post-milestone self-reflection and post-milestone dialogue.

Post-Milestone Self-Reflection

Too often, learners receive their milestone results at the end of a course but are not given any meaningful opportunities to self-reflect on these results. In contrast, one instructor we spoke with, Dr. Lesa Tran Lu of Rice University, created the following self-reflection for learners to complete after a mid-term chemistry exam. This self-reflection requires learners to evaluate their own learning strategies. Note that the self-reflection includes a rationale. It also focuses learners' attention on exam items that are commonly missed ("questions 3 and 5"). Although learners can earn credit for their completion of this self-reflection, it is not a milestone.

> ### Chemistry Course Post-Exam Self-Reflection Example
>
> Reviewing your exam and correcting misunderstandings in your answers are key exercises in learning chemistry. Thus, you will have the opportunity to earn back points on your exam by reflecting upon your answers to a question on Exam 1.
>
> ***Instructions*** Review questions 3 and 5 on the exam, choose ONE question upon which to reflect, and answer the following questions (if you scored perfectly on both Questions 3 and 5, please choose another question to reflect upon):
>
> - Assess the accuracy and logic of your own response: briefly explain whether the reasoning presented is logical, noting what information is correct or incorrect and providing correct logical reasoning and explanation where needed.
> - What conceptual shortcomings prevented you from answering the question correctly? Try to focus on the concepts, rather than the math.
> - If you feel like you lost points because of carelessness, not being able to express yourself clearly, not knowing how to approach a problem, or not pacing yourself during the exam, how do you plan to address these challenges?
> - Overall, what could you have done differently to better prepare for the exam? Or, what will you do differently as you prepare for the next exam?
>
> Of course, you should reflect upon all of the exam questions, but you are only required to submit your reflection on one question. You may refer to the exam key, consult your own notes, and discuss this assignment with your classmates, TAs, and instructors. However, you must turn in your own work.

If your course is in a discipline or program that requires tests, establishing a way for learners to use feedback on tests is essential. We suggest scheduling final exams and other milestones before the end of the course (if allowed by the institution) and adding self-reflection at the end of the course. This strategy gives you enough time to give feedback on the milestone and gives learners enough time to reflect on the feedback.

Post-Milestone Dialogue

A post-milestone dialogue is a dialogue between the learner and the instructor, focusing on the learner's performance on the milestone. The dialogue can involve a written format (e.g., e-journal) or an oral format (e.g., virtual conference).

The dialogue begins with instructor feedback on the learner's performance on the milestone. The learner self-reflects on the feedback, and then the instructor responds to the learner's self-reflection. Although this approach can involve a larger time investment on the part of the instructor, the dialogue can be streamlined by creating a database of typical feedback on various aspects of learners' work and then using relevant feedback for each learner. In addition, you may want to ask questions that prompt learners' self-reflection, such as:

- What did you do well?
- What needs improvement?
- What questions do you have about the feedback?

The Appendix contains additional feedback prompts for learner self-reflection.

As with the post-exam reflection example offered earlier in the chapter, you may decide to give learners credit for their participation in a post-milestone dialogue. However, participation in the dialogue is not a milestone.

In summary, feedback is only useful if learners understand it and attempt to apply it to their future learning. Prompting learners to self-reflect on the feedback and to engage in dialogue about the feedback is consistent with adult learning principles.

Review the Theories of Personality instructor's decisions about how learners will use feedback.

Theories of Personality Example:
Learners' Use of Feedback

Learners will benefit from self-reflecting on the formative feedback they receive on their dialogue posts. In my feedback, I might ask questions such as, "What did you learn from the feedback you received?" and "How will you approach the next case differently, based on the feedback you received?" Learners will write their self-reflection in an e-journal, and I will respond to the self-reflection. However, although I will give learners credit for this action, the e-journal self-reflection and dialogue will not be a milestone.

Now determine how learners will use the feedback they receive in your learning activity.

Application:
Determine Learners' Use of Feedback

Decide how your learners will self-reflect and/or dialogue about the feedback they receive. Such self-reflection and dialogue can be informal (e.g., "think about these questions") or formal (e.g., "write a paragraph"). Jot down your notes in your *course log*.

FEEDBACK TOOLS

Providing feedback on milestones can be quite time-consuming, considering the volume and complexity of the work that learners may produce. In this section, we explore the pros and cons of rubrics, discuss how to improve rubrics, and present an alternative feedback tool. You, in turn, will create or revise a feedback tool for your learning activity.

Rubrics: Pros and Cons

One of the most common strategies for evaluating and providing feedback on these activities is a rubric. We discuss pros and cons of rubrics as well as an alternative you can consider.

Rubrics are feedback tools that describe learners' achievement of a milestone. Most commonly seen in the realm of teaching writing, rubrics typically indicate the characteristics that must be present in learners' work in order to achieve a certain grade. Rubrics can improve consistency of feedback by increasing objectivity. When thoughtfully constructed, rubrics clearly communicate expectations to learners and can save you time in grading (Goggins Selke, 2013). In addition, rubrics align with most learning management systems (LMSs) and with higher education grading practices in general.

However, there are pitfalls. Rubrics can reduce learner creativity and individuality. Instructors using rubrics may also find that the rubric scores on individual milestones do not actually reflect the learners' overall growth and performance in the course (i.e., either over-represent or under-represent learners' performance).

Notes from Our Journey:
The Rubric Challenge

We have long struggled with the use of rubrics. In fact, to be blunt, rubrics have been the bane of our existence. Here are some of the key challenges we have faced:

- Writing a rubric that our learners understood: If the learners hadn't yet learned the skills, how could they understand the rubric?
  - In many cases, our learners had not been exposed to the skills and had no idea of the meaning of what we were asking. For example, learners might be told that they were responsible for correct comma placement when they had never learned about comma placement. These types of issues can be particularly troublesome for English language learners but also appear troublesome for some native English speakers.
- Determining the number of grading levels: Did we need five levels that corresponded to grades A–F, or was it enough to have three or four levels with points for each level and a grade based on total number of points?
  - We found that four or five levels were most difficult because it was impossible to accurately differentiate between the middle levels. We resorted to such unhelpful approaches as defining the top level as a paper with no more than two errors, the next level as three or four errors, and so forth.
  - We asked ourselves if there was a real difference between two errors and three errors. Were some errors more important than others? How are qualitative features captured in a quantitative measurement environment?
- Deciding the amount of detailed description to provide for each aspect of performance: We found that too much description led to confusion for our learners and ourselves.
  - Our learners didn't know where to focus their efforts. Clearly, our learners could not focus on everything, but if we weren't going to pay attention to all that we described, why did we include certain aspects of performance in the rubric?
- Milestone summative grade not matching our assessment of the quality of work: Generally, we found that when we used rubrics, the grade indicated by the rubric was higher than our assessment of the quality of work.
  - Even by adjusting our choice of level on the rubric, the grade indicated by the rubric was often higher than indicated by the actual quality of the work. This disconnect between the rubric score and our qualitative assessment led to much frustration on our part.

And so, we journeyed from using these point-based rubrics to using alternative methods, such as checklists and feedback dialogues. Our focus shifted from judging learners' work to helping learners improve their skills and understanding of the course information. This shift matched our view of our role as facilitators of learning, resulting in less frustration and dread of grading.

From the learners' perspective, rubrics can be overwhelming if they involve evaluation of too many aspects of performance. Similarly, when various aspects of performance are grouped together within a single rubric category (e.g., "writing skills"), a rubric score on this category doesn't give learners a clear sense of what they need to do to improve.

Creating Better Rubrics

To create better rubrics, one option is to make rubrics much more fine-grained and to couple the rubrics with other forms of feedback, such as detailed comments on a portion of a written milestone. Another option is to modify the rubric so that learners receive feedback on individual characteristics of each grading criterion (rather than lumping several criteria together). A third alternative is to use rubrics for determining summative grades only after formative rubric feedback on related work has been provided.

We generally do not use wide ranges of points in our rubrics, as that provides too much subjectivity in grading. Instead, when we do use rubrics, we often use a three-point rating scale for criteria. We have found that defining the middle category or categories on a rubric requires the most thought, as performance is less clear-cut in the middle. Unless you have clear indicators of numerous levels of performance, we recommend that you begin with three levels. The Appendix contains an example of a writing rubric that can be used for both formative and summative feedback.

Your Travel Journal:
Rubrics

Consider a rubric you currently use and ask yourself a few questions about how well your rubric works. Jot down your notes in the space provided.

Do learners improve after receiving feedback on the rubric?

Does the rubric provide objective information about learners' performance, or is there a degree of subjectivity involved in the rubric?

Is the rubric intended for formative feedback, summative feedback, or both?

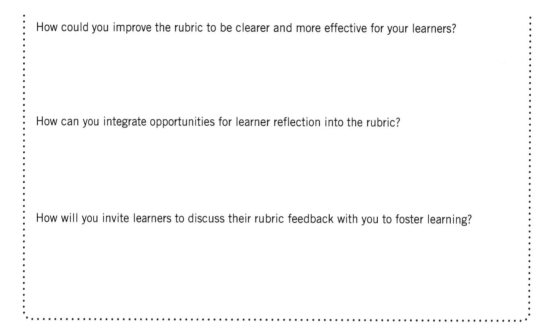

How could you improve the rubric to be clearer and more effective for your learners?

How can you integrate opportunities for learner reflection into the rubric?

How will you invite learners to discuss their rubric feedback with you to foster learning?

Milestone Checklists

We acknowledge that rubrics are extremely popular in higher education. However, some authors (e.g., Wilson, 2006) have called for an alternative to rubrics, especially when providing formative feedback on complex skills such as writing. Our own approach veers from the norm, in that we use traditional rubrics only on a very limited basis. Instead, one strategy that we have found useful is to create a detailed milestone checklist of characteristics that indicate attainment of a milestone. Learners receive a copy of the checklist to review their own (and others') work, and the checklist can be used for both formative and summative feedback.

The milestone checklist is a succinct tool that does not attempt to rate learners' milestone attainment on a scale (as in the case with many rubrics). The checklist includes opportunities for the instructor to point out specific places in a learner's work where the characteristic is present (or is not present but needs to be), as well as suggested actions for improvement (e.g., reviewing certain course material, accessing additional resources in the course, visiting a tutorial or writing center, etc.). This approach makes attainment of the milestone the expectation. If there are characteristics that learners have not yet demonstrated, then the learners and the instructor have information about what they need to focus on in order to reach the milestone.

Let's return to our example. The instructor decides to create a milestone checklist for the case analysis and interpretation milestones (formative and summative). Table 9.2 presents an example of a milestone checklist with feedback provided in the comments section.

Table 9.2 Example of a milestone checklist

Milestone checklist for case analysis and interpretation	
Instructions: This checklist provides guidance on the written case analysis and interpretation. If all of the milestone criteria are checked, your work provides evidence that you have fully reached the milestone! If a characteristic has an arrow, you will need to continue working on that area to reach the milestone. Comments are provided to help you improve. Please see the comment(s) under any milestones that are unchecked.	
Criteria for writing	**Comments**
✓ The paper is free from grammatical errors.	
✓ The paper is free from spelling errors.	
✓ The paper is free from punctuation errors.	
✓ The paper is well-organized.	
✓ The paper uses appropriate language and avoids jargon.	
➤ Source material is paraphrased or quoted correctly.	Include page numbers with quotations.
✓ In-text citations use the appropriate format.	
➤ References use the appropriate format.	Use ampersand (&) before the last author's name. Provide page numbers for all articles, using the format pp. 1–10.
Criteria for critical thinking and topic knowledge	**Comments**
➤ Relevant theoretical concepts are identified.	Review the concept "observational learning" and consider how this concept applies to the case.
✓ Application of theoretical concepts to the case is logical.	

With this checklist, learners know what they need to work on to improve. This tool is particularly useful when paired with qualitative comments on a learner's work (or portion of the work).

If the checklist is being used for summative purposes and a grade is needed, scores or weights can be assigned to each criterion on the checklist. We recommend an "all or nothing" approach to scores/weights for a criterion. For example, if the learner meets a criterion, the learner receives the full number of points for that criterion. If the learner does not meet the criterion, the learner does not receive any points for that criterion. This reduces subjectivity in assigning scores to criteria. Assuming that learners have had previous opportunities to practice the relevant skills and receive feedback, then this approach is fair.

Now create or revise a feedback tool (rubric, checklist, or feedback dialogue) for your learning activity.

Application:
Create or Revise a Feedback Tool

Look at your summative milestone for the learning activity. In your *course log*, create or revise a feedback tool (e.g., rubric, checklist, feedback dialogue) that you will use to give learners feedback on the milestone. Include both topic knowledge and skill areas for that summative milestone in your feedback tool. Use the same tool for formative milestones in the same learning activity, modifying the tool as needed.

Travel Advisory:
Semiotics of Feedback

As with all communication, feedback has semiotic meaning to learners. Consider how your learners will interpret and respond to harsh feedback. Similarly, consider whether your learners will be able to understand and use excessive feedback on a milestone (e.g., a paper completely covered in corrections). Some learners may need more in-depth feedback on a smaller number of areas, especially on formative milestones.

LEARNING ACTIVITY UPDATE

Now that you have made various decisions about resources in the previous chapter and about feedback in this chapter, you are ready to update your learning activity.

Review the instructor's updated learning activity, with resources, characters, and additional information about feedback added.

	Theories of Personality team educational video on assessment

Purpose:

The purpose of this learning activity is for you to apply theories of personality to a written case analysis and interpretation within a psychotherapy clinic setting.

Milestones:

- Dialogue posts and responses (formative)
- Final case analysis and interpretation (summative)

Setting:

Welcome to the Integrative Psychotherapy Clinic! In this activity, you and a partner are interns who are rotating through three departments led by three theorists: Dr. Freud's Psychoanalytic Department, Dr. Skinner's Behavioral Department, and Dr. Bandura's Social-Cognitive Department. In each theorist's department, you will learn to apply key theoretical concepts to clinical cases. Your job is to self-reflect on what you learn, discuss with your partner how theories apply to cases presented in the clinic, and use your learning to analyze and interpret a case from all three theoretical perspectives in the Integration Department.

Skill areas:

- Critical thinking
- Writing

Resources:

- Videos on psychoanalytic, behavioral, and social-cognitive theories of personality, with self-reflection questions
- Summary documents for theories and case examples, with self-reflection questions
- Annotated handout on APA style and writing tips
- APA style website
- Website on case analysis and interpretation
- Cases 1, 2, and 3
- Detailed week-by-week instructions for the learning activity
- Support and tips from Carl and Karen, the senior interns (i.e., two characters)

Actions and feedback:

- Duration: three weeks
- Case 1: Psychoanalytic vs. behavioral theories – self-reflection and written dialogue; e-journal reflection on feedback
- Case 2: Behavioral vs. social-cognitive theories – self-reflection and written dialogue
- Case 3: Integration of theories – final case analysis and interpretation
- Your instructor will provide feedback on each dialogue and on your final case analysis and interpretation.

Now update your learning activity.

Application:
Update Your Learning Activity and Write Instructions

Review all of your notes on the learning activity (milestones, purpose statement, actions, resources, and feedback) in your *course log*. Keeping your course theme in mind, update your learning activity and write instructions for the activity.

Your instructions can be as detailed as the learning activity requires. We recommend that you write the instructions for the entire activity to see how the activity flows and what might need to be adjusted. You can divide the instructions into parts (e.g., weeks) later, if your learning activity stretches across two or more weeks. Keep in mind how the wording you choose will affect your students.

Milestone:
Learning Activity

You have completed your second milestone: A learning activity that is ready for your course.

Call a Colleague:
Your Learning Activity

Seek feedback on all of the elements of your learning activity: milestone(s), purpose statement, actions, resources, and feedback. Jot down your notes in the space provided.

FEEDBACK: SUMMARY

In this chapter, you explored various feedback options, including formative and summative feedback, peer feedback, and what learners will do with the feedback they receive. You considered the pros and cons of rubrics and contemplated using a milestone checklist. You created a feedback tool and finalized your learning activity.

You are now ready for *Chapter 10: Course Structure*.

10 Course Structure

COURSE STRUCTURE: INTRODUCTION

The course structure consists of an itinerary for your course and the use of modules to organize and present items within your course.

In this chapter, you will complete several actions:

- draft an itinerary
- create additional learning activities and add them to your itinerary
- create a learner feedback survey
- list module titles
- choose images for your modules
- create your module layout.

ITINERARY

An itinerary contains a detailed description of what learners will do and when. This process is similar to building a course schedule in your syllabus. The difference is that you start by scheduling one learning activity and then decide whether to schedule additional activities in the itinerary, rather than starting with an entire course schedule of topics and then deciding what activities will suit those topics.

We continue with our example of the Theories of Personality course. Table 10.1 presents an initial itinerary for this course.

Table 10.1 Itinerary draft for Theories of Personality course: one learning activity scheduled

Week	Topics	Actions and milestones	Feedback opportunities
1	Psychoanalytic and behavioral theories	Self-reflection on videos and handouts	

Table 10.1   *(cont.)*

Week	Topics	Actions and milestones	Feedback opportunities
1 (cont.)	Psychoanalytic and behavioral theories	Dialogue on psychoanalytic and behavioral theories applied to case 1 (formative milestone)	Peer feedback on posts Instructor formative feedback on dialogue
2	Behavioral and social-cognitive theories	E-journal self-reflection on instructor feedback on case 1 dialogue Self-reflection on videos and handouts Dialogue on behavioral and social-cognitive theories applied to case 2 (formative milestone)	Instructor feedback on e-journal self-reflection Peer feedback on posts Instructor formative feedback on dialogue
3	Integration of theories	Self-reflection on previous self-reflection notes, dialogues, and feedback received Individual case study analysis and interpretation of case 3 (summative milestone)	Instructor summative feedback on case study analysis and interpretation
4	To be determined		
5	To be determined		
6	To be determined		
7	To be determined		

This learning activity takes three weeks. The schedule is manageable, and both the instructor's and the learners' workload is not overwhelming. The rest of the class time (weeks 4–6) is available for an additional learning activity focused on the second cluster of topics.

Once you have drafted your itinerary, you will have a better sense of how much time is available for additional learning activities. If you find that most of the available course time is taken up with the first learning activity, you will either need to scale back this learning activity or else create additional learning activities that are brief. This broadening and narrowing process is part of the iterative nature of course creation!

Before you draft your itinerary, we show you the next two steps in the process so that you can see how creating an itinerary and creating additional learning activities go together in an iterative way.

Review the instructor's decision process about creating additional learning activities.

Theories of Personality Example:
Second Learning Activity

My itinerary currently contains one learning activity (see Table 10.1). This activity is the most important because it introduces learners to some of the major theories of personality and gives learners practice with two of the skill areas – critical thinking and writing. However, I still need a learning activity for the other topics and summative milestone: the team educational video presentation on a controversial personality assessment issue. After taking into account the first learning activity, there is enough time left for this milestone.

My second learning activity will require the team to choose a topic from a list I provide, conduct research as a team, and create a brief educational video that presents their research. Because this is an online course, I will tell teams that they can produce a video out of several individual clips from team members, but that they must work as a team to plan the contents of the video. Teams will present their videos in an online educational video showcase, and teams will respond to other teams' videos with questions and comments. Finally, learners will individually reflect on the course, their team experience, and the work that they produced by completing another self-reflection in their e-journal.

Review the instructor's second learning activity. Note that the activity reflects decisions that the instructor would make by following the complete process for creating a learning activity.

	Theories of Personality team educational video on assessment	
Purpose: The purpose of this learning activity is for your team to create an educational video that will teach your fellow psychotherapy clinic interns about a controversial aspect of personality assessment.	*Milestone:* • Team educational video (summative)	
Setting: Each team chooses a personality assessment specialist, who is researching a controversial issue in personality assessment. After researching the chosen issue, your team will create an educational video to teach your fellow interns about that issue during a video showcase.	*Skill areas:* • Critical thinking • Teamwork	
	Resources: • Videos on trait and humanistic theories, with self-reflection questions and transcripts	

(*cont.*)

Actions and feedback:	*Resources* (cont.)
• Duration: seven weeks • You will choose a team and specialist who will provide your team topic. • After reading and reflecting on the resources related to your topic, you will have a virtual meeting with your team to discuss your plan for researching the topic and creating the video. • Team members will research the topic and create individual segments for the video, which the team will combine into a single video. • Your team will share your video with other teams in the video showcase and respond to other teams' videos with questions and comments. • Your final step is to self-reflect on the course, your team experience, and the work you have produced, and to write your self-reflection in your e-journal.	• Summary documents for assessment instruments, with self-reflection questions • List of personality assessment topics (choose one topic) • Video on creating an educational video, with transcript • Detailed week-by-week instructions for the learning activity • Support and tips from Dr. Specialist (a character)

**Theories of Personality Example:
Final Itinerary**

I would like for learners to start working as a team at the beginning of the course, rather than waiting until mid-course. I decide to start the second learning activity in week 1 by having learners choose teams, but I will spread this learning activity out over the seven weeks. Spreading it out will also give learners time to read and view the relevant resources for their topic prior to creating the video. I schedule this learning activity in my itinerary (see Table 10.2).

Finally, having peeked at the next step in the process (*Chapter 11: Course Start Here*), I decide that I need to build in orientation and team building, so I add a brief orientation-related learning activity to the first week.

Table 10.2 illustrates the final itinerary for the Theories of Personality course. Both learning activities are included, along with an orientation activity. Some weeks involve actions for multiple learning activities, but these actions complement each other and have the same theme. Thus, the two learning activities are experienced as a cohesive course.

Table 10.2 Final itinerary for Theories of Personality course

Week	Topics	Actions and milestones	Feedback opportunities
1	Orientation	Complete orientation activity. Choose team and select a partner within your team.	Instructor formative feedback on orientation activity
2	Psychoanalytic and behavioral theories	Self-reflection on videos and handouts. Dialogue on psychoanalytic and behaviorist theories applied to case 1 (formative milestone).	Peer feedback on posts Instructor formative feedback on dialogue
3	Behavioral and social-cognitive theories	E-journal self-reflection on instructor feedback on case 1 dialogue. Self-reflection on videos and handouts. Dialogue on behavioral and social-cognitive theories applied to case 2 (formative milestone).	Instructor feedback on e-journal self-reflection Peer feedback on posts Instructor formative feedback on posts and replies
4	Integration of theories Psychoanalytic personality assessment	Self-reflection on previous dialogue posts and replies. Case study analysis and interpretation of case 3 (summative milestone). Self-reflection on readings. Choose team topic and begin research.	Instructor summative feedback on case study analysis and interpretation
5	Trait theories, humanistic theories, and personality assessment	Self-reflection on readings. Finalize research and create video.	

Table 10.2   (*cont.*)

Week	Topics	Actions and milestones	Feedback opportunities
6	Educational video presentation showcase	Post video in showcase (summative milestone); reply to two other teams' videos with a question. Respond to other teams' questions about your video.	Peer feedback on video Instructor summative feedback on video
7	Reflection on course	As a team, discuss and respond to other teams' questions; also discuss how your team worked together. E-journal self-reflection on course, team experience, and milestones.	Peer feedback on teamwork

 Travel Advisory:
Sequencing and Timing of Learning Activities

The sequencing and timing of learning activities depends on the activities themselves and on the topics of your course. For example, in some courses (such as the course depicted in Table 10.2), it makes sense to have two separate but related learning activities occurring simultaneously. In other courses, it might be better to have one learning activity for a period of time, followed by another learning activity, and so forth. Some courses use a single learning activity throughout the entire course (see, for example, the Business Simulation in *Chapter 7: Learning Activities*). Look at your topic clusters to help you determine the best sequencing and timing of learning activities.

Now it's time for you to draft an itinerary that includes your first learning activity.

 Application:
Draft Your Itinerary

You will need the details of your learning activity and knowledge of your course time frame (e.g., full-semester; half-semester; two weeks, etc.) to draft your itinerary.

Create your itinerary in your *course log*. You are just scheduling one learning activity for now. You will add learning activities as needed once you see how your first learning activity fits into your itinerary. At the same time, we recommend that you think ahead and consider what other learning activities you might want to include (based on the summative milestones you originally selected), to ensure that there is enough time for each activity.

Here are some tips for scheduling a learning activity in your itinerary:

- Include all of the actions that learners need to complete.
- Ensure that learners do not have to complete too many actions during the same time frame (e.g., one week).
- If you have more than one milestone for the learning activity, space out the milestones to ensure that learners have enough time to complete any prior actions and enough time to review your feedback before the next milestone is due.
- As you create additional learning activities, you may discover that the amount of time needed for each learning activity will change, depending on how many actions are involved. Keep in mind that this initial itinerary is a draft.

Now that you have a draft of your itinerary with one learning activity scheduled, you can determine how many (if any) additional learning activities are needed.

Application:
Create Additional Learning Activities and Update the Itinerary

Return to your course map. What topic clusters have not yet been covered? Do you need additional learning activities to cover these topics? If so, go through the process of creating one or more additional learning activities by reviewing Chapters 7–9.

As you create additional learning activities, schedule these learning activities in your itinerary. You can use the itinerary as a detailed course schedule in your course and/or include an abbreviated version in your syllabus. Carefully consider how much learners can realistically accomplish in your course.

Be careful not to overload learners with too many activities. However, as we discuss in the next *Exploring the Terrain*, learning activities that are realistic, relevant, and meaningful tend to be perceived by learners as a reasonable amount of work.

Exploring the Terrain:
Learner Perceptions of Workload

According to Kember (2004), determining the learner workload in a course presents a challenge. A traditional measure of workload is the number of hours a learner spends in class plus the number of hours the instructor deems an appropriate amount time that students should spend outside of class on the course (homework/independent study). This measurement is questionable because the time spent outside of class on the course is a "guess-timate" by the instructor. In addition, in an online course, there is no set amount of time the learner spends in formal "class." Thus, learners' perceptions of workload must also be taken into account.

Kember (2004) undertook a case study to examine five undergraduate learners' perceptions of workload at a university in Hong Kong. Kember (2004) reviewed the learners' seven-day activity diaries, analyzed questionnaire data measuring their perception of workload, and interviewed each learner. In addition, Kember and Leung (2006) continued to explore factors that influenced learners' perception of workload using data from the same questionnaire with 3,320 undergraduate students (response rate 59 percent).

Key findings from both studies were similar and included the following:

- Workload perception and amount of time reported in class and studying were not directly related.
- A disjointed curriculum led to the perception of higher workloads, whereas a coherent curriculum led to the perception of manageable workloads. Note that we believe that this holds true for a course as well as a curriculum. Ensuring that the connections among the topics are clear and coherent will help students perceive the course workload as manageable.
- Workload was not perceived as excessive if the course was considered stimulating.
- Perceived high workload led to an increased tendency to use a surface approach to learning, whereas workloads that are seen as reasonable led to deeper learning approaches.
- Types of assessment had an impact on learning approaches. When frequent tests were used, students spent more time individually memorizing the material, which seemed to adversely impact morale and class cohesion and led to the complaint of a high workload and a surface approach to learning. On the other hand, projects that tested understanding and active student engagement led to more class cohesion, no complaints about workload (even though the students reported more hours of work), and a deeper approach to learning.

Learners' perception of a reasonable workload is influenced by instruction that is connected, coherent, and, thus, promotes understanding. If learners' interest is stimulated, they will put more time and effort into engaging in deeper learning and perceive the workload to be manageable. However, once learners experience too much stress and pressure, their learning will suffer. In a carefully crafted course, less is more.

 Your Travel Journal:
Your Final Itinerary

You have updated your itinerary. Now self-reflect on the following questions. Jot down your responses in the space provided.

What topics have you included, and why?

What topics did you leave out, and why?

Is the time frame for actions and milestones reasonable, given learners' contexts?

What functions do self-reflection, dialogue, and application serve in each activity, and are these actions connected in a coherent way?

Will the milestones give you evidence of learners' topic knowledge and skill area abilities?

Do you have enough time to give feedback on milestones?

 Call a Colleague:
Your Final Itinerary

Call a colleague to discuss your itinerary. Jot down your notes about any comments/suggestions that your colleague offered about your learning activities and itinerary that you will consider incorporating.

Learner Feedback Surveys

Now that you have finalized your learning activities, you may want to think about how you will obtain learner feedback on these activities. We recommend that you create a brief learner feedback survey for this purpose. A learner feedback survey is an anonymous survey about learners' experiences in the course. It generally has a small number of items (no more than five) and can include items about the course in general and items about the specific learning activities. A learner feedback survey is an effective way to gauge learners' reactions and address any concerns about the course early on.

Items can gauge learners' responses to:

- self-reflection, dialogue, and application
- realistic, relevant, and meaningful learning activities
- instructor presence
- collaboration with peers in the course
- inclusiveness through text and images.

Note that we recommend placing the learner feedback survey early in your course, when there is still time to respond to learners' concerns. In addition, early placement will ensure that this survey does not compete with the official end-of-course evaluation.

Review the learner feedback survey that the instructor creates for Theories of Personality.

Theories of Personality Example:
Learner Feedback Survey

You have just participated in a learning activity on theories of personality. Please respond to the following questions. Your responses will be anonymous.

What did you find useful about the learning activity? What did you enjoy?

What were your concerns about the learning activity?

What suggestions do you have for improving this learning activity?

Now create a learner feedback survey for your course. It can focus on a specific learning activity, your course in general, or both. However, keep the survey short.

 Application:
Create a Learner Feedback Survey

In your *course log*, create questions for a learner feedback survey. You can include this survey after a learning activity and/or mid-course. If you plan to examine changes in your learners' experiences in the course or across courses, use the same survey questions at each point.

Itinerary: Summary

Creating your itinerary has been the first step in creating the course structure, as the itinerary informs the organization and presentation of the elements of your course.

The next part of creating the course structure involves making decisions about how to organize and present items in your course. By using text and visual layout, you will make your course more than a list of isolated "to-do" links.

COURSE MODULES

Shedroff (2001) notes that there is no one way of organizing course information. The key is to provide a logical structure that makes sense to your learners, is easy for them to follow, and progresses from more basic to more complex information and skills.

When thinking about the organization of information, imagine that this workbook didn't contain chapters or sections. The information contained in the workbook would feel like one long stream, and you might feel at a loss to know what the natural starting and stopping points were. Similarly, if an online course contains a seemingly never-ending list of item links with no information about which items go together, then learners can feel overwhelmed and unable to see the "big picture" of the course. To address this issue, you need a strategy for organizing your items.

Modules are one way of organizing items in your course. A module can be defined in several ways: by a unit of time (e.g., week), topic, chapter, unit, genre, or learning activity, or in other ways that are logical for your course. The definition depends in part on institutional norms, the length of your course, and whether your course will serve as a master course for various sections of the same course with varying time frames. Regardless of how modules are defined for your course, be consistent in what you call them. We call them modules.

Travel Advisory:
Learning Management System Terminology

As we noted in Chapter 1, this workbook does not provide instructions for working with a specific LMS. That said, we have found that most LMSs include the following components (albeit with varying names):

- items – files and links (e.g., resources, actions, milestones);
- labels – tools for describing items;
- modules – folders that hold related items.

We use these three terms in this chapter for ease of communication, but we recommend that you consult with your LMS support team for guidance on how these components work in your institution's LMS.

Number and Title of Modules

The number of modules is dictated by the specifics of your course. However, as a starting point, consider creating one module per unit of time (e.g., week) in your course. Module titles may be related to the topics covered in the modules or to some aspect of the learning activity.

Review the instructor's modules.

Theories of Personality Example:
Module Titles

This is a list of modules for the seven-week course. There is one module per week.

Module 1: Orientation
Module 2: Psychoanalytic and behavioral theories of personality
Module 3: Behavioral and social-cognitive theories of personality
Module 4: Integration of theories; psychoanalytic personality assessment
Module 5: Trait theories, humanistic theories, and personality assessment
Module 6: Educational video presentation showcase
Module 7: Reflection on the course

Now list your module titles.

 Application:
List Your Module Titles

Create a list of your module titles in your *course log*. Module titles are typically related to the topics in that module.

Now that you know the number and titles of your modules, you can decide what the layout of your module will be.

MODULE LAYOUT

The module layout is the way you want your module to look. The layout includes the selection and placement of images in the module, the use of labels (i.e., descriptions of files and links), and the organization of items within the module. How learners respond to your module layout is strongly influenced by semiotics.

Images in Modules

The images you choose for the modules communicate information. A meaningful image in the module can represent the learners and the theme. For example, an image can depict the learner as a future professional in the discipline. Since the purpose of images is to convey information, check for cultural meaning that may not be familiar to your learners. In addition, you may use icons in the module to help your learners identify repeated actions and resources at a glance, similar to how we have used icons in this workbook.

Review the instructor's decision process for images in modules.

Theories of Personality Example:
Images

I want to make my course as realistic as possible. Thus, I need the following images:

- photos of the main theorists;
- icons that represent concepts in the personality theories (e.g., brain icon);
- images for the two senior intern characters;
- images and text for clinic elements (e.g., "Psychoanalytic Department").

I will check all images I select for copyright laws and will work with my LMS support team to make sure the images are sized appropriately.

Now choose images for your modules.

Application:
Choose Images for Your Modules

Consider where you might want to use images in your module. Find or create images and save them in your *course log*. Be aware of copyright laws and other guidelines for using open-source images. In addition, review learner concerns about inclusion in the Appendix.

Consider what items or item types (e.g., documents; self-reflection tasks) recur in your course. Will it help your learners recognize these recurring items if you use an icon in the label where you describe the item? If so, find or create your icons and save them in your *course log*. Continue to be aware of copyright laws and other guidelines for using open-source images. See the Appendix for additional guidelines on using images.

Labels in Modules

Many items appear in an LMS as links. However, links do not inherently convey what learners should do with the information found in the linked item. To describe items and links, you can use a label. However, your choice of words for the label can make a huge difference in how learners respond to the items and links. Throughout this workbook, we have emphasized the importance of semiotic awareness – understanding the meaning and tone of the words and images you use. Words can have hidden meaning. Words evoke emotion. The wording of a label describing a learning activity can be perceived by the learner as impersonal and even daunting if it is unclear, very formal, or harshly worded, such as a terse ultimatum to complete by a deadline. (Yes, deadlines are necessary, but there are choices of how deadlines are presented to the learner.)

You create the tone of your course through the words you choose. You can be professional while creating warmth, fun, empathy, or other emotions to engage the learner while also being clear, concise, and professional. Consider the words and tone you would use in a face-to-face class, then use the same words and tone when you create a label. You can also include white space to help make the label easier to read.

Item Organization within Modules

The organization of items within the module is determined by the learning activity/activities occurring in the module. Because you have created all of your learning activities, it is likely that you are very clear on the items each module will contain. However, you will need to check the logic of the items and their order in each module. As you arrange the items in each module, try to see the items from the learners' perspectives: Does the order of presentation make sense, and will learners see how each item contributes to their learning?

Module Components

Creating a module layout involves visualizing what the module will look like. Table 10.3 presents the initial layout for the sixth module of the Theories of Personality course. See if you can determine what is missing.

Table 10.3   Initial module layout for Theories of Personality course

Module 6: All work must be completed by the October 15th deadline.
• Finalize your team video.

• Showcase presentation link
   ○ Post video in showcase discussion forum.
   ○ Reply to two other teams' videos with a question.
   ○ Respond to other teams' questions about your video.

Start early to make the deadline. No excuses for late work will be accepted. If your technology does not meet online course standards, it is your responsibility to contact the IT department.

The style of writing in Table 10.3 is clear and concise, but it isn't very friendly, and it shows an instructor who has been frustrated by late work. In addition, there is minimal use of white space, and the instructions provide only the bare minimum of information needed. Adult learning principles are not clearly evident in the layout.

To remedy this issue, we suggest that a module layout include the following components:

- brief introduction to the module, including topics covered and relevant skill areas
- prior learning that will be activated
- resources and actions learners will take (with relevant items and links)
- milestone(s) and feedback
- connection between current learning and future learning
- scenario, if applicable
- other theme-related images and text.

Now contrast the example you have just seen in Table 10.3 with a revised layout for the same module depicted in Table 10.4.

Table 10.4   Revised module layout for Theories of Personality course

Module 6: Educational video presentation showcase	
	This Week's Rotation: Video Showcase Congratulations! You have reached your final clinic rotation: the video showcase in which all teams present their educational videos and give each other feedback. In this module, you will demonstrate the teamwork that went into creating your video. You will learn about various controversies in personality assessment by viewing your peers' videos. You will also sharpen your critical thinking skills by asking and responding to questions about the videos.
Dr. Specialist's Words of Wisdom: You are a vital member of your team! If you need help with creating your video, reach out to your team and let them know. Start early to make the October 15th due date.	To get started, click on the link to the showcase. The link contains resources and instructions for the activity. Educational Video Presentation Showcase
Module feedback In this module, you will receive your instructor's feedback on a milestone: the team educational video presentation. You will also receive other teams' feedback on your video.	**A look ahead** Although this is the last clinic rotation, you have one more week in your internship. The questions and feedback you receive on your team educational video presentation will inform your self-reflection in the final module.

Notice the friendly wording. The theme is evident in the module, through the use of images, scenario, and character (Dr. Specialist). The introduction contains a brief description of the topics, skill areas, and learning that will occur in the module. Actions and resources are included in a link, and feedback is described. There is also a reference to previous learning (i.e., the teamwork that went into the video) and future learning ("a look ahead").

You now have everything you need for your modules. It is time to create your module layout.

 Application:
Create Your Module Layout

Contact your LMS support staff to discuss what options are available to you in your LMS for module layout and uploading images.

In your *course log*, create a visual depiction of your layout for a single module. Keep in mind what is possible in your LMS. Your layout will give you a common look for the modules in your course and will make the task of uploading items into your LMS easier.

Call a Colleague:
Your Module Layout

Ask a colleague for an opinion on your module layout. Possible points of discussion follow. You may want to jot down your notes directly on a copy of your module layout.

- Is your module introduction succinct and clear?
- Are items organized in a logical way?
- Is your tone friendly but professional?
- Is your use of images getting too busy or even overwhelming?
- Is your theme evident in your module layout?

COURSE STRUCTURE: SUMMARY

In this chapter, you created an itinerary, created additional learning activities as needed, created a learner feedback survey, listed module titles, chose images for your modules, and created a module layout.

You are now ready to continue to *Chapter 11: Course Start Here.*

11   Course Start Here

COURSE START HERE: INTRODUCTION

You are now ready to complete the last and, arguably, most critical part of your course: *Start Here*. You may be wondering why this endeavor has been left for last. It probably seems a bit backward to end the process with the beginning of the course. In fact, we are often told to "start at the beginning and work our way through to the end." The rationale for creating *Start Here* last is that you need not only a clear view of your course destination but also a clear picture of the path you will follow to reach the end result – successful learner understanding of the course destination. So, the first opportunity your learners have to engage with your course and each other is the last thing you create.

Notes from Our Journey:
The Workbook Start Here – A Lesson Learned

At the beginning of our journey, we were confident that we knew where we were going and what our readers would need to do to achieve the workbook destination; therefore, we confidently, and to our mind quite logically, created the workbook *Start Here* first. We were also very excited to get started and produce *something*! "After all," we thought, "we know what we want to cover in the workbook and how we want to organize the information. What could be easier than beginning with *Start Here*?"

About three-quarters of the way through the process of creating this workbook, we reviewed our initial *Start Here* and discovered that a significant portion had to be rewritten, which was a shock, although it shouldn't have been. If we had reined in our initial enthusiasm to get something done and mindfully given thought to the implications of the iterative, organic nature of our Change-adept Course Creation Process, we would have remembered that ongoing change is a natural part of this process. When comparing our initial workbook map to our final workbook map (*Chapter 5: Course Map*; Figure 5.1), you can easily see substantial change from the initial conception to the final creation.

Once we stopped and considered that the purpose of the workbook *Start Here* is to welcome and orient readers to the workbook, we realized our *Start Here* must reflect the information in the final workbook. Toward that end, the re-creation of our *Start Here* came after the *Prepare*, *Create*, and *Revise* sections were completed.

Based on what we learned, we moved *Chapter 11: Course Start Here* chapter to the end of the *Create* section, thus saving you frustration of a major rewrite of your course *Start Here*.

Travel Advisory:
Iterative Course Creation Process

As you create your *Course Start Here*, you may need to make some, most likely minor, changes to the other parts of your course as the iterative nature of the Change-adept Course Creation Process continues.

In this chapter, we will guide you through the process of creating *Start Here* for your course, using both welcome and engagement strategies and orientation strategies. We will provide you with strategies and techniques similar to the ones we used in the workbook *Chapter 1: Start Here*. As a reminder, in the workbook *Chapter 1: Start Here*, we did the following:

- welcomed readers to the workbook with a welcome letter
- presented our theme of a journey
- introduced ourselves
- described the contents of the workbook
- outlined the workbook destination, skill areas, and milestones
- oriented you to the workbook format and features
- provided you with some initial resources
- included a diagram of the Change-adept Course Creation Process
- presented the workbook map
- engaged you in some preliminary actions (*Your Travel Journal* and *Call a Colleague*).

In order to welcome, engage, and orient your learners, you will need to draw on what you have learned and applied as you created your course. Once your *Course Start Here* has been created, you will be ready to create your complete course in your learning management system (LMS).

 Travel Advisory:
Start Here Rationale and Terms

Start Here is a common term used in online courses to signal to the learners that this part of the course includes information that they will need as they begin their online course – an introduction to the instructor and fellow learners, and orientation to the course, resources (e.g., syllabus, textbook, other essential material), and academic support (e.g., tutoring center, disability services, counseling services). You or your institution may want to use a different term to refer to *Start Here*, e.g., Orientation or Introduction to the Course.

WELCOME AND ENGAGEMENT STRATEGIES

Welcome and engagement strategies are part of the learning environment and promote the learners' feelings of inclusion by incorporating adult learning assumptions and the learning process. Table 11.1 includes a summary of some welcome and engagement strategies. Using these strategies can enhance learners' confidence, engender a feeling of belonging, and foster a sense of community as the learners enter the course. We know that learners' sense of community is a powerful predictor of learner engagement.

Table 11.1 Welcome and engagement strategies

Welcome and engagement strategies	Purpose
Welcome letter/video	Introduces the instructor to learners; puts a "friendly face" on the course; establishes the instructor's presence, and makes the instructor relatable.
Introductory group activity	Builds group cohesion among learners; gives practice with discussion tools; may be used to discuss the rules of netiquette and expectations for responses.
Course café and virtual group meeting space	Provides an ungraded forum for course questions that the learners and/or the instructor can answer. You may want to start the course café by posting FAQs based on previous learners' questions. You may want to set up virtual group meetings at the beginning of the course to make sure that everyone can access and use the virtual group meeting tools.
Instructor information	Provides contact information for the instructor. For example, you may want to include email, office hours, office phone number, and cell phone number. Include whether you will respond to a text, how quickly you will respond to a text or email, and what hours are acceptable to text or call.
Introductory survey	Gathers information about course-relevant aspects of learners (e.g., prior experience with the course topic, feelings related to the course topic, why the topic is important to the learner, learner's relevant background).

Take a moment to consider how these strategies include and integrate the adult learning principles that include our view of learning (cognitive, social, and emotional); the learning process, adult learning assumptions, and semiotics for inclusion of diverse learners. Remember that the more you integrate these elements into your *Course Start Here*, the more effectively you will welcome and engage learners.

Welcome Letter/Video

The welcome letter/video introduces the instructor and presents a bit of information about the course. It is not a substitute for an orientation video or syllabus; rather, it is the first point of contact that learners have with the course and the instructor and thus should be inviting and relatively informal.

Let's revisit the Theories of Personality course. The instructor has written a welcome letter for learners.

Theories of Personality Example:
Welcome Letter

Welcome to PSY 2310: Theories of Personality. My name is Dr. Doctor and I am delighted to be working with you this semester. Prior to becoming a faculty member, I worked as a clinical psychologist for 10 years, and I continue to maintain a private practice. I enjoy teaching psychology students and watching you grow into confident, capable professionals.

In this online course, you will find that the learning activities will prepare you to understand personality the way psychologists do. Throughout this course, you will form a virtual team of interns working at the fictional Integrative Psychotherapy Clinic. Your team will encounter realistic cases of patients that psychologists would work with. Using course resources, you will apply theories of personality to your understanding of the patients depicted in the cases. In addition, you and your team will research a special topic in personality assessment and create an educational video presentation that you will share with your fellow interns.

To succeed in this course, log in to this course daily. It is a fast-paced course, and I will communicate frequently. Be sure to check your institutional email daily or forward your institutional email to your personal email, as frequent communication is essential for this course. Read the syllabus, check the course calendar, meet the deadlines, participate in the discussions with your peers and me, and contact me earlier rather than later if you have questions or issues. I'm here to help you succeed.

I look forward to working with you this semester. Let's get started!

Dr. Doctor

Office: (111) 888-5555
Email: doctord@college.edu

Travel Advisory:
Welcome Letter

This letter could also be recorded as a video with the instructor delivering the welcome message. If you use a video, you will need to provide a transcript or closed captioning for greater learner accessibility.

As you write your welcome letter, consider what elements were present in the letter above. Did you feel welcome and engaged? What adult learning principles were included? What seemed to work in this letter and what would you change?

Now create your welcome letter.

Application:
Create Your Welcome Letter

In your *course log*, write a welcome letter for your course.

Introductory Group Activity: Getting to Know You

In many courses, an introductory group activity is used to build the learning community. An introductory group activity can put all learners on an equal footing, foster expectations of interdependency (a critical component for swift trust; Meyerson, Weick, & Kramer, 1996), and invite learners to immediately share:

- information about their personal and professional backgrounds and past experiences with the course topics (cognitive)
- feelings about their experiences with certain types of learning activities, such as group projects (emotions)
- something fun or interesting about themselves (social).

Two examples of "Getting to Know You" group activity formats are provided. The first example provides a basic version of this introductory group activity.

"Getting to Know You" Group Activity Instructions
1. Introduce yourself to the class, share one reason that you are taking this course, and identify one topic on the syllabus that interests you. Explain why that topic is of interest to you.
2. Read and reflect on your peers' responses. Then reply to two peers whose posts differ from yours in some way. Choose someone who doesn't have a reply until everyone has at least one reply. Share your reaction to your peers' posts and ask a follow-up question.
3. Reply to those who replied to your original post by responding to their questions.

This example fosters dialogue early in the course by requiring learners to ask each other questions as part of their response to each other's posts in the group activity. However, the instructions for the initial post – "introduce yourself to your peers" – often elicits rote answers. Consider changing the wording to insert surprise and a bit of fun that can generate more novel responses while providing you with similar information.

One of the authors of this workbook changes the question but elicits the same type of information. The second example illustrates this twist on the "getting to know you" group activity from the Theories of Personality course. Although the example is especially fitting for a course on personality, it can be used in any course.

Theories of Personality Example:
"Getting to Know You" Group Activity Instructions

1. Choose one animal, bird, fish, or insect that you think best describes your personality, and describe why. Then share one interesting thing about yourself. Use your imagination!
2. Read and reflect on all your classmates' responses. Look for patterns of similarities and differences across your course peers.
3. Reply to two peers who described something different from you. For each person, comment on the similarities and differences between your response and their response and ask a question about something your find interesting. Choose someone who doesn't have a reply until everyone has at least one reply.
4. Reply to the people who replied to your original post by responding to their comments and questions.

Note that in both of these examples, learners have to follow up with each other's responses. This approach helps create a sense of connection and belonging and can foster self-reflection as the learners respond and ask questions of peers. This type of introductory group activity is more than just an exchange of pleasantries; learners get to know each other a bit better and gain practice with asking and answering questions based on their reflection on what they read.

Now create an introductory group activity.

Application:
Create an Introductory Group Activity

In your *course log*, create instructions for a "Getting to Know You" activity. Try to be creative/fun, as learners have been exposed to these types of activities throughout their years at school. Remember to word your instructions with semiotics in mind. In addition, remembering that your learners are adults may lead you to more interesting or engaging discussion activities.

Course Café and Virtual Group Meeting Space

When learners are working in groups, they need a space where they can exchange ideas, post and reply to each other's questions about information and activities, and coordinate their work. There are many external (i.e., cloud-based) spaces that learners can use to post and share their work as well as participate in virtual meetings. However, it is best if you create a space in the LMS for students to post their work and communicate asynchronously (e.g., course café) and/or synchronously (e.g., virtual meetings). By using the LMS, all work is available to the group and to you in the event of a mishap. In addition, learner privacy is maintained.

The *course café* provides an asynchronous space where learners can post questions and comments at any time and receive answers from each other and from you. The café gives learners a reason to log on to the course on a regular basis. It is also a space where learners can converse about topics not directly related to course activities. Although the space is informal, it is important that you monitor learners' posts and respond as needed to prevent misinformation and ensure netiquette rules are followed. In other words, you act as the moderator. Posts to the course café can provide you with insight into what learners are thinking and the questions they have, which can allow you to take proactive action if necessary.

A *virtual group meeting space* can be set up for small groups to meet. The virtual meeting is synchronous. If you include group or team projects in your course, we highly recommend that you arrange a synchronous group "get together" at the beginning of the course where you familiarize the learners with how to access the virtual meeting space, test their computers' video and audio, and help them learn to use the tools available. This initial learner experience of participating in a virtual meeting encourages learner connection and group belonging and reduces issues learners might have when they begin to work on their projects. You may choose to leave the group space open at all times for learners to use throughout the course or limit access to only certain days and times.

Review the Theories of Personality instructor's description of the course café (in this case, "clinic café") and virtual team meeting.

Theories of Personality Example:
Clinic Café and Virtual Team Meeting

Throughout this course, the Clinic Café discussion board will remain open for you to share your ideas and questions with the class and with your senior interns, Carl and Karen. Please check this discussion board daily, and Carl and Karen will respond to questions regularly.

In addition, a virtual meeting room has been created for your educational video presentation team. It is open 24/7 for meetings. Your team can decide when you need to meet, but you should hold at least two synchronous meetings.

Please record each meeting and submit any questions you have about your group project and/or the course to me by email or through the Clinic Café.

Now create an invitation to your course café.

Application:
Create an Invitation to the Course Café

In your *course log*, write an invitation to learners encouraging them to post to the course café. Create FAQs about the course that you will post on the Course Café. Using these techniques can encourage learners to visit the café at the beginning of the course as you try to establish learners' habits of using the spaces within the course to better support learning.

In addition, create a virtual meeting announcement.

Application:
Create a Virtual Meeting Announcement

In your *course log*, write an announcement that you will send to learners about attending a virtual meeting. Be sure to include the benefits of using the virtual meeting space throughout the course.

Instructor Information

Instructor presence is a critical part of engaging and retaining your learners. Your presence can be felt in the way you present information about yourself to your learners. You can include a link to your CV, your professional website, and/or any other information that learners may find useful. We recommend using a friendly and engaging, yet professional, tone. At a minimum, this section should include instructions on how to reach you, your preferred method of communication, your response time to emails and other communications, and any other instructor expectations that require emphasis.

We recommend that the information in the instructor information section be duplicated elsewhere (e.g., in the syllabus and/or course policies). Providing access to information in various places addresses the use of semiotics for inclusion of diverse learners. For example, some learners might not choose to access the instructor information section in *Start Here*, but will read the syllabus!

Travel Advisory:
Your Contact Information

Carefully consider the options you give students on how to contact you. Do you want to give them your cell phone number? If so, what hours are you willing to respond to texts and take phone calls? Remember that learners may have unpredictable hours, so you need to set expectations at the beginning of the course.

Note that no example is presented for the Theories of Personality course, as this information would be highly instructor-specific. You can create your instruction information now.

Application:
Create Your Instructor Information

In your *course log*, create a list of relevant information about how to communicate with you, your expectations about communicating with you, and other important information you want learners to know. Pay attention to the words and tone you use in conveying the information.

Introductory Survey

An introductory survey can provide information about your learners' contexts and their initial experiences with the course topic and their initial course experiences. An introductory survey is a helpful way to gather data unavailable to you as you created the course. Although you kept your learners' presumed contexts in mind as you created the course, you can't be sure that you accurately envisioned your learners. By using an introductory survey, you can capture key information that will help you better understand who is taking your course and what their needs may be.

Once your learners have responded to the survey, we recommend providing a summary of the survey results to your learners. Posting the summary sends three important messages:

- You read your learners' responses.
- You are interested in your learners.
- You can use the summary as an opportunity for a learning activity. The summary can be used to reinforce the group identity and help establish connections among the learners. This type of activity serves to develop connections among the learners and foster the appreciation of differences, leading to inclusion among the learners in the class.
  - As part of the summary, you may ask learners to reflect on the similarities and differences among their peers, and the value that those similarities and differences bring to strengthen the overall learning in the course.
  - Ask learners to post their thoughts and reply to a peer's post. For something different, you could ask your learners to meet virtually to discuss their thoughts on the findings of the summary, and post their thoughts as part of a discussion board.

Do not overload your learners with too many questions. A brief survey with thoughtfully chosen questions yields the best results. Again, a summary of the survey results should be shared with the learners.

Let's look at the questions that the Theories of Personality instructor generated for an introductory survey.

Theories of Personality Example:
Introductory Survey

I brainstorm some possible questions for my introductory survey:

- What is your experience with the topics of this course?
- List two challenges that you expect to encounter in this course.
  - How can you meet those challenges?
- List two strengths that you have that will help you be successful in this course.
  - How can you leverage those strengths to meet your potential challenges?
- Are you looking forward to taking this course or would you rather be taking another course? Why?
- What are the 2–3 most important things you expect to learn in this course?
  - What makes these items so important to you?
- What ways do you think you can apply what you expect to learn in this course?
- What questions do you have for me and for others in this course?
- What are some ways I can help you be successful in this course?

After reviewing these questions, I decide that my survey will have three questions:

- What is your experience with the topics of this course?
- What questions do you have for me and for others in this course?
- What are some ways I can help you be successful in this course?

Now you can create an introductory survey.

Application:
Create an Introductory Survey

In your *course log*, create introductory survey instructions and questions for an introductory survey.

Your Travel Journal:
Your Welcoming and Engagement Strategies

Consider the following questions on your welcoming and engagement strategies and jot down your ideas in the space provided.

How do you want your students to feel as they go through the *Course Start Here* section?

Which welcoming and engagement strategies are you most likely to use and why? Less likely and why?

Which of the strategies do you think are most likely to engage your students in the learning process of your course? (Keep in mind both expected and unexpected outcomes that you have experienced in the past.)

How will you be present in the course?

What other ideas do you have to welcome and engage your students?

Call a Colleague:
Your Welcoming and Engagement Strategies

Share your welcoming letter, "getting to know you" group activity, course café information, virtual meeting, instructor information, and introductory course survey with a colleague. Ask them to share their approach to welcoming and engaging their learners at the beginning of a course and provide feedback on what you have created. Jot down notes from your conversation below.

ORIENTATION STRATEGIES

Orientation strategies promote learner readiness to participate in the course. The orientation provides the learners with information on the organization and structure of the course, the "rules" on policies and procedures, your expectations, and how to navigate the course. In Table 11.2, you will find a list of commonly used *Course Start Here* orientation strategies.

Table 11.2 Orientation strategies

Orientation strategy	Purpose
Orientation video	Provides general information of the course; usually overlaps with the syllabus but provides the "highlights" of the course that learners might gloss over in the syllabus.
Introduction to course theme and icons	Orients learners to the course theme and icons used to reinforce the theme. Includes a "key" or "legend" to recurrent images or icons to define their meaning. Presents the visual element of the course to draw learners in.
Syllabus	Presents a course contract between the instructor and the learner that includes relevant details about the course and instructional schedule. The breadth and depth of information in a syllabus are often determined by institutional policies.
Course summary	Includes the "highlights" of the syllabus.
Policies (use of technology, plagiarism, netiquette, etc.)	Links to institutional policy webpages or other documents.
Course calendar	Presents a "quick glance" look at the course as a whole, as well as due dates for all milestones.
Supplementary resources	Provides information for learners who are less prepared for the course with supplementary information to increase learners' readiness to learn the topics.

Table 11.2   (*cont.*)

Orientation strategy	Purpose
Academic supports	Provides links to tutoring, disability services, and other institutional academic learner supports; may also include professional websites and study strategies.
Information about reflection, dialogue, and feedback	Provides an overview of the form and function of self-reflection, dialogue, and feedback in the course; presents information about communication expectations, including synchronous communication requirements, if any. Provides instructions for how groups/teams will be formed and how they will work together. Also describes the instructor's approach to feedback.
Quizzes • Start Here Course Topics Quiz • Treasure Hunt Quiz	• The Start Here Course Topics Quiz allows you and your learners to evaluate their knowledge of the course topics. • The Treasure Hunt Quiz informs you and the learners about their navigation skills and how well they can find key components of the course (e.g., expectations, policies, due dates, resources).

In this section, you will create the orientation items for your *Course Start Here*. We do not provide examples for the Theories of Personality course because the orientation items will be highly specific to your course.

Orientation Video

An orientation video is more in-depth than a welcome video. Whereas a welcome video provides a brief introduction to the course and to the instructor, an orientation video walks learners through key elements of the course, demonstrates how to navigate the course, and shows how to use key features of the LMS. The orientation video is important for all learners since each course has its own idiosyncrasies.

Application:
Create Your Orientation Video

In your *course log*, create a script/storyboard for your orientation video. When you are ready to create the video, contact your IT department for consultation.

Introduction to Course Theme and Icons

Just as we did in the workbook *Start Here*, your *Course Start Here* is a great place to introduce the course theme and any icons you will be using throughout the course. Think back to the workbook *Start Here* and consider how the theme of a journey was introduced to you. Similarly, if you are using a theme for your course, we recommend introducing the theme (including any scenario that runs throughout your course, if applicable) and explaining why you chose this theme/scenario.

Hand-in-hand with the theme are the course icons. Recall the icon key that was presented in the workbook *Start Here* and the subsequent use of the icons throughout the workbook. These icons helped to reinforce the theme of a journey and set the stage for a coherent and familiar visual format throughout. You can do the same as part of your *Course Start Here*. If you use icons, we strongly recommend that you include an icon key to introduce your learners to the intended meaning of each graphic.

Application:
Create an Icon Key

In your *course log*, create an icon key with a description of each icon's meaning.

Syllabus

A full discussion of the *syllabus* is beyond the scope of this book! Many institutions provide templates to ensure that common information is provided to all learners, as syllabi are increasingly viewed as an official course document that serves as a contract between the learner and the instructor, and ultimately between the learner and the institution. When the syllabus is viewed as a contract, it can be perceived as a legal document that results in long, detailed descriptions of policies, rules, and expectations, to name a few. Our general recommendations for online course documents (e.g., semiotics, formatting considerations) apply to the syllabus.

Application:
Create Your Syllabus

In your *course log*, create your syllabus. If your institution provides a template or requires inclusion of certain information, be sure to meet those requirements. For examples and information on how to create high-quality syllabi, search for reliable sources that focus on higher education.

Course Summary

Because of the complexity of many syllabi, we recommend that you create a Course Summary in your *Course Start Here* that highlights and summarizes the most important information contained in the syllabus that you want learners to know. These highlights may include the course destination, milestones, skill areas, learning activities, course map, course and institutional policy summaries, or any other information you choose. Be sure to reference back to the location of the details in the syllabus, and state that if there is any discrepancy between the information in the Course Summary and the syllabus, the syllabus is the official source. If you include too much information in this summary, you will lose the usefulness of providing quick, easy-to-read course highlights.

Application:
Create Your Course Summary

In your *course log*, create a Course Summary that you will use in your course. A list of items you might consider including are listed in the previous discussion.

Policies

Policies help establish the "rules" that guide learners' behavior, your behavior, and the interaction between you and the learners. There are two types of policies: course policies and institutional policies. You should address both in your syllabus.

Course policies are those policies that are specific to your course (e.g., the grading policy, how to contact you, how quickly you will respond, what happens when a paper is late, how to schedule a conference call/video with you, the process for handling group conflict during a project). In addition, there are relevant institutional policies (e.g., academic integrity/plagiarism, dropping a course, student problem escalation). For institutional policies, we recommend that you list key policies that apply to learners, include a brief summary of each, and provide a link to the actual policy.

In addition to policy inclusion in your syllabus, we recommend including a summary of key course and institutional policies in your Course Summary discussed previously, and include the location of the more detailed information in the syllabus. Learners should be reminded that the course syllabus serves as the official source for course policies, and the institutional policies are the official source for any institutional policy.

Travel Advisory:
Policy Links

Institutional policy links will need to be checked before the beginning of each course to ensure that the links work. This issue is an annoying fact of digital life.

Application:
Describe Policies and Identify Links

In your *course log*, list your course policies and relevant institutional policies. Concisely state your course policies. List the relevant institutional policies, a brief description, and the direct link to the policy.

Course Calendar

Many syllabi include a week-by-week course calendar. We have also seen a calendar presented directly in *Course Start Here*. In contrast, we recommend putting all due dates in your LMS's course calendar tool and directing learners to the LMS calendar by providing a link.

Notes from Our Journey:
Using the LMS Course Calendar

The reason we strongly recommend using the LMS course calendar is to avoid learner confusion (and yours) in the event a due dates changes. We have experienced this confusion when we had due dates in multiple places (syllabus, within each learning module, on the *Start Here* page) and then had to change a due date. Confusion reigned and emails flew, resulting in unnecessary learner and instructor frustration. It was not pretty!

Our advice, based on experience, is to keep due dates only in the LMS calendar, and let the learners know that the "official" due dates reside only in the LMS calendar. By following this policy, due dates are much easier to change and communicate, alleviating frustration and anxiety for all. In fact, we have had learners tell us how grateful they were to have one calendar that included all due dates. Our learners said that it helped them better plan their time by making the due dates for the entire course visible in one place.

Application:
Create Your Course Calendar

In your *course log*, create your course calendar. Include the due date and time for each milestone. Depending on the types of learning activities and to help your learners plan their time, you may also want to include when interim actions should be completed, even if these do not require that work be submitted to you. Providing this information can be especially helpful for group members working on a project.

Supplementary Resources

Perhaps one of the most important but also most often overlooked orientation strategies in an online course is determining what background information learners need to know before they are ready to engage with the course topics. Instructors often assume that learners will be ready to learn the current topics by virtue of having successfully passed prerequisites for the course. However, we have found that prerequisites do not always ensure learners' readiness. Learners vary widely in their background knowledge, and we rarely have access to their grades or other performance indicators from previous, relevant courses. Thus, it is helpful to consider what information learners need to know prior to starting your course, and then provide supplementary resources to help fill in potential gaps in learners' knowledge.

Identifying/creating supplementary resources can be quite an undertaking, and you may feel that it is an unreasonable demand on your time to find resources for learners who are unprepared to succeed. However, the good news is that many of these resources already exist online; thus, simply providing links to a well-curated assembly of resources, along with suggestions for their use, will often suffice. The key is to anticipate your learners' potential gaps and then identify resources that you can direct them to as needed. In addition, you can provide supplementary resources on the skill areas that your learners will be developing in your course and direct learners' attention to these resources in the appropriate learning activities.

We recommend that these background resources be placed together in a folder or other specific location and clearly labeled as "supplementary," along with a description of their purpose. For example, if you are teaching a course that has significant writing requirements, you could include a folder with links to online writing tutorials and resources.

Travel Advisory:
Supplementary Resources for Inclusion

Providing for the needs of your learners is part of creating a course that is inclusive of diversity, helps promote a growth mindset for you and your learners (Claro et al., 2016), and may encourage learner persistence leading to completion of your class and, perhaps, to graduation. If your learners complete a Start Here Course Topics Quiz, you will have a good indicator of their baseline level of knowledge and can identify appropriate resources. Note that if you discover that most or all of your learners need a supplementary resource, you should move that resource into the relevant learning activity and make it a required resource.

Application:
Identify Supplementary Resources

In your *course log*, identify any supplementary resources that you believe learners might need.

Academic Supports

Learners benefit from knowing the institutional academic supports available to them and how to access those supports. Thus, we recommend including links to support services and information such as the institution's library, tutoring services, student services, registrar, academic calendar, and last day to withdraw without penalty. In addition, in some courses it can be useful to include links to professional organizations and other resources to encourage learners to network and gain more specialized information about their profession.

Application:
Identify Academic Supports

In your *course log*, create a list of institutional academic supports that are available at your institution. Include a brief description and contact information. If your institution provides information on study strategies (e.g., from the tutoring services center), or if you have found helpful websites that provide study tips for your discipline, include this information as well.

Information about Self-Reflection, Dialogue, and Feedback

To encourage learners' buy-in to the central role of self-reflection and dialogue in the course, you can explain why these actions are important and provide examples of how self-reflection and dialogue will help learners in the course as well as in their everyday lives. One strategy for introducing the role of self-reflection is to include a brief reflection that begins to elicit learners' cognitive and emotional responses to the course. For example, you can ask learners to reflect on their feelings about the course destination or their ideas about how they might apply what they learn to their personal and/or professional lives.

Application:
Create an Initial Self-Reflection Prompt

In your *course log*, describe self-reflection. Explain why self-reflection is important in your course. Write a self-reflection prompt for your learners that you will use in your *Course Start Here*.

You have already given some thought to how to introduce learners to collaboration and engage learners in dialogue in the Introductory Group Activity in this chapter. It is also helpful to describe your approach to feedback and how you expect learners to use the feedback you provide. This description is more than just proving a grade range chart (i.e., 93–100: A; 90–92: A–; etc.). Rather, it explains the form that feedback will take (e.g., comments, rubrics, etc.), type of feedback (formative or summative), the source of feedback (instructor, peers), and how you expect learners to apply the feedback they receive. Information about feedback should be included in the syllabus and in the Course Summary.

Application:
Describe Your Feedback Approach

In your *course log*, describe how you will give feedback on milestones. Also describe what you expect learners to do with the feedback they receive.

Start Here Course Topics Quiz

We recommend that if you want to establish a baseline for your learners' prior cognitive knowledge about the course topics, use a short quiz with automatic feedback. If you use a quiz, make sure your learners know that the purpose of the quiz is to establish a baseline to help you decide what to emphasize in the course. We recommend making this a formative, ungraded activity.

Do not overwhelm the learners with too many questions. Use the "critical few" approach to selecting the questions. A summary of results of the quiz should be shared with the learners.

Application:
Create a Start Here Course Topics Quiz

In your *course log*, create a brief quiz assessing learners' baseline knowledge of the course topics.

Treasure Hunt Quiz

We often integrate a low-stakes "Treasure Hunt" quiz, using multiple-choice questions, on how to navigate the course and find information in *Course Start Here*. This quiz serves as a self-check for learners to ensure that they understand the most important information about the course and where to find it. It also gives you feedback on areas where learners may need reminders about the location of information or the information itself.

Quiz items may include questions about policies, grading, due dates, other information you deem important, and where specific information is located. We recommend that you give learners multiple attempts to take the quiz so they make a perfect score. The purpose of the Treasure Hunt Quiz is for learners to review the material until they know the answer — and to know where to find the answers if they forget later in the semester!

Application:
Create a Treasure Hunt Quiz

In your *course log*, write the questions for your Treasure Hunt Quiz.

Your Travel Journal:
Your Orientation Strategies

Consider the following questions and jot down your notes in the space provided.

What necessary knowledge/skills do your learners sometimes lack when they begin your online course?

From your perspective, what is the importance of providing an orientation for your learners?

As you review the orientation strategies suggested for your *Course Start Here*, which seem to be the most relevant for your course and why?

Which orientation strategies seem less relevant for your learners and your course and why?

What other orientation ideas do you have?

Call a Colleague:
Feedback on Your Orientation Strategies

You have created many orientation items for your Course *Start Here*. We recommend that you call a colleague for feedback on at least some of the items you have created. In particular, you might ask your colleague for feedback on your syllabus and essential information summary. In addition, ask your colleague to share their syllabus and other information and techniques they use to orient their learners at the beginning of the course. Jot down your notes and ideas in the space provided.

Table 11.3 summarizes the *Start Here* strategies and techniques that you explored and applied throughout the chapter. Now that you have created items for each of these strategies, take a moment to review what you created for each, and reflect on what you hope to accomplish by using the strategy in your *Course Start Here*. If you decide not to include a specific strategy in your *Course Start Here*, save what you created, as you may decide to use it in a subsequent course.

Table 11.3 *Course Start Here* checklist

Check each item that you decide to use in your *Course Start Here*.

Check items that apply	Welcoming and engagement strategies
	Welcome letter/video
	Introductory group activity
	Course Café and virtual meeting space
	Instructor information
	Introductory survey
	Orientation strategies
	Orientation video
	Introduction to course themes and icons
	Syllabus
	Essential course information summary
	Policies
	Course calendar
	Foundational resources
	Academic supports
	Information about self-reflection, dialogue, and feedback
	Start Here Course Topics Quiz
	Treasure Hunt Quiz

**Application:
Create Your Course in Your LMS**

You are now ready to put all of your course items into your LMS! Gather all of your item files and notes from your *course log*. Consult with your LMS support staff for guidance on how to upload and arrange files.

Milestone:
Your Complete Online Course

You have reached the workbook destination: a complete online course!

Call a Colleague:
Feedback on Your Online Course

Give your colleague access to your course, and ask for feedback. You may want to ask for specific feedback on areas where you have questions, you may want general feedback, or you may want both. The choice is yours. Jot down your notes in the space provided.

COURSE START HERE: SUMMARY

You have learned about the two sets of strategies that are included in *Course Start Here*: welcome and engagement strategies and orientation strategies. You have used the strategies to create the relevant *Start Here* items for your course. You have also created your course in your LMS.

Your journey is almost complete!

You will now proceed to the **Revise** section, which contains *Chapter 12: Course Evaluation and Revision.*

REVISE

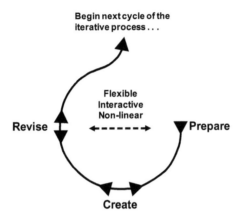

Change-adept Course Creation Process. Copyright 2019

The final section in this book contains only one chapter, but this chapter embodies the iterative nature of the Change-adept Course Creation Process. *Chapter 12: Course Evaluation and Revision* contains a step that instructors sometimes overlook. Overlooking revision is understandable, since creating a fully online course is such a huge accomplishment that it can be tempting to bask in its glow and put off thinking about changes until later.

However, we have found that it is important to develop a plan for evaluating and revising the course before we teach it because life gets very busy once a course is active. If we postpone developing an evaluation and revision plan, then there is never quite enough time to actually develop the plan, and opportunities for useful course feedback to inform course revision are missed.

To that end, the final part of the process will involve creating an evaluation and revision plan that you can use to determine when and what changes are needed.

12   Course Evaluation and Revision

COURSE EVALUATION AND REVISION: INTRODUCTION

As you have experienced throughout this workbook, revising your course has been an ongoing part of the Change-adept Course Creation process.

- You have frequently checked your course and modified elements as you developed new ideas and understandings about what will work best for your learners.
- You have reviewed your topics, milestones, and learning activities to ensure that they lead to the course destination, making adjustments as needed.
- You have also reviewed your resources with attention to adult learning principles and revised them to maximize their impact.
- You reviewed your course and all its elements in terms of adult learning principles.

Why, then, is additional revision needed? We suggest two reasons. First, it is helpful to look at the course as a whole, to make sure that the various parts all work together and that there are no major gaps. Second, you never know exactly how well a course will work until learners actually take the course. Once learners are enrolled, you can begin the process of revising the course based on the feedback you receive.

In this chapter, we will begin with a review of the course as a whole. We then move into revising the course while learners are enrolled and discuss the circumstances that might necessitate such revision. We close with the process of revising a course after it has been offered, viewing various sources of feedback in the context of a systematic course evaluation and revision plan.

Travel Advisory:
Minor and Major Revisions

One distinction we have found helpful is to think of revisions as either minor or major. Minor revisions include things like correcting typos, modifying instructions for clarity, changing one or two images, and so forth. Major revisions are more substantial and may involve changes to structure, topics, or activities. Minor revisions are less time-consuming and can improve learners' immediate experience of the course; thus, it is useful to complete minor revisions as they come up.

In contrast, major revisions may require more time and thought; they typically will improve future learners' experience of the course. Therefore, major revisions benefit from occurring on a cycle (e.g., once per year).

REVIEW OF COURSE ELEMENTS

To begin, we encourage you to go through your course and examine each component. If you have organized your course into modules, you can complete this step module-by-module.

Application:
Review Each Module

Review each module you have created. Complete the checklist below by checking any items you need to revisit. In your course log, describe any revisions needed for those items.
Module Title:

Revisit?	Review items
	Module introduction included
	Relevant milestones stated
	Resources include a variety of formats, if appropriate
	Resources appear in order of use and are linked to actions
	Actions appear in order of completion
	Self-reflection, dialogue, and application are connected within learning activities
	Learning activities include relevant, realistic, and meaningful applications to learners' personal/professional lives
	Learning activity instructions are detailed and accurate
	Feedback strategies are stated, with link to relevant tool(s) such as rubric or checklist
	Images and wording reviewed for semiotics
	Course theme is integrated, if applicable
	All links are accurate and active

Application:
Review Course as a Whole

Now take a look at your course as a whole. Complete the checklist below by checking of any items you need to revisit. In your course log, describe any revisions needed for those items.

Revisit?	Review items
	Start Here includes welcoming and engagement strategies
	Start Here includes orientation strategies
	Start Here includes updated syllabus
	Course calendar is updated
	Course policies are prominent
	Other resources and supports are posted/linked
	Modules are organized logically
	Appropriate LMS features are enabled

COURSE REVISION OF LIVE COURSE

Sometimes instructors are reluctant to make changes to a course once it has begun. However, there are times when major revisions are needed while learners are enrolled. Given that the syllabus is often considered a contract for the course, we generally recommend that you not make any revisions that would affect the integrity of the syllabus. The following circumstances may necessitate major revisions during the course, though you will need to check your institution's policy on making changes to a syllabus while the course is being taught.

Lack of Learner Readiness

Although you considered your learners' contexts when creating your course, it is impossible to anticipate everything there is to know about your learners. Even if you have included a learner survey in Start Here, there may still be unexpected factors that crop up as the course progresses. Once the course is underway, you might discover that your learners are not as prepared as you thought they would be. If this is the case, you might have to modify learning activities to better meet your learners' needs.

We see this occur frequently with skill areas such as writing, quantitative reasoning, and information literacy. It is a good idea for you to be prepared to direct learners to supplementary resources if you discover that learners need help in these areas. Doing so can involve uploading or linking supplementary resources to your course (e.g., in *Start Here*), posting a course announcement about these items, and encouraging individual learners to use these resources through individual communication.

In some circumstances, you may discover that many of your learners have not mastered prerequisite information necessary for your course. Therefore, some re-teaching of prerequisite information may be needed. Such re-teaching can occur through online tutorials, synchronous small-group sessions, and supplementary learning activities. In this case, you will need to state clearly whether learners' participation in the re-teaching activities is optional or required, and what the expected outcome of participation (or non-participation) will be.

In addition, clarifying your role in re-teaching is essential. Some instructors prefer to engage in re-teaching themselves, while others prefer to refer learners to tutoring services with a clear referral request. Regardless of which you prefer, it is good to have a clear plan for helping learners who are not ready for a learning activity. Such an approach is preferable to the frustration you and your learners will experience in trying to "get through" a course that they are not ready for.

Feedback-Related Changes

In *Chapter 10: Course Structure*, you created a learner feedback survey for use after a learning activity, mid-course, or at another point before the end of a course. We recommend that you review and summarize the feedback as soon as you receive it, post the summary for your learners, and explain what changes you are making (if any) as a result of the feedback.

Despite well-laid plans, you may discover that one or more of your learning activities is not producing the expected results, is unclear to learners, and/or garners negative feedback from learners. If you obtain feedback once the learning activity is complete, then you will need to make notes for future revision. However, if you obtain feedback earlier, then you may need to modify the activity to be more effective. Modifications might include clarifying instructions, changing the time frame of the activity (e.g., giving learners more time to complete certain parts), and providing additional explanations about the benefits of the activity.

Unexpected Events

Sometimes unexpected events (such as an environmental catastrophe or institutional change) may throw your course off track. In such cases, we recommend focusing on learners' needs and identifying the most essential knowledge and skills that you want them to obtain in the course. You may then need to substantially revise the learning activities to provide a reasonable amount of work for learners who have been affected by the unexpected events. Once again, we emphasize that if you think you need to revise your syllabus, be sure to consult your institution's policies.

The bottom line with regard to course revisions while learners are enrolled is that flexibility is key and communication with your learners paramount! Adult learners want and need to know the revised plan and changed expectations. Although you have carefully created all of your learning activities to be effective, sometimes activities miss the mark. It is important to determine the cause of such disappointing outcomes. Is it something as simple as unclear instructions? Are learners unprepared to succeed on the activity? Or does the entire activity itself need an overhaul? By reflecting on what is going well and what needs improvement, you will demonstrate flexibility in your approach.

COURSE EVALUATION

After learners have taken your course, you have enough information to identify areas where revision is necessary. The revision process begins with course evaluation.

Course evaluation is the systematic review of a course's strengths and areas for improvement, with a focus on the teaching and learning experience and on learners' attainment of milestones. Conducting a course evaluation puts you in a better position to undertake an informed revision of your course.

Strategies for evaluating your course can include:

- analyzing learners' work to determine attainment of milestones
- analyzing learner behaviors in the course
- surveying learners on things such as engagement and satisfaction
- discussing your course with colleagues
- self-reflecting on your course
- obtaining peer review of your course
- using course rubrics to determine how your course compares to established standards.

Travel Advisory:
Being Open to Course Evaluation

Instructors are often wary of evaluation, as they may be concerned that too much scrutiny of their course will lead to criticism and/or having to overhaul a course that they have worked hard to create. Evaluation is also linked in many instructors' minds with "teaching evaluations" – which are sometimes used punitively rather than as a developmental tool.

In contrast, we view evaluation as a necessary and exciting part of the Change-adept Course Creation Process. Evaluation involves careful consideration of the aspects of a course (and your instructional approach) that are going well, as well as aspects that may benefit from being refined. As with face-to-face courses, online courses need to be revised regularly – not just in terms of updating content but also in terms of responding to new learner needs, integrating new technology (where appropriate), and modifying activities and milestones to better engage and motivate learners. Course evaluation provides you with an opportunity to learn and grow! By building evaluation into your course creation process, you will have greater ownership of the outcomes of evaluation. You may also be in a better position to explain and respond to any challenges that arise, such as negative learner feedback or problematic group behaviors.

Your Travel Journal:
Course Evaluation

Before evaluating your course, consider what you hope to learn from the evaluation. Jot down your questions and other notes in the space provided.

SOURCES OF COURSE FEEDBACK

Once you have made a list of your questions, identify some existing sources of feedback on your course. In addition to learners' work, you probably have access to your institution's course/teaching evaluations. You may also have access to data collected in your learning management system (LMS). You might need to create some additional tools to evaluate specific components of your course (such as a mid-course survey). In this section, you will explore various ways of gathering and analyzing data for a more complete evaluation of your course.

Notes from Our Journey:
Our Evaluation Plan

In designing this workbook, we evaluated the effectiveness of our approach throughout. Our evaluation plan had three main components:

- Feedback from colleagues on the information in the workbook. This feedback helped us tweak the workbook to ensure it was relevant and useful to you.
- Tools to help you discuss and reflect on the workbook information. Your own reflections are an important source of information about how well the book is working.
- Milestone checkpoints to help you gauge whether the book has helped you reach the workbook destination.

Only one of these sources of feedback (i.e., feedback from colleagues) was immediately available to us. However, the tools that we incorporated into the book provide an additional (albeit indirect) source of feedback.

One thing you will have experienced with this book is that we had you evaluate your progress early and often through self-reflection and dialogue tasks. Similarly, you and your learners may benefit from early course evaluation. Rather than waiting until a course is finished to determine its strengths and areas for improvement, you might want to take an early and regular look (e.g., weekly) at how the course is functioning and at how learners are responding. This action allows you to improve your course for your current learners.

We will present several sources of course feedback, along with strategies for analyzing and using each type of feedback to make revisions:

- milestone performance
- learner behaviors in the course
- learner interaction quantity and quality
- surveys
- self-reflection and discussion
- peer review of your course and use of a course rubric.

One thing you will find is that all of these sources of feedback involve data. Every course produces a wealth of data. However, some instructors are more comfortable than others with data analysis. Some instructors avoid using data because they feel unsure of their analytical skills or feel that quantitative data does not provide a complete picture of what is happening in the course. Others are reluctant to change their approach (even if the data suggests a change is warranted). Still other instructors feel overwhelmed by the amount of data available and thus would prefer to use their own impressions about the effectiveness of their course. Do any of those descriptions sound familiar to you?

We have found that many courses are never subjected to rigorous evaluation, which results in a huge missed opportunity to improve those courses. Although instructor impressions are a valuable source of data, other data can shed light on areas that impressions might overlook. Remember: Feedback is information. When we reflect on the feedback and discuss it with others, then we are in a better position to improve our courses.

 Your Travel Journal:
Course Data

Reflect on your own approach to course data. Jot down your reflections in the space provided.

Do you resist looking at data? If so, how can you rise to the challenge of using course data to improve your course?

Are you more comfortable with quantitative or qualitative information? How can you incorporate both as you review your course?

If you are already comfortable with data analysis, what sources of data do you look at? What sources of data might you add to your analysis?

What resources are available at your institution to assist with gathering and analyzing course data?

Milestone Performance

In our view, a good course strives to help all students succeed. Although there will be some variability in terms of learners' performance, a successful course helps learners develop greater knowledge about the course topics and accomplishing the milestones.

Note that our perspective differs from the view that in a good course, some learners will necessarily fail (which is often the attitude that underlies grading on a curve or never "giving" A grades). Similarly, we do not share the view that a good course "weeds out" learners who are deemed "poor" candidates for a major and/or profession. Although an analysis of learners' goodness-of-fit with a major and/or profession is important, one or two early learning activities – or even a course – are probably not the best way to conduct this analysis.

Because we believe that courses should be designed to help all learners achieve the milestones of the course, we suggest that learners' performance on milestones should be routinely analyzed. Analysis of learners' work involves looking at learners' performance vis-à-vis some set of criteria. In other words, to what extent did learners truly reach the milestones of the course by demonstrating the expected knowledge and performing at the expected level within each skill area? A course can be engaging, motivating, and provide an excellent learner experience, but if learners do not achieve the milestones, then the course is not effective.

To begin, look at the milestones that best answer the questions you have posed for your course evaluation. For example, if your main question is whether learners are attaining all the specified milestones for the course (and at what level of proficiency), then you will need to gather data from all milestones. If, on the other hand, you are looking at a specific milestone (perhaps one that learners have struggled with in the past), you will just need to look at that milestone.

Once you have selected the milestones that address a particular question, you can look at both quantitative data (e.g., scores on a rubric) and qualitative data (e.g., your comments on learners' milestones). If you have a small number of learners, you may want to look at all of your learners' performance. If you have a large number of learners, you may select a representative sample (e.g., a subset of learners' work that includes both high- and low-performance examples).

Although this review of data may seem like a large task, you can make it more efficient if you set up a system for gathering data on milestones, such as a spreadsheet into which you can download quantitative and qualitative data from your LMS. Furthermore, rather than waiting until the end of a course to analyze all data, you might want to evaluate learners' performance right after they have completed the milestone. Conducting a post-milestone review is an excellent teaching strategy, as it allows you to provide additional resources to address areas where learners need help.

For example, if any learners perform poorly on an early milestone, you may need to provide these learners with extra guidance to help them attain later milestones.

Learner Behaviors in the Course

Because the LMS generally does not provide you with a direct source of feedback about learners' attentiveness and engagement (given that you typically cannot see and hear learners while they are in the course), it is helpful to find alternatives to determine whether learners are engaged. Engagement is a prerequisite for learning. If learners are not reading/viewing the resources, for example, they will not have the background information needed to develop knowledge on the topic through tasks. Tracking learner behaviors can help to measure overall course effectiveness as well as identify learners who need intervention.

Learner behaviors include any observable behaviors that indicate engagement in the course. Such behaviors include accessing resources, creating dialogue posts that exceed the minimum requirements, emailing the instructor, and submitting work early or on time.

Most LMSs provide some tracking tools for identifying learners at risk and for analyzing learner participation, such as the number of views per resource. Although an in-depth discussion of how to use these tools is beyond the scope of this workbook, you may benefit from exploring these tools through your institution's LMS support staff.

Alternatively, you can use a more holistic approach: Take a look at overall participation rates for various course features and identify which features are most (and least) accessed. You can also review one or two basic learner behaviors through your course's learner tracking area or grade center (such as the most recent course access date) to identify learners who are not sufficiently accessing and participating in the course.

Given our premise that learning occurs within dialogue, it is important to evaluate both the quantity and the quality of learner-to-learner interaction in a course. For example, learners' level of participation in asynchronous written dialogues or synchronous dialogues that the instructor observes (either live or by video recording) can be examined according to a rubric or other set of criteria.

 Your Travel Journal:
Evaluating Learner Behavior

Consider what learner behaviors you might evaluate and how you might evaluate those behaviors. Jot down your notes in the space provided.

Surveys

One of the best ways to know how learners are experiencing a course is to ask them! By evaluating learners' experience with a course, you can identify areas of the course that need clarification, strengthening, or even major modification.

Surveys are helpful tools for gathering data on learners' thoughts, feelings, and perceptions. Surveys can include those that you develop as well as institutional course evaluation surveys.

As we discussed in *Chapter 10: Course Structure*, it is helpful to create one or more anonymous learner feedback surveys to embed into your course. The survey can include questions on course organization and navigation, accessibility, learner support, ease of technology use, and other structural aspects of the course. The survey can also include questions on clarity of expectations, content, learning activities, and other items.

You may choose to include questions about learners' perceptions of your availability, usefulness of feedback, and other aspects of your role as the instructor. However, note that the way in which these questions are worded may heavily influence learners' responses (especially among learners who are concerned about pleasing you, the instructor). We recommend that you ask general, open-ended questions about more sensitive areas, such as "What could I do as your instructor to make this course better for you?" or even a more generic question such as "What would make this course better?" and ensure that learner responses are truly anonymous.

You will benefit from reviewing and analyzing the survey results soon after learners complete the survey, which will give you enough time to make minor revisions to the course and/or your own approach to better meet learners' needs.

Institutional course evaluation surveys can also provide a wealth of information, particularly when response rates are high enough to suggest that the results are representative of all (or most) learners' experience. You can improve your response rate by explaining to learners why the course evaluation is important, reassuring learners that their responses will be anonymous, and emphasizing that you take their responses seriously and use the feedback to determine what works well and what needs enhancing each semester. It is also helpful to send out reminders close to the time when the course evaluations are due and put the due date on the course calendar. We encourage you to look at both the quantitative and the qualitative data that a course evaluation provides (if applicable). You will benefit from reviewing both items about the course itself as well as items about your own effectiveness as an instructor. Even though course evaluations often have a negative connotation, they can be an incredibly effective tool for assessing your online course.

Your Self-Reflection and Dialogue

Given that self-reflection and dialogue are at the heart of our view of learning, you might not be surprised to see these activities woven into course evaluation as well! Just as your learners grow in knowledge by thinking about their learning and discussing it with others, you too will grow as you self-reflect on and discuss your work with others.

Discussing your course with colleagues before, during, and after teaching the course is a helpful way to get professional feedback. Many instructors are reluctant to share their work with others, either out of a concern for being critiqued or else for proprietary reasons. However, we encourage you to share your successes and challenges with others who are creating online courses, keeping an open mind about the feedback you receive. You might discover that a colleague has a useful way of approaching an issue that you are facing. You might also find that others appreciate your insights into various course creation and instructional challenges.

Consider forming an online course creation and teaching group with colleagues at your institution and/or elsewhere. Regularly engage in "show and share" sessions, where you show what you are working on in your course and share your input with others. Or, if you prefer, establish a working partnership with another instructor at your institution. Meet regularly to discuss your work and to look at examples of good online courses together. Brainstorm ideas, try them out, and then come back to discuss the results with your partner. Share your reflections on what has worked and what needs to change.

Peer Review and Course Rubrics

Peer review involves having another person (e.g., a colleague) systematically review and provide feedback on your course according to a course rubric. Peer review can take the evaluation process to the next level by involving an objective evaluator and a set of objective criteria.

Your institution may already have a course rubric or evaluation form that you can use as-is or modify to meet your needs. If not, there are numerous course rubrics available online, including those developed by other universities, LMS companies, and organizations that provide external review of online courses. These rubrics overlap significantly. You may want to search for "online course rubric" for ideas and then work with colleagues to develop a rubric that will work for you.

Once you have familiarized yourself with the rubric, you can review your own course and determine how it measures up in each area of the rubric. Be honest! If you find that there are areas that you could enhance, now is the time to do so.

Following self-review, your course can be submitted to a peer reviewer. Keep in mind that the reviewer will likely need to see an active course to fully evaluate such qualities as learner interaction and instructor feedback. However, you will need to maintain your current learners' confidentiality by giving the peer reviewer a "blind" copy of the course. You can work with your LMS support staff to obtain the "blind" copy.

Some LMSs and online learning organizations provide opportunities for you to be peer reviewed by an external reviewer. Consider whether this option would work for you and whether an external reviewer might offer additional insights to supplement those of reviewers from your institution.

YOUR EVALUATION AND REVISION PLAN

Now that you have reviewed various types of evaluation strategies, consider which ones will work for you. You can create an evaluation plan, including the source of feedback, what data the source provides, and how the data will be used to revise the course.

In addition, consider how you want to structure your revision cycle. We noted at the beginning of this chapter that minor revisions should usually be completed right away, whereas more major revisions may occur every one to two years. Think about your course information and how often it needs to be updated. For example, courses based on current events, developments in the field, and other up-to-the-minute information will likely require a more frequent revision cycle, particularly in terms of resources. In contrast, courses that present fewer recent developments in the field may not need resource updates as frequently. However, all courses benefit from regular revision of learning activities!

Table 12.1 presents an example of an evaluation and revision plan that includes a list of feedback sources, what data each source will produce, and how the data will be used to inform course improvements.

Table 12.1   Example of an evaluation and revision plan

Sources of feedback	Data	How data will be used
Learners' case analysis and interpretation papers	Common errors in writing	Develop/refine writing skills checklist and re-teaching resources in writing.
Learners' attainment of milestone criteria	Percentage of learners who achieved each milestone's criteria	Review milestones with lower achievement and determine whether learning activity modifications are needed to increase achievement.

Table 12.1 (*cont.*)

Sources of feedback	Data	How data will be used
Quality of learner interaction	Written dialogue posts – depth of responses	If responses do not show depth, re-examine strategies and prompts used for fostering reflection and dialogue. Clarify activity rationale and instructions.
Colleague feedback	Comments on a course review rubric	Look at strengths and weaknesses on the course review rubric. Discuss comments with a colleague to get more information.
Learner feedback on end-of-course survey	Learner self-reported learning and suggestions for improving the course	Review overall learners' data, look for patterns, and reflect on which suggestions may be useful. If learners report low achievement of milestones, consider whether this report matches instructor's rating of learners' achievement of milestones, and why.

Application:
Create Your Evaluation and Revision Plan

To create your evaluation and revision plan, consider what sources of feedback you will use, what data each source will provide, and how you will use those data to evaluate and (if needed) revise your course. Also plan how frequently you will revise your course, including both minor and major revisions.

Sources of feedback	Data	How data will be used

Like everything you have done in this book, revision is part of an iterative process! You may change this plan many times.

Milestone:
Evaluation and Revision Plan

You have completed another milestone. You now have a solid plan for evaluating your course and revising it regularly.

Call a Colleague:
Dialogue on Course Evaluation and Revision

Talk with a colleague about the process of course evaluation and revision. Share your plan and get feedback. Be open to ideas, and ask your colleague to participate in your evaluation plan. Consider asking your colleague to help you form an online course creation and teaching group as a source of support and feedback as you teach your course. Jot down your discussion notes in the space provided.

COURSE EVALUATION AND REVISION: SUMMARY

In this chapter, you reviewed your course and considered changes that might be needed before offering it to learners. You considered circumstances under which you might need to revise the course while learners are enrolled. You also created an evaluation and revision plan to gather data with an eye to course improvements. Most importantly, you spoke with a colleague about your plan and considered establishing an ongoing support network as you teach the course.

You have completed your first cycle of the Change-adept Course Creation Process! We encourage you to celebrate your accomplishment with your colleagues.

You are now ready for a final reflection in the Epilogue.

Epilogue

Congratulations, you have reached your destination! You have created an online course and placed it in your LMS.

To reach this destination, you learned about and applied foundational adult learning principles: our view of learning, the learning process, adult learning assumptions, and semiotics for inclusion of diverse learners. You followed the Change-adept Course Creation Process: prepare, create, and revise. Throughout the process, you engaged in self-reflection and dialogue with your colleagues to create an online course that addressed your adult learners' needs.

Along the way, you participated in learning activities that led to the accomplishment/ completion of the following milestones:

- Course Map (Chapter 5)
- Learning Activity (Chapter 9)
- Online Course (Chapter 11)
- Course Evaluation and Revision Plan (Chapter 12).

You have accomplished so much, yet one final milestone remains: to complete your end-of-journey self-reflection.

 Your Travel Journal:
End-of-Journey Self-Reflection

We suggest that you review the workbook and your self-reflections. In particular, look at the initial self-reflection you completed in Chapter 1. Consider what has changed and what has stayed the same over the course of your journey. In the space provided, jot down your reflections.

Now that you have completed your course, what are your thoughts and feelings about what you have learned about adult learning and the Change-adept Course Creation Process?

What do you consider valuable, new, and/or significant that you will continue to do as you create and revise online courses?

What would you do differently the next time you create or revise a course?

Which of your ideas and practices have changed during your online course creation journey?

What advice would you give a colleague who is creating an online course for the first time?

How might you share your knowledge of creating online courses with others?

We wish you all the best as you continue to develop your skills to create successful online courses that support adult learners' needs. Although we have referred to this as the workbook destination, in reality it is a rest stop before you begin the next phase.

The journey continues!

Appendix

APPENDIX CONTENTS

The Appendix contains the following resources associated with the relevant chapters:

- Addressing learners' concerns about inclusion (Chapters 3 and 11)
- Learning activity purpose statement examples (Chapter 7)
- Complete business simulation: an example (Chapter 7)
- Human growth and development learning activity: an example (Chapter 7)
- Virtual role-play examples (Chapter 7)
- Tips for working with different types of resources (Chapter 8)
- Examples of feedback prompts for self-reflection (Chapter 9)
- Rubric example (Chapter 9)

ADDRESSING LEARNER CONCERNS ABOUT INCLUSION

Review Table A.1 for some suggestions you can use to address concerns your learners may have as they begin the course. Particularly relevant to addressing these concerns is the use of semiotics to promote the inclusion of diverse learners discussed in *Chapter 3: Learning Principles* and *Chapter 11: Course Start Here*.

Table A.1 Addressing learner concerns about inclusion

Learner concerns	Ways to address learner concerns
Am I welcome in this course? Will I be supported by the instructor? By my peers?	The language you use throughout your course and particularly in your initial communications with your learners is of great importance. A friendly tone of voice, invitation to participate in the course, encouragement to ask questions, the use of second person "you" rather than the more formal third person "the student" are all ways to help alleviate anxiety and to establish an inviting, inclusive learning environment. Give your learners options on how to contact you (text, email, virtual office hour meetings, phone), so they can choose the medium they feel comfortable using. Set office hours for various times and on different days to make it easy for your learners to contact you. Also, let your learners know that they can schedule times to talk outside of scheduled office hours. Encourage peers who are working together to exchange multiple ways to contact each other. Make it easy for your learners to contact you and their peers in the course, and respond promptly when contacted.

Table A.1   (*cont.*)

Learner concerns	Ways to address learner concerns
Do those people in the picture look like me?	If your learners do not feel connected to at least some of the images you have chosen, they may feel disconnected from the course. By not feeling that they belong, they may opt out of the course or struggle for the duration.
Does that icon have meaning for me?	Given the ubiquity of icons used in software, many icons have developed nearly universal meaning. Other icons may need to be explained or include short reminder words as they are used in the course. Also think carefully about how similar icons may send different messages. For example, you may use a book as an icon to represent "read." Think about whether the book should be open or closed. What might be the implicit meaning of the icon if the book is open compared to if the book is closed?
Does that word have meaning for me?	As instructors, we have an in-depth knowledge and clear understanding of the words, particularly jargon and acronyms, associated with our discipline. Our learners do not possess our level of nuanced knowledge. For example, in statistics the word "significant" has a very specific meaning that refers to likelihood that a finding may be generalized to the population under consideration. However, in common usage "significant" means "important."
How can I find out what this article is saying?	It is your responsibility to be mindful of your learners' level of understanding. Choose resources that match their level, or create summaries or prompts to support learners' understanding. If the material is too difficult or confusing, learners may give up or manage to muddle through without developing the understanding necessary to be successful in the course. Be prepared to provide supplemental resources to learners needing additional support, and be available to answer questions.
Is that narrative or story relevant to me?	Narratives and stories can be powerful ways to connect learners' experiences to the content. Beware of mentioning people or events from history unless you provide an introduction to them, why they are important, and connect how they are relevant to the point or topic under discussion. Sometimes childhood tales are used to make a point. Make sure that the point is clear even if the learner is not familiar with the story. Many childhood stories are culturally grounded. Look for ways to link the story or narrative to the learners' experiences.

Table A.1   *(cont.)*

Learner concerns	Ways to address learner concerns
Am I offended by the word, image, narrative/story, video?	Watch for biased wording and potentially upsetting video content and images that may seem hostile to or exclude certain groups. If even one learner feels excluded for any of these reasons, learning for everyone is impeded. Asking someone else to review your course for unintentional biases and assumptions can be helpful.

LEARNING ACTIVITY PURPOSE STATEMENT EXAMPLES

Table A.2 includes some additional examples of learning activity purpose statements from different disciplines. More information can be found on creating learning activity purpose statements in *Chapter 7: Learning Activities*.

Table A.2   Additional examples of learning activity purpose statements

Learning activity purpose statement *The purpose of this activity is:*	Topic(s)	Summative milestone	Theme
... for you to apply your knowledge of chemical reactions by writing a lab report describing the results of an experiment conducted in a simulated chemistry lab.	Chemical reactions	Written lab report	Simulated chemistry lab
... for you to apply your knowledge of the US Civil Rights movement by presenting a group research project to a tour group visiting a US history museum traveling exhibit.	Research process steps and US Civil Rights movement	Group research project presentation	US history museum traveling exhibit
... for you to apply product design principles to a redesign project at a tech start-up company.	Product design principles	Redesign project	Tech start-up company

COMPLETE BUSINESS SIMULATION: AN EXAMPLE

The simulation learning activity is the full example of the overview presented in Chapter 7. The example shows the learning activity including actions, skills, and milestones week by week.

CC	**District managers' group project for Corporation Corp, Inc.**

Purpose:	*Milestones:*
The purpose of this learning activity is for you to work together as a managers' group to apply what you learned about organization change and organizational culture at the beginning of the course to a business situation using actual data collected from a company, and to individually reflect on your experience.	• District summary of employee data (formative) • Written cross-functional district managers' recommendation report (summative) • Written individual self-reflection paper (summative)

Setting:	*Skill areas:*
You work for a district office that is part of Corporation Corp. Your team includes the district manager, plus managers from five functional departments that will be represented: dispatch, customer service, maintenance, drivers, and accounts payable/accounts receivable.	• Data interpretation • Teamwork • Writing

Overview of actions and feedback:	*Resources:*
• Duration: six weeks • Your instructor will assign you to one of the six managers' roles. Depending on the number of learners in the class, some functional departments may not be included. This decision will be up to the instructor. • You will represent your functional department in two synchronous virtual meetings to review the data, discuss the district culture, and write a report to recommend changes to address employee concerns and meet the COO's challenge to the district. • You will review and comment on other manager groups' recommendations.	• Challenge from the COO. • Employee survey data summaries by functional department and district-wide (used with permission of the company). • Employee listening session data summaries by functional department and district-wide (used with company permission). • General description of the situation in each functional department and district-wide. • Cameron, K. S. & Quinn, R. E. (2006). *Diagnosing and changing organizational culture: Based on the competing values framework* (rev. ed.). San Francisco, CA: Jossey-Bass. • Organizational Culture Assessment Instrument (Cameron & Quinn, 2006). • Other summaries and reports generated by individual group members and the group as a whole.

(cont.)

• You will self-reflect on your experience throughout the process and write a final self-reflection paper. • Your instructor will provide summative feedback on the two milestones. • In the role of COO liaison, your instructor will provide summative feedback on the milestone at the end of the activity.	

Background:

All employees in your district were asked to complete an anonymous employee survey to help management better understand employee attitudes toward their work and the company. After the surveys were completed, a summary of the overall district survey results was given to all employees, and a summary of each functional department employee survey results was given to the relevant department. Employees were then asked to participate in listening sessions to discuss the survey results for their functional department. Notes were taken during the listening sessions, and a summary of the listening session findings was distributed to the employees of that functional group.

In addition, the district has been given a challenge from the COO. Although the COO stated that the district had the highest EBIT and margins, he is concerned that other indicators show that people and equipment were being worked too hard. He issued a challenge to the district to become even better. The district manager has decided that the best approach to meet the COO's challenge and address any issues that surfaced from the employee surveys and listening sessions is to create a cross-functional managers' group to identify ways to improve the district and meet the COO's challenge.

As a manager of your functional group, you have been asked by the district manager to participate in a meeting of district functional group managers.

Week 1

Your role. You are the manager of a functional group who has been asked by the district manager to participate in a cross-functional managers' group that has been tasked with recommending changes to the district's culture that address employee concerns identified from employee survey and listening session data and meet the COO's challenge to the district.

Learning activity - Part 1: Preparing for the first managers' meeting

Instructions:
• Form cross-functional managers' groups that include one manager from each functional group plus the district manager.

(*cont.*)

Week 1

- Post your contact information in your managers' group folder.
- Establish a time and day to meet synchronously, and post group member contact information.
- Individually read the resources.
- In preparation for the group meeting:
  - ○ Review the employee survey data and the employee listening sessions data for your function. If you are the district manager, review the data for the district as a whole.
  - ○ Summarize the similarities and differences between the two data sources and identify any ambiguities and anomalies between the survey data and the listening session data. Write an employee data summary for your function and post to your manager group's folder.
  - ○ Read other functional managers' summaries of employee data for their function.
  - ○ Be prepared to discuss.

Resources:
- The COO's challenge to the district
- General description of the situation in the district and functional area
- Functional area employee data from the employee survey summary
- Functional area employee data from the listening sessions summary

Milestone: None (actions prepare you to reach the milestones).

Skill areas: data interpretation, teamwork, writing

Week 2

Learning activity – Part 2: First cross-functional managers' group meeting (synchronous)

Instructions:
- In preparation for the first cross-functional managers' group meeting, review the employee survey data and listening session data for your function.
- During the cross-functional managers' group meeting (synchronous):
  - ○ Identify and agree on roles and responsibilities.
  - ○ Share your views of the COO's challenge to the district.
  - ○ Look for similarities and differences among the data for the functional groups and discuss ambiguities and anomalies found in the data.
  - ○ Based on the information listed above, develop a common view of the data for the district.
  - ○ Together write a district summary of the employee data. Observe APA formatting, grammar, and mechanics including citing sources and references. The summary should be written clearly and concisely.
  - ○ Post the district employee data summary to your group's folder. This summary will be used to inform the discussions in the second meeting.

(*cont.*)

Week 2
• After the meeting, individually reflect on how well the members worked together, your contribution to the group, and any changes that you experienced in your views or feelings during the meeting discussions. Save your notes on your reflection. You will use your notes to create your final reflection at the end of this learning activity.
Resources: • Functional and district-wide employee survey data summaries and functional listening session data • Review COO's challenge to the district
Milestone: District employee data summary (formative)
Skill areas: data interpretation, teamwork, writing

Week 3
Learning activity – Part 3: Preparing for second cross-functional managers' group meeting
Instructions: In preparation for the second meeting: • Review the COO's challenge and the district employee survey data summary. • Review Cameron and Quinn's Competing Values framework. • Based on the COO's challenge to the district and the district summary of the employee data, complete the Organization Culture Assessment Instrument (OCAI) for current and preferred culture for your function. • Post your OCAI culture graph results in your group's folder. • Review other managers' OCAI culture graph results and be prepared to discuss.
Resources: • District summary of employee data • COO's challenge to the district • Cameron, K. S. & Quinn, R. E. (2006). *Diagnosing and changing organizational culture: Based on the competing values framework* (rev. ed.). San Francisco, CA: Jossey-Bass. • Organizational Culture Assessment Instrument (OCAI) (Cameron & Quinn, 2006).
Milestone: None (actions prepare you to reach the milestones).
Focus areas: data interpretation, teamwork

Week 4
Learning activity – Part 4: Second cross-functional managers' group meeting (synchronous)

(*cont.*)

Week 4

Instructions:
• During the meeting:
  ○ Review the individual cross-functional managers' OCAI graphs, and create a composite graph of the current and desired culture for the district.
  ○ Based on the employee data, the culture results, and the COO's challenge, develop recommendations on how to move the district from the current culture to the desired culture, while maintaining what is working well.
  ○ Together, write a report of your cross-functional managers' recommendations and rationale. Remember what you learned at the beginning of the course on organizational change and apply relevant strategies. Include relevant information from peer-reviewed articles that informed your recommendations and cite. Be sure to discuss how the recommended changes will help the district meet the COO's challenge. Use APA formatting including citations and references. The report should be clearly and concisely written. Review the report for grammar and mechanics.
  ○ Post the district cross-functional managers' recommendation report to the discussion board.
• After the meeting, individually reflect on how well the members worked together, your contribution to the group, and any changes that you experienced in your views or feelings during the meeting discussions. Add these notes to your previous notes. You will use your reflection notes to create your final reflection at the end of this learning activity.

Resources: • District cross-functional group summaries • Cameron, K. S. & Quinn, R. E. (2006). *Diagnosing and changing organizational culture: Based on the competing values framework* (rev. ed.). San Francisco, CA: Jossey-Bass. • Organizational Culture Assessment Instrument (OCAI) (Cameron & Quinn, 2006). • Resources on organizational change introduced during the first half of the course. • American Psychological Association. (2010). *Publication manual of the American Psychological Association* (6th ed.). Washington, DC: Author.
Milestone: district cross-functional managers' recommendation report
Skill areas: data interpretation, teamwork, writing

Week 5
Learning activity – Part 5: Responding to other cross-functional managers' group recommendation reports
Instructions: • Each individual in the course will read two other district cross-functional managers' recommendation reports posted on the discussion board, provide comments on each group's recommendations, ask clarifying questions, and identify similarities and differences among the other two groups' recommendations and their group's recommendation, and discuss how well each of the district's recommendations addressed the COO's challenge. • Members for each group will reply to the comments and questions on their report.

(cont.)

Week 5
Resources: • Two other district cross-functional managers' recommendation reports
Milestone: None (actions prepare you to reach the milestones).
Skill areas: data interpretation, writing

Week 6
Learning activity – Part 6: Self-reflection on the project
Instructions: • Self-reflect on what you learned from this experience as a whole. Use your past two reflections to inform your final reflection. Consider what you learned about yourself, what worked well for you, and what you might do differently next time you are part of a group. What changes in yourself and in others did you notice as you participated in the process? Discuss how the simulation and your experience might apply to an actual situation. Your self-reflection should be thoughtful and well written. Use APA style and formatting. Review your paper for correct grammar and mechanics. Include citations and references as relevant. • Post your reflection as an individual activity.
Resources: • American Psychological Association. (2010). *Publication manual of the American Psychological Association* (6th ed.). Washington, DC: Author.
Milestone: individual self-reflection paper on what you learned
Skill areas: writing

Additional Suggestions

To make this simulation even more authentic, you could accentuate the fact that learners are part of a real experience by adding an image of a meeting room in the discussion area. A character could guide learners by providing tips and important reminders. Or you could have the character be a top manager who drops in to add a question to the weekly discussion board.

HUMAN GROWTH AND DEVELOPMENT LEARNING ACTIVITY: AN EXAMPLE

This learning activity provides an additional example for *Chapter 7: Learning Activities*. This learning activity example shows the actions, skills, and milestones. Note the difference between the Human Growth and Development Activity and the previous Business Simulation Learning Activity.

Case discussion for school ISD

Purpose: The purpose of this activity is for you to collaborate as a team in recognizing developmental challenges, generating evidence-based hypotheses, and identifying how you would gather additional information to answer questions.	*Milestones:* • Case discussion posts and replies (formative) • Two-page paper (summative)
Setting: You are part of a newly created team in your local school that has been formed to support families in need. Each team will work with one of the families identified as needing assistance.	*Skill areas:* • Generating evidence-based questions and hypotheses • Teamwork
Overview of actions and feedback: • Duration: five weeks • You and your team have been assigned to assist one family. You will read the case study report that describes the challenges that the family as a whole and each family member faces. • Each team member will be the facilitator for a team dialogue that focuses on one family member. Each team member will choose a family member in a different stage of development. • Each team member will respond to the facilitator's post. • Remember that development is cumulative. As you serve as facilitator, keep in mind the possible influence of other family members (and their stage of development) as well as the influence of earlier stages of development on the designated family member. • The final two weeks are focused on self-reflection on the case, the dialogue, and the issue of culture in development. • You will receive feedback on each post and reply from your instructor.	*Resources:* • Chapters 1–5 of the *Human Growth and Development* textbook (developmental stages) for team dialogue. • Chapter 6 of the *Human Growth and Development* textbook (culture and development) for whole-class dialogue. • Case study for your team.

Week 1: Dialogue on infancy and early childhood

Facilitator: Identify cognitive, physical, and/or social-emotional aspects of your designated family member (youngest child) that might be a cause for concern. Choose one of the challenges and identify at least two hypotheses about what might be contributing to this challenge. Cite two sources as evidence.

Team members: Choose one of the hypotheses that the facilitator has presented and explain why you do or do not agree with this hypothesis as a potential explanation. Identify an additional hypothesis. Cite one source as evidence.

Facilitator: Respond to your team members' new hypotheses, noting whether or not you agree with these possibilities and why. Identify what additional information you would need to determine which of the hypotheses is/are correct, and a plan for how you would gather that information.

Team members: Read the facilitator's final post and reply with an explanation of why you agree or disagree with the facilitator's information-gathering plan.

Instructor feedback: The instructor will summarize each team's discussion and will provide individual formative feedback on each learner's strengths, as well as areas for improvement.

Week 2: Dialogue on middle childhood

Facilitator: Identify cognitive, physical, and/or social-emotional aspects of your designated family member (middle child) that might be a cause for concern. Choose one of the challenges and identify at least two hypotheses about what might be contributing to this challenge. Cite two sources as evidence.

Team members: Choose one of the hypotheses that the facilitator has presented and explain why you do or do not agree with this hypothesis as a potential explanation. Identify an additional hypothesis. Cite one source as evidence.

Facilitator: Respond to your team members' new hypotheses, noting whether or not you agree with these possibilities and why. Identify what additional information you would need to determine which of the hypotheses is/are correct, and a plan for how you would gather that information.

Team members: Read the facilitator's final post and reply with an explanation of why you agree or disagree with the facilitator's information-gathering plan.

Instructor feedback: The instructor will summarize each team's discussion and will provide individual formative feedback on each learner's strengths as well as areas for improvement.

Week 3: Dialogue on adolescence
Facilitator: Identify cognitive, physical, and/or social-emotional aspects of your designated family member (oldest child) that might be a cause for concern. Choose one of the challenges and identify at least two hypotheses about what might be contributing to this challenge. Cite two sources as evidence.
Team members: Choose one of the hypotheses that the facilitator has presented and explain why you do or do not agree with this hypothesis as a potential explanation. Identify an additional hypothesis. Cite one source as evidence.
Facilitator: Respond to your team members' new hypotheses, noting whether or not you agree with these possibilities and why. Identify what additional information you would need to determine which of the hypotheses is/are correct, and a plan for how you would gather that information.
Team members: Read the facilitator's final post and reply with an explanation of why you agree or disagree with the facilitator's information-gathering plan.
Instructor feedback: The instructor will summarize each team's discussion and will provide individual summative feedback on each learner's strengths as well as areas for improvement.

Week 4: Reflection on culture and development
Team: Read one other team's complete case study and written dialogue thread, compare it to your own team's case study and thread, and generate a hypothesis about why your own team's discussion was different from the other team's discussion. Summarize your observations and your hypothesis in a two-page paper, referencing the role of assumptions and biases about culture in your observations.
Instructor feedback: The instructor will provide summative feedback on your paper.

Additional Suggestions

If you set this learning activity in any institution and use documents that come from or mimic actual files and forms used, you provide the learners with an experience that gives them confidence that they can perform in a real situation. Images may include photos and icons that evoke developmental stages of human growth and development. Consider using characters that represent knowledgeable employees for each segment of this learning activity.

VIRTUAL ROLE-PLAY EXAMPLES

Table A.3 shows how virtual role-play can be used in a variety of disciplines. These examples supplement *Chapter 7: Learning Activities*, and additional information is presented.

Scenario-based dialogues can occur in the context of virtual role-play, which involves learners taking roles within a virtual space. Role-play is helpful for professional courses (e.g., business, education, counseling, nursing and allied health), but it can also be meaningful as a part of learning activities in other disciplines that require interpersonal skill practice, such as communications, language, political science, psychology, and science.

Virtual role-play requires that learners use synchronous communication software that allows them to interact in real time. Ideally, this software also allows a recording function so that learners can record their role-play, review and reflect on it, and submit it to the instructor for evaluation.

To be effective, the role-play must be sufficiently structured. This structure involves giving learners a scenario and parts to play. It can also require giving learners instructions about what knowledge and skills they should demonstrate and how learners will be evaluated.

Self-reflection and dialogue are essential following a role-play, particularly because role-play activities can bring up numerous emotions for all involved. We advise you to keep role-plays brief and focused. Provide reflection prompts that participants can respond to immediately after the role-play while the experience is still fresh.

Here are examples of role-play scenarios that can be integrated into online courses within various disciplines. Depending on the purpose of the activity (e.g., skill practice or assessment of skills in a highly realistic scenario), instructions for each player in the role-play might not be shared with other role-players.

Table A.3   Virtual role-play scenarios

Discipline	Role-play scenario and instructions for primary role	Instructions for additional role(s)
Counseling	You are meeting a client for a first counseling session. Conduct a clinical interview while demonstrating basic therapeutic skills.	You are seeking counseling for symptoms of depression and anxiety. You report some but not all of these symptoms as your presenting problem. You are open during the rest of the interview except when describing your psychosocial history.
Education	You are meeting with your administrator to discuss your students' test scores. Present a summary of the scores, students' strengths and areas for growth, and your plan for addressing growth areas in the next six weeks.	You are a supportive principal. You have lots of questions about the data and are concerned about the presence of numerous areas where students are lagging behind the district average.
Journalism	You are interviewing two lawyers about their current high-profile harassment case. Ask the three questions that your viewers most want to know the answers to.	You are two lawyers representing a client in a high-profile harassment case. You are both motivated to present your client in the best possible light and are reluctant to answer questions about your client's history. One of you wants to gain the spotlight and dominate the conversation.

Table A.3 (*cont.*)

Discipline	Role-play scenario and instructions for primary role	Instructions for additional role(s)
Management	Two employees have been referred to your human resources office because of a conflict. Mediate a discussion between them with the goal of resolution.	You are two employees who have been involved in an ongoing conflict and now are in mediation with human resources. You are currently furious with each other and initially refuse to talk.
Communications/ public relations	You are working for a business that needs to restore its public image after a series of public relations problems. Interview the CEO to identify communication strategies for corporate leadership when speaking with the press.	You are the CEO of a business with a series of public relations problems. Your marketing team wants to restore the business' public image, but you don't want to accept personal responsibility for any of the problems.
Nursing	You are working in an emergency room. Obtain the chief complaint and take a health history from a patient who has just been triaged to your evaluation room.	You are in the emergency room. You are currently experiencing a kidney stone (but don't know this) and have diabetes, high blood pressure, and high cholesterol.
Allied health	You are meeting with a child for an occupational therapy session focused on handwriting.	You are a six-year old child with low grip strength and poor fine motor control. You have a low level of cooperation.
Political science	You are running for chairperson of the city council and are holding a press conference. Be prepared to discuss your plan for managing the council and handling the city's $10 million budget deficit.	You are three members of the press attending the press conference of a candidate for chairperson of the city council. The city currently has a $10 million budget deficit. You want to get the best scoop for your news outlet about this candidate's management and budget plan.
Language	You are dining in a casual restaurant in Italy for the first time. You are eager to practice your Italian language skills. Request a table for one, ask for the menu, order your favorite dishes, and converse with the waiter in Italian.	You are the waiter at a casual restaurant in Italy. You have been instructed by your management to speak English to anyone you perceive to be a non-native Italian-speaking customer.

TIPS FOR WORKING WITH DIFFERENT TYPES OF RESOURCES

Tips for Working with Resources includes text, images, video and audio, website resources, and slide presentations and provides greater detail to supplement the information in *Chapter 8: Resources*. Before making your final selection of the resource you will use and to help guide your selection or creation of a resource, review the appropriate table for additional information.

For ease of use, each type of resource is addressed in a separate table – Table A.4 focuses on text-based resources, Table A.5 focuses on working with images, Table A.6 addresses audio and video resources, Table A.7 looks at the use of websites as resources, and Table A.8 provides information on slide presentations. We end with accessibility considerations.

Table A.4 Tips on text-based resources

Resource type	Tips for selecting or creating text-based resources
Text (online and hardcopy)	Whether selecting or creating a text resource, look for/include the following: • short "chunked" paragraphs, bullets, tables, and headers to break up dense text; • white space to make the information more readable; • professional terminology defined clearly; • clear explanations that avoid colloquialisms and jargon; • callouts, sub-headers, or other formats that mark important points or pose thought-provoking questions; • default and automatic headers usage ensures uniform fonts and spacing; • visual uniformity of fonts; • text that offers a brief commentary on key concepts; • a statement of the scope and use of the document that acts as a cognitive prompt so the learner thinks about how to approach the resource; • avoid using all caps – all caps indicates yelling; • wording choice that is clear, concise, and interesting; • inclusive language, like "you" instead of "students or learners"; • follow your institution's policy and legal copyright law when selecting resources.

Table A.5   Tips for working with images as resources

Resource type	Tips for selecting or creating images as resources
Images	Images can be resources when used to provide information. When selecting or creating images, consider the following: • Images give information *(a picture is worth 1,000 words)*. Your course software will probably allow you to insert images. Check with your institution's IT support to verify. • Tables, graphs, diagrams, and charts can be used to visually represent and summarize essential course information. • The meaning your image conveys to diverse learners may differ from your intended meaning. Consider diverse interpretations. • Be very careful when using humorous images. Humor is individually and culturally bound and may unintentionally offend or exclude some learners. • Review images to ensure that they add to the overall visual impression of uniformity, connection and continuity, clarity of information, professionalism, and credibility. • Images may not appear as you intend on all devices. Color and size are important considerations. • Follow copyright laws. Images used for education purposes are not automatically copyright-free. If you take pictures of people, check whether you need signed permission. Be sure to follow all privacy laws and policies of your institution.

Table A.6   Tips for working with video and audio media

Resource type	Tips for selecting or creating video and audio resources
Media – video & audio	Video and audio media provide additional resources you may select or create: • Check with your institution's library for video and audio sources available for use in your online course. • If you select video media on a website, carefully review it for advertising and other videos that appear in proximity to the video you have selected. • Check affiliations and sources of the video to make sure your institution approves. • Ensure that the video has closed caption and transcript options available. • Ensure that audio includes a transcript. • Check audio levels for any audio media or videos your students will view. • Check links each semester to ensure that they work. • If you use video or audio of your learners, guest speakers, or others, follow your institutional policies including release forms and student privacy. • Follow your institutional policies on copyright usage and follow copyright laws.

Table A.7   Tips for using websites as resources

Resource type	Tips for selecting websites as resources
Websites	Carefully explore any websites you are considering using as resources. Use the following questions to guide your decision on using websites as resources. *Reviewing the website* • Does the information contained in the website align with the course topics and milestones? • Is the website easy to navigate? • Is the information of interest contained in an easy-to-access section of the website? • If the learner needs to navigate to other sections to find all the relevant information, is it easy for the learner to return to the original location? • Does the website provide a positive learning experience that targets the course topic(s) and milestones? • Does the structure of the website information support adult learning principles? *Preventing potential issues* • Check links each semester to ensure that they work. • Are learners' information and privacy protected when they access the website (e.g., is the website secure, does the learner need to sign in and provide personal information, does it meet your institutional policies on student privacy)? • Does the website have any ads or information in proximity to your targeted information that is questionable? • Is the producer/author reliable? • Does the website have any affiliation that would be negative for you or your institution? • Does the website meet the level of visual and functional quality appropriate for your course and institution? Note: some government documents and resources require copyright permission to use. Follow your institutional policies and the law on copyrighted materials.

Table A.8 Tips for working with slide presentations

Resource type	Tips for selecting or creating slide presentation resources

Presentation files	Ask yourself why you are using a presentation as a resource and how many slides it will take you to present the information. If you have more than 15 slides to present, consider breaking your resource into parts with fewer slides.
	Below are additional ideas to consider as you review previous slide presentations or create new slide presentations.
	• Place text and graphics consistently on the slide to establish form and expectation.
	• Use white space to ensure that your slides are easy to read and to keep your slides from looking too busy.
	• Use slide backgrounds that are simple; avoid busy or dark backgrounds.
	• Make sure the text color is easy to distinguish from the background.
	• Don't make your textboxes too wide. The eyes have to travel farther across each line.
	• Remember that you aren't projecting on a wall, so you can reduce your font, especially the title.
	• The title should be the same size as or only slightly bigger than the font in the slide. Use a font size that is comfortable to read on a laptop.
	• To find ways to keep the slide presentation from being one-way lecture notes, you can edit the slides by adding questions that help your learners interact with the slides through reflection and discussion. For example, use questions that
	  ○ provide a transition or segue way to the next slide and create anticipation;
	  ○ ask about past experience, applications to real life, or future work;
	  ○ prompt reflection;
	  ○ have your learners post their answers and discuss with peers.

Here is an example of an ineffective slide followed by an effective slide. Look at the difference between the two slides and review one of your slide presentations. Look at some of your previous slides and consider what you are doing well and what you might want to change to ensure the information on your slides is clear and engaging.

Ineffective Slide

This Title is Bigger than Needed	
• There is often a lead sentence that shouldn't be bulleted. • There is a little white space. • The information is too dense to be effective. • Information *(A single word can be meaningless.)* • Consider the learners' needs. Are you using green or red background with gray font that might not be seen clearly with some vision challenges? • If the font is too big to see on the screen, or too small, it can be hard to read. Since you are not projecting this on a wall, the font can be smaller for easier reading and printing, but remember that it must be legible on other devices and in print. • Too many bullets make the slide overwhelming.	Graphic may be too big, too small, or not copyright safe. The graphic may not accurately represent content. Nothing leads the learner into the next slide.

Effective Slide

This Title Is a Good Proportion	

An intro sentence doesn't need a bullet.
 	
  • There isn't too much information.
  • There are few words and bullets.
  • Meaning is complete.
 	
The slide appearance adds clarity and meaning.
 	
  • White space makes learners focus on content.
  • No senseless background design.
	Meaningful graphic goes here and is copyright safe.
	
	(Segue or question can go here.)

Accessibility Considerations

Discussing ways to ensure course accessibility for your learners is outside the scope of this workbook. While software and equipment (assistive technologies) are constantly changing, creating a course that is accessible to all learners is of the utmost importance and speaks directly to the need to use semiotics to promote the inclusion of diverse learners.

To ensure that your course is accessible to all your learners, check with the disability services office at your institution for the most recent information and guidelines on accessibility. In addition, check with your IT support staff for specific information on accessibility features supported in your LMS. Note that assistive technology is changing rapidly. Below is a list of some of the accessibility concerns that you will want to be familiar with and address:

- Documents should be created so they can be read by screen readers.
- Place labels or headers above links or groups of links that describe and/or explain the information contained in the link. Describing links assists learners who use screen readers.
- Include alternative text (alt text) labels for images. Alt text provides a description of an image included in your course. There are guidelines on how to create effective alt text descriptions for images.
- For longer text, use a font with a serif or foot like Times New Roman because it helps lead our vision to the next letter. Use sans serif without feet like Helvetica, Arial, or others for titles and shorter text. It's easy to read and is available on most devices.
- Script font can be hard to read for those learners for whom English is their second language.
- Light-color font, red and green, and other color combinations can be hard to see for those learners with colorblindness.

EXAMPLES OF FEEDBACK PROMPTS FOR SELF-REFLECTION

It can be challenging to provide feedback to learners that prompts their self-reflection on actions taken and formative and summative milestones accomplished. In Table A.9, we present examples of feedback that you can use to encourage your learners to consider more than just the correctness of the action or milestone. These examples supplement the information provided in *Chapter 9: Feedback*.

You may also consider how to provide feedback that mirrors what a learner might experience in a work situation. The more realistic the feedback, the more relevant and meaningful the learner will find it. You may also use a character or group of characters to offer specialized feedback. There is an authority granted to characters by students that overrides the obviously fake set up of a person who isn't really there. People are willing to let the character hold authority as part of the role-play they are participating in as learners (Reeves, 2004).

Table A.9   Feedback prompts for self-reflection

Focus of feedback	Examples
Learners' participation in dialogue (oral or written)	• I noticed that you were quiet/did not post very often during much of the discussion but spoke up/became more active when the group began discussing ___. What prompted the change in your interest? • It looks like ___ is an issue that you feel strongly about. What personal experiences have shaped your beliefs about this issue? • The group had a heated debate but worked through disagreements to find a common understanding. What helped your group to reach consensus?

Table A.9   (*cont.*)

Focus of feedback	Examples
Learners' self-reflection tasks	• What would your group recommend to address _____ issue in _____ setting? • I am interested in your comments about _____. What personal experiences have shaped your ideas and opinions? • I understood your response about ___ but was confused about ___. Consider whether you are explaining your position fully or whether additional information could clarify your position.
Learners' milestones	• I was excited to see you identify _____ in your paper, as I see this as a sign of real insight. • I found myself a little confused by your statement that _____. Can you restate what you mean in another way? • You both took great care to understand each other's concerns during the dialogue. How do you think that consulting with a colleague about questions and concerns in the future might be similar to your experience in this activity? How might it be different?
Learners' emotional responses to an activity	• What contributed to the feelings you experienced in response to the video? • How can you use your emotional reaction to the video as a way to better understand ethics? • Your group quickly came to a consensus about the ethical issues in the video. What will you do when you confront an ethical issue that elicits more disagreement among your group in the future?
Learners' performance on tests/quizzes	• Which problem set item did you find most difficult, and why? What could you do differently? • How would you gauge your performance on the test? • What quiz material did you feel least confident about, and why? • After taking this test, what is one question you have about the material? • What is one topic that you are excited about in this course, and why? • What are your feelings toward the course material so far?

RUBRIC EXAMPLE

Chapter 9: Feedback introduces rubrics as one way to provide learner feedback. Table A.10 shows an example rubric for a written milestone. This rubric has three categories of performance: proficient (which requires that all criteria be met), developing (one or more of the criteria is met), and "conference required," meaning that the learner must schedule a conference with the instructor to discuss the learner's performance.

Table A.10 Example of a rubric for a written milestone

Criterion	Proficient	Developing	Conference required
Audience and purpose	The writer demonstrates attention to the audience and purpose of the work and maintains a scholarly tone throughout.	The writer generally attends to the audience and purpose of the work but may occasionally lapse into non-scholarly writing habits (e.g., use of colloquialisms or jargon)	Audience and purpose are unclear.
Thesis statement	The work includes a clear, focused, and inviting thesis statement.	The work includes an identifiable thesis statement, but the thesis is somewhat confusing, disconnected from the rest of the essay, or unfocused.	Thesis statement is missing or not identifiable.
Organization	The work contains an introduction, body, and conclusion, with information that is well-organized and relevant to the topic of the essay. Transitions are varied. Examples are clearly connected to the relevant point(s).	The work contains an introduction, body, and conclusion, but has irrelevant information and/or lack of smooth transitioning between paragraphs. Examples are included, but not always clearly connected to the relevant point(s).	The work is missing an introduction and/or conclusion and includes no examples.

Table A.10   (*cont.*)

Criterion	Proficient	Developing	Conference required
Paragraph structure and style	The work incorporates paragraphs that are unified (i.e., all sentences within the paragraph relate to the main idea of the paragraph), are logically organized (i.e., sentences are ordered in a way that flows and makes sense), demonstrate conciseness of expression (i.e., no "wordiness" or rambling), and that use clear, accurate language.	Paragraphs have sentences that are logically organized but may include choppy sentences, unnecessary wordiness, unclear wording, or lack of supporting detail.	Paragraph meaning cannot be determined due to organizational or word choice issues.
Grammar and mechanics	The work demonstrates nuanced understanding of grammatical and mechanical rules, with *minimal errors* within the writing checklist categories.	Although there may be several errors in grammar and/or mechanics, these do not interfere with readability.	Errors in grammar and/or mechanics interfere with readability.
APA style	Citations and references are accurately formatted, and headings and all other aspects of the paper formatting are accurate.	There are minor errors in the citations and references, headings, and/or other aspects of the paper formatting (e.g., running head or headings).	There are major errors in APA style, such as missing citations and improper inclusion of elements in references.

Table A.10 *(cont.)*

Criterion	Proficient	Developing	Conference required
Source material	Source material is credible, relevant, and current; peer-reviewed scholarly journal articles predominate (i.e., at least the minimum number of required sources are from peer-reviewed journals). Examples and evidence are original/novel and show clarity of purpose and voice.	Source material is credible, relevant, and current, but non-peer-reviewed scholarly sources (e.g., books or book chapters) predominate. Examples and evidence are generic or exclusively quoted from source material.	Source material is not scholarly; Internet sources (other than electronic journal articles) are used exclusively.
Suggestions for improvement			
Summary of learner's content knowledge			

References

Allcock, S. J., & Hulme, J. A. (2010). Learning styles in the classroom: Educational benefit or planning exercise. *Psychology Teaching Review, 16*(2), 67–79.

Americans with Disabilities Act of 1990, Pub. L. No. 101-336, 104 Stat. 328 (1990). As amended, 2008. Retrieved from ada.gov/pubs/adastatute08.htm.

Anderson, L. W., & Krathwold, D. R. (Eds.). (2001). *A taxonomy for learning, teaching, and assessing: A revision of Bloom's taxonomy of Educational Objectives.* New York: Longman.

Argyris, C., Putnam, R., & Smith, D. M. (1985). *Action science: Concepts, methods, and skills for research and intervention.* San Francisco, CA: Jossey-Bass.

Bartunek, J. M., Gordon, J. R., & Weathersby, R. P. (1983). Developing "complicated" understanding in administrators. *Academy of Management Review, 8*(2), 273–284.

Bates, A. W. (2019). *Teaching in a digital age: Guidelines for designing teaching and learning* (rev ed.). BC Open Textbooks. Retrieved from http://opentextbc.ca/teachinginadigitalage.

Bloom, B. S., Engelhart, M. D., Furst, E. J., Hill, W. H., & Krathwold, D. R. (1956). *Taxonomy of educational objectives: The classification of educational goals. Handbook I: Cognitive domain.* New York, NY: David McKay Company.

Boud, D. (1991). *Implementing student self assessment* (2nd ed.). Sydney: HERDSA.

Branson, R., Rayner, G., Cox, J., Furman, J., King, F., & Hannum, W. (1975). Interservice procedures for instructional systems development: Executive Summary, Phase I, Phase II, Phase III, Phase IV, Phase V. (TRADOC Pam 350-30 NAVEDTRA 106A). Ft. Monroe, VA: U.S. Army Training and Doctrine Command (NTIS No. ADA 019 486 through ADA 019 490). Retrieved from http://dtic.mil/dtic/tr/fulltext/u2/a019488.pdf.

Brill, J. M., & Hodges, C. B. (2011). Investigating peer review as an intentional learning strategy to foster collaborative knowledge-building in students of instructional design. *International Journal of Teaching and Learning in Higher Education, 23*(1), 114–118.

Brookhart, S. M. (2019). A perfect world is one with no grades. *ASCD Express, 14*(31). Retrieved from http://ascd.org/ascd-express/vol14/num31/a-perfect-world-is-one-with-no-grades.aspx

Buzan, T., & Buzan, B. (1993). *The mind map book.* London: British Broadcasting Corp.

Canning, E. A., Muenks, K., Green, D. J., & Murphy, M. C. (2019). STEM faculty who believe ability is fixed have larger racial achievement gaps and inspire less student motivation in their classes. *Science Advances, 5*(2), 1–7.

Cantillon, P., & Sargeant, J. (2008). Giving feedback in clinical settings. *British Medical Journal, 337,* 1292–1294.

Carroll, S. (2017). Meta-learning: Teaching students how to learn builds success for life. *The National Teaching and Learning Forum, 26*(4), 1–4.

Clancy, A., & Vince, R. (2019). "If I want to feel my feelings, I'll see a bloody shrink": Learning from the shadow side of experiential learning. *Journal of Management Education, 43*(2), 174–184.

Clark, D. R. (2015). ADDIE timeline. Retrieved from http://nwlink.com/~donclark/history_isd/addie.html.

Claro, S., Paunesku, D., & Dweck, C. S. (2016). Growth mindset tempers the effects of poverty on academic achievement. *Proceedings of the National Academy of Sciences, 113*(31), 8664–8668.

Clement, N. D., & Lovat, T. (2012). Neuroscience and education: Issues and challenges for curriculum. *Curriculum Inquiry, 42*(4), 534–557.

Coffield, F., Moseley, D., Hall, E., & Ecclestone, K. (2004). *Learning styles and pedagogy in post-16 learning: A systematic and critical review.* London: Learning and Skills Research Centre.

Coghlan, D., & Brannick, T. (2014). *Doing action research in your own organization* (4th ed.). Los Angeles, CA: Sage.

Dale, E. (1969). *Audiovisual methods in teaching.* New York, NY: Dryden Press.

de Bruyckere, P., Kirschner, P. A., & Hulshof, C. D. (2015). *Urban myths about learning and education.* San Diego, CA: Elsevier.

Dewey, J. (1916). *Democracy and education: An introduction to the philosophy of education.* New York, NY: Macmillan.

Dewey, J. (1938). *Experience and education.* New York, NY: Free Press.

DiCarlo, S. E. (2009). Too much content, not enough thinking, and too little FUN! *Advances in Physiology Education, 33,* 257–264.

Drew, A. J. (2014). Teaching international business across multiple modes of delivery: How to maintain equivalence in learning outcomes. *Journal of Teaching in International Business, 25,* 185–199.

Ehrlinger, J., & Shain, E. A. (2014). How accuracy in students' self perceptions relates to success in learning. In V. A. Benassi, C. E. Overton, & C. M. Hakala (Eds.). *Applying science of learning in education: Infusing psychological science into the curriculum* (pp. 142–151). Washington, DC: Society for the Teaching of Psychology. Retrieved from http://teachpsych.org/ebooks/asle2014/index.php.

Eyler, J., & Giles, D. E., Jr. (1999.) *Where's the learning in service learning?* San Francisco, CA: Jossey-Bass.

Gannon-Cook, R., & Ley K. (2015). Overlooking the obvious: How to use semiotics and metaphors to reinforce e-learning. *Participatory Educational Research, 2*(3), 109–121.

Garrison, D. R., Cleveland-Innes, M., & Fung, T. S. (2010). Exploring causal relationships among teaching, cognitive and social presence: Student perceptions of the community of inquiry framework. *Internet and Higher Education, 13,* 31–36.

Geake, J. (2008). Neuromythologies in education. *Educational Research, 50*(2), 123–133.

Gergen, K. J. (1994). *Toward transformation in social knowledge* (2nd ed.). Thousand Oaks, CA: Sage.

Gergen, K. J. (2009). *Relational being: Beyond self and community.* New York, NY: Oxford University Press.

Gergen, K. J., & Thatchenkery, T. (2004). Organization science as social construction: Postmodern potentials. *Journal of Applied Behavioral Science, 40*(2), 228–249.

Girash, J. (2014). Metacognition and instruction. In V. A. Benassi, C. E. Overson, & C. M. Hakala (Eds.). *Applying science of learning in education: Infusing psychological science into the curriculum* (pp. 152–168). Washington, DC: Society for the Teaching of Psychology. Retrieved from http://teachpsych.org/ebooks/asle2014/index.php

Goggins Selke, M. J. (2013). *Rubric assessment goes to college: Objective, comprehensive evaluation of student work.* Lanham, MD: Rowman & Littlefield.

Goodwin, B., & Miller, K. (2012). Good feedback is targeted, specific, timely. *Educational Leadership, 70*(1), 82–83.

Harrow, A. J. (1972). *A taxonomy of the psychomotor domain: A guide for developing behavioral objectives.* New York, NY: David McKay Company.

Hull, G. A., & Nelson, M. E. (2005). Locating the semiotic power of multimodality. *Written Communication, 22*(2), 224–261.

Hussey, T., & Smith, P. (2002). The trouble with learning outcomes. *Learning in Higher Education, 3*(3). 220–233.

Immordino-Yang, M. H., & Gotlieb, R. (2017). Embodied brains, social minds, cultural meaning: Integrating neuroscientific and educational research on social-affective development. *American Educational Research Journal, 54*(1S), 344S–367S.

Kagan, S. (2005). Rethinking thinking: Does Bloom's taxonomy align with brain science? *Kagan Online Magazine.* Retrieved from http://kaganonline.com/free_articles/dr_spencer_kagan/289/Rethinking-thinking-does-blooms-taxonomy-align-with-brain-science.

Kember, D. (2004). Interpreting student workload and the factors which shape students' perceptions of their workload. *Studies in Higher Education, 29*(2), 165–184.

Kember D,. & Leung, D. Y. P. (2006). Characterising a teaching and learning environment conductive to making demands on students while not making their workload excessive. *Studies in Higher Education, 31*(2), 185–198.

Kirschner, P. A., & van Merrienboer, J. J. G. (2013). Do learners really know best? Urban legends in education. *Educational Psychologist, 48*(3), 169–183.

Kisfalvi, V., & Oliver, D. (2015). Creating and maintaining a safe space in experiential learning. *Journal of Management Education 39*(6), 713–740.

Knowles, M. S., Holton III, E. F., & Swanson, R. A. (2005). *The adult learner: The definitive classic in adult education and human resource development* (6th ed.). Boston, MA: Elsevier.

Koc-Januchta, M., Hoffler, T., Thoma, G., Prechtl, H., & Leutner, D. (2017). Visualizers versus verbalizers: Effects of cognitive style on learning with texts and pictures – an eye-tracking study. *Computers in Human Behavior, 68,* 170–179.

Kolb, D. A. (1984). *Experiential learning: Experience as the source of learning and development.* Upper Saddle River, NJ: Prentice Hall.

Krathwold, D. R., Bloom, B. S., & Masia, B. B. (1964). *Taxonomy of educational objectives. Book II: Affective domains.* New York, NY: David McKay Company.

Kuechler, W., & Stedham, Y. (2018). Management education and transformational learning: The integration of mindfulness in an MBA course. *Journal of Management Education, 42*(1), 8–33.

Lalley, J. P., & Miller, R. H. (2007). The learning pyramid: Does it point teachers in the right direction? *Education, 128*(1), 64–79.

Langer, E. J. (1989). *Mindfulness.* Cambridge, MA: Da Capo Press.

Langer, E. J. (1997). *The power of mindful learning.* Cambridge, MA: Da Capo Press.

Langer, E. J. (2000). Mindful learning. *Current Directions in Psychological Science, 9*(6), 220–223.

Lapakko, D. (1997). Three cheers for language: A closer examination of a widely cited study of nonverbal communication. *Communication Education, 46,* 63–67.

Lapakko, D. (2007). Communication is 93% nonverbal: An urban legend proliferates. *Communication and Theater Association of Minnesota Journal, 34,* 7–19.

Levinson, D. J. (1986). A conception of adult development. *American Psychologist, 41*(1), 3–13.

Liu, X., Magjuka, R. J., Bonk, C. J., & Lee, S. (2007). Does sense of community matter: An examination of participants' perceptions of building learning communities in online courses. *Quarterly Review of Distance Education, 8*(1), 9–24.

Martinez, A. E. (2006). What is metacognition? *Phi Delta Kappan, 87*(9), 696–699.

McNiff, J., & Whitehead, J. (2002). *Action research: Principles and practice* (2nd ed.). New York, NY: Routledge.

Mead, G. H. (1934/2015). *Mind, self, & society: The definitive edition.* Chicago, IL: University of Chicago Press.

Mehrabian, A., & Ferris, S. R. (1967). Inference of attitudes from nonverbal communication in two channels. *Journal of Consulting Psychology, 31*(3), 248–252.

Merriam, S. B., & Bierema, L. L. (2014). *Adult learning: Linking theory and practice.* San Francisco, CA: Jossey-Bass

Merriam, S. B., & Brockett, R. G. (2007). *The profession and practice of adult education: An introduction.* San Francisco, CA: Jossey-Bass.

Merriam, S. B., Caffarella, R. S., & Baumgartner, L. M. (2007). *Learning in adulthood: A comprehensive guide* (3rd ed.). San Francisco, CA: Jossey-Bass.

Meyerson, D., Weick, K. E., & Kramer, R. M. (1996). Swift trust and temporary groups. In R. M. Kramer & T. R. Tyler (Eds.). *Trust in organizations: Frontiers of theory and research* (pp. 166–195). Thousand Oaks, CA: Sage.

Mezirow, J. (1991). *Transformative dimensions of adult learning.* San Francisco, CA: Jossey-Bass.

Monahan, N. (2015, October 12). More content doesn't equal more learning. *Faculty Focus.* Retrieved from http://facultyfocus.com/articles/curriculum-development/more-content-doesnt-equal-more-learning.

Montessori, M. (1948/1973). *From childhood to adolescence, including erdkinder and the function of the university* (The Montessori Educational Research Center, trans.). New York: Schocken.

National Academies of Sciences, Engineering, and Medicine (NASEM). (2018). *How people learn II: Learners, contexts, and cultures.* Washington, DC: National Academies Press.

National Research Council (NRC). (2000). *How people learn: Brain, mind, experience, and school – expanded edition.* Washington, DC: National Academies Press.

Nicol, D. J., & Macfarlane-Dick, D. (2006). Formative assessment and self-regulated learning: A model and seven principles of good feedback practice. *Studies in Higher Education, 31*(2), 199–218.

Nicol, D., Thomson, A., & Breslin, C. (2014). Rethinking feedback practices in higher education: A peer review perspective. *Assessment & Evaluation in Higher Education, 39*(1), 102–122.

Nilson, L. B. (2003). Improving student peer feedback. *College Teaching, 51*(1), 34–38.

O'Connor, A. B. (2006). *Clinical instruction and evaluation: A teaching resource* (2nd ed.). Sudbury, MA: Jones and Bartlett.

Pratt, D. D. (1988). Andragogy as a relational construct. *Adult Education Quarterly, 38*(3), 160–181.

Reeves, B. (2004). Benefits of interactive online characters. Unpublished manuscript, Center for the Study of Language and Information, Stanford University.

Rhodes, T. (2010). *Assessing outcomes and improving achievement: Tips and tools for using rubrics.* Washington, DC: Association of American Colleges and Universities.

Robert Jr., L. P., Dennis, A. R., & Hung, Y. C. (2009). Individual swift trust and knowledge-based trust in face-to-face and virtual team members. *Journal of Management Information Systems, 26*(2), 241–279.

Rohrer, D., & Pashler, H. (2012). Learning styles: Where's the evidence? *Medical Education, 46*, 630–635.

Rovai, A. P. (2007). Facilitating online discussions effectively. *Internet and Higher Education, 10*(1), 77–88.

Sankey, M. D., Birch, D., & Gardiner, M. W. (2011). The impact of multiple representations of content using multimedia on learning outcomes across learning styles and modal preferences. *International Journal of Education and Development using Information and Communication Technology, 7*(3), 18–35.

Saunders, S., & Kardia, D. (1997). Creating inclusive college classrooms. Retrieved from http://crlt.umich.edu/gsis/p3_1.

Schenck, J., & Cruickshank, J. (2015). Evolving Kolb: Experiential education in the age of neuroscience. *Journal of Experiential Education, 38*(1), 73–95.

Scheuermann, J. A. (2018, February 5). Group vs. collaborative learning: Knowing the difference makes a difference [Web log post]. Retrieved from http://facultyfocus.com/articles/course-design-ideas/group-vs-collaborative-learning-knowing-difference-makes-difference.

Schinske, J., & Tanner, K. (2014). Teaching more by grading less (or differently). *CBE Life Sciences Education, 13*(2), 159–166.

Schlegel, M. J. (1995) *A handbook of instructional and training program design.* Springfield, VA: Eric Document Reproduction Service. Retrieved from http://files.eric.ed.gov/fulltext/ED383281.pdf.

Schoenfeld, A. H. (2016/1992). Learning to think mathematically: Problem solving, metacognition, and sense making in mathematics (reprint). *Journal of Education, 196*(2), 1–38.

Schon, D. A. (1983). *The reflective practitioner: How professionals think in action.* New York, NY: Basic Books.

Shea, P., Li, C. S., & Pickett, A. (2006). A study of teaching presence and student sense of learning community in fully online and web-enhanced college courses. *The Internet and Higher Education, 9*, 175–190.

Shedroff, N. (2001). *Experience design 1.* Indianapolis, IN: New Riders.

Shelley, D. J., Swartz, L. B., & Cole M. T. (2007). A comparative analysis of online and traditional undergraduate business law classes. *International Journal of Information and Communication Technology Education, 3*(1), 10–18.

Shireman, R. (2016). *The real value of what students do in college* [report]. The Century Foundation. Retrieved from http://tcf.org/content/report/the-real-value-of-what-stu dents-do-in-college/?agreed=1.

Simon, E. (2018, November 21). 10 tips for effective online discussions. *EduCause Review*. Retrieved from http://er.educause .edu/blogs/2018/11/10-tips-for-effective-online -discussions.

Singh, H., & O'Boyle, M. W. (2004). Interhemispheric interaction during global–local processing in mathematically gifted adolescents, average-ability youth, and college students. *Neuropsychology, 18*(2), 371–377.

Snyman, M., & van den Berg, G. (2018). The significance of the learner profile in recognition of prior learning. *Adult Education Quarterly, 68*(1), 24–40.

Stacey, R. (2000). The emergence of knowledge in organizations. *Emergence, 2*(4), 23–39.

Stacey, R. (2001). *Complex responsive processes in organizations: Learning and knowledge creation*. New York, NY: Routledge.

Subramony, D. P., Molenda, M., Betrus, A. K, & Thalheimer, W. (2014). The mythical retention chart and the corruption of Dale's cone of experience. *Educational Technology, 54*(6), 6–16.

Taylor, D. C. M., & Hamdy, H. (2013). Adult learning theories: Implications for learning and teaching in medical education: AMEE guide no. 83. *Medical Teacher, 35*(11), e1561–e1572.

Taylor, V. F. (2018). Afraid of the deep: Reflections and analysis of a role-play exercise gone wrong. *Journal of Management Education, 42*(6), 772–782.

Tobin, T. J., & Behling, K. T. (2018). *Reach everyone, teach everyone: Universal design for learning in higher education*. Morgantown, WV: West Virginia University Press.

US Department of Education, National Center for Educational Statistics. (2018). Table 311.5 Number and percentage of students enrolled in degree-granting postsecondary institutions, by distance education participation, location of student, level of enrollment, and control and level of institution: Fall 2015 and fall 2016. Retrieved from: http://nces .ed.gov/programs/digest/d17/tables/dt17_311 .15.asp?current=yes.

Weick, K. E. (1995). *Sensemaking in organizations*. Thousand Oaks, CA: Sage.

Weick, K. E., & Roberts, K. H. (1993). Collective mind in organizations: Heedful interrelating on flight decks. *Administrative Science Quarterly, 38*(3), 357–381.

Weick, K. E., Sutcliffe, K. M., & Obstfeld, D. (2005). Organizing and the process of sensemaking. *Organization Science, 16*(4), 409–421.

Weinstein, Y. (2019, February 16). Memorizing versus understanding [Web log post]. Retrieved from http://learningscientists.org/ blog/2018/2/16-1.

Whitman, G., & Kelleher, I. (2016). *Neuroteach: Brain science and the future of education*. New York, NY: Rowman & Littlefield.

Wiggins, G. (2012). Seven keys to effective feedback. *Educational Leadership, 70*(1), 10–16.

Willingham, D. T. (2018). Does tailoring instruction to "learning styles" help students learn? *American Educator, 42*(2), 28–32, 43.

Wilson, B. G., Ludwig-Hardman, S., Thornam, C. L., & Dunlap. J. C. (2004). Bounded community: Designing and facilitating learning communities in formal courses. *International Review of Research in Open and Distance Learning, 5*(3), 1–19.

Wilson, M. (2006). *Rethinking rubrics in writing assessment*. Portsmouth, NH: Heinemann.

Index

For EU product safety concerns, contact us at Calle de José Abascal, 56–1°,
28003 Madrid, Spain or eugpsr@cambridge.org.